30 DAY GOURMET's BIG Book of Freezer Cooking

Nanci Slagle and Carol Santee

30 Day Gourmet Press

The *Big Book of Freezer Cooking* may be purchased for educational, business, or sales promotional use. For more information please contact: *Special Markets Department*, 30 Day Gourmet Press, PO Box 272, Brownsburg IN 46112 or e-mail office@30daygourmet.com

30 Day Gourmet, Inc.
PO Box 272
Brownsburg IN 46112

Email: office@30daygourmet.com
Website: www.30daygourmet.com

Photography by Nexis Technical Services, Carol Santee, Charissa Birnbaum, Nanci Slagle, Tammy Davis

Cover photo credits:
Easy-Reach refrigerator/freezer courtesy of Amana and Maytag Corporation

Library of Congress Control Number: 2010921402

Slagle, Nanci and Santee, Carol
      30 Day Gourmet's Big Book of Freezer Cooking
      Nanci Slagle and Carol Santee. – Brownsburg, IN: 30 Day Gourmet Press, ©2012.

ISBN-10: 0-9664467-7-1
ISBN-13: 978-0-96644677-7
1. Cooking   2. Title

Pictured on front cover:
      Chicken in Cherry Sauce (page 84)
      Tuscan White Bean Soup (page 139)
      Beef Kabobs (page 64)
      Italian Chicken Bites (page 189)
      Crunchy Peanut Butter Ice Cream Cups (page 202)

Visit Us on the Web!

Our website, www.30DayGourmet.com, is a great resource for even more freezer cooking information. You can check out the Cooks' Corner message boards, find hundreds of great recipes, read hints and tips from other cooks, share your own freezer cooking recipes with other cooks, and meet some really nice people! Use this login information to access our Members section of the website:

- user name: recipes

- password: macaroni

Chewin' THE NEWS   Subscribe to Chewin' the News, our monthly newsletter full of news, ideas, free recipes, tips, and more. It's a wonderful free resource for freezer cooking.

   Find the 30 Day Gourmet fan page on Facebook® to discover more about freezer cooking and connect with other freezer cooks.

What others are saying about 30 Day Gourmet:

Cooks, Parents & Families say:

The best part about 30 Day Gourmet cooking is how much my husband brags about our full freezer to all of our friends. As a working mom, this has been a god-send. My kids love the recipes.

teacher from Iowa

Although we are a small family, I was glad to see that is not a problem because your system isn't just geared to "large" families. This is a true FAMILY cookbook. Thank you for easy-to-read instructions and ingredients I can pronounce.

dual career family from New York

Just awesome! I'm a whole new person come 6 p.m.

homeschool mom from Florida

After researching all the "once-a-month" cooking books out there, yours is BY FAR the most complete, organized and thorough program we have found.

cooking couple from Indiana

My 18 year old son and I made several meals for him to put in single serving sizes and take to his college apartment. He finds this to be a quick and easy way to have home-cooked meals.

working mom from Ohio

My friend and I are having a great time with this. Our husbands are proud of us and our kids aren't hungry anymore. We're not running through the drive-thru or making a meal out of soccer field food. Thank you for inspiring us!

It's well worth it and we're hooked.

busy mom from Missouri

Penny Pinchers say:

This cookbook is the best money I have ever invested!

frugal family from Washington

I recently compared my budget from a "before 30 Day Gourmet" year to an "after 30 Day Gourmet" year. What a surprise! I had cut our grocery spending by almost $1000!!! Thanks for the wonderful book!

computer analyst from California

Great book! It's the only way I cook anymore! I just love the recipes. No one can believe they have been pulled out of the freezer and I am saving LOTS of money!

daycare provider from Virginia

Seniors & Singles say:

Your method works well for retirees who do not want to spend every day thinking of what to cook when we have more fun things to do. The 6 person meal gives us 3 meals in the freezer. I have enjoyed your recipes so much and tell everyone who will listen about this method of cooking!

retired secretary from Texas

As a single person, freezer cooking has been great for me! Making it all ahead and packaging it in single-serving sizes has saved me so much time and money.

aerobics instructor from Nevada

I just started my daughter-in-law in freezer cooking and she loves it! I had been cooking this way for years but your cooking manual made it easier to teach her how to do it.

active grandma from Michigan

Table of Contents

Table of Contents

30 Day Gourmet's *BIG Book of Freezer Cooking*

by Nanci Slagle and Carol Santee

Nanci is the President of 30 Day Gourmet, Inc. and an original founder of the company. She is a graduate of Cedarville University with a BA in English Education and works as a high school English teacher and Drama Director. Nanci and her husband of 30 years have four children and reside near Indianapolis, Indiana.

Meet Nanci: When I discovered freezer cooking in 1993, I had been married for 14 years and was the mother of four children ages 8, 5, 3 and 1 month. I was also a "crisis cook" who didn't think about dinner until the last possible moment. We ate fast food dinners. We ate cereal dinners. We ate my husband's "breakfast for supper" specials. And we ate a lot of hot dogs and boxed macaroni and cheese dinners. Sound familiar?

In my early days of freezer cooking, I tackled the then-daunting task with a good friend. Together, through trial and more than a few errors, we figured this thing out. In the beginning, we got together once a month and assembled 25-30 entrées for each of us. After a few years, we began cooking every three months. Our 2-day cooking marathons netted us each about 75 freezer meals. As our family sizes, schedules and tastes changed, we found that the "system" we had developed was adaptable enough to "flex" along with us.

Fast forward to 2012. I am now a high school English teacher with two children on their own, one in college, and only one still at home. I no longer have long cooking marathons but instead do mini-sessions every 3-4 weeks. Freezer cooking is still the best way I have found to feed my family great home-cooked food without having to stress over the "dinner chore".

Carol is the author of 30 Day Gourmet's *Freezer Lunches To Go* and *Healthy Freezer Cooking* eBooks. She is a computer information specialist and a work at home mother. Carol and her husband of 25 years have three children and reside near Columbus, Ohio.

Meet Carol: Our family was introduced to 30 Day Gourmet in 1999 by my sister-in-law. When visiting her house, I saw the Meal Inventory Worksheet posted on her refrigerator and asked her about the system. At the time, I was working full time and found it difficult to find the time to put a delicious and nutritious meal on the table every night. Our family jumped in gung-ho and cooked for 30 days the first time out! We realized that it saved us time and money but I soon found out it helped me in many other ways. It allowed me to spend more time with my family and less in the kitchen. Planning meals in advance also helped me take control of our food purchases.

I left the workforce in 2001 to become a stay at home mom. This move forced our family to evaluate our food expenses. This was the start of our cooking based on "What's on Sale". It was also the beginning of what would eventually become *Freezer Lunches To Go* as we learned how to create a freezer cooking alternative to school lunches.

Today, I work for 30 Day Gourmet editing and formatting ebooks, writing newsletters, and answering questions from fellow freezer cooks. I have one child living on his own and two in college. I now cook alone based on "What's on Sale" and enjoy creating new freezer cooking recipes to share in our monthly newsletter.

Freezer Cooking Rewards

The rewards of freezer cooking are numerous and each cook's #1 may be different but here are the ones we hear over and over:

Reward #1 - It's flexible and fits my lifestyle.

Face it. Our lives these days are busy. It's unrealistic to think that we can meet the dinner challenge the same way that our mothers and grandmothers did. Many of them knew by 9 a.m. every morning what they were serving for dinner that night. Not in today's homes! With hectic jobs and busy kids' schedules, most of us don't even start thinking of a plan until late afternoon. 30 Day Gourmet's plan means you can still put together a great meal – all from your freezer. Seniors and singles. Work-outside-the-home moms and work-at-home moms. Grandmas, teachers, accountants, even truck drivers! This works for everybody!

Reward #2 - It saves me lots of money!

Eating out or going to the grocery store today for tonight's dinner can be very costly. A family of 4 can easily spend $25+ on a fast food dinner or pre-packaged frozen dinners. Using 30 Day Gourmet's plan will lower your food bills! Our cooks average $6.00 for each main dish recipe (4-6 servings) and many spend even less. Think of what you could save! And tell us you don't have a better place to spend that money.

Reward #3 - It's healthier.

Using the recipes in this book means you'll be cooking "from scratch" which also means that you'll be cutting way back on the unhealthy ingredients found in processed foods. Unlike lots of other freezer cookbooks, we provide nutritional information for every recipe in this book and on our website. This makes substitutions easy which helps when you are cooking for special diets.

Reward #4 - I love the fresh, home-cooked taste.

You'll eat few "pre-packaged" and even fewer "drive-thru" foods. Will you miss them? Don't worry about losing flavor. Learning to package your freezer foods correctly takes care of that. There's no skimping on taste with 30 Day Gourmet's recipes!

Reward #5 - I'm enjoying a greater variety of foods.

At 6 p.m. most of us can only think of 2 or 3 entrées we know how to make! Not anymore! With a little planning, 30 Day Gourmet cooks freeze a wide variety of great-tasting foods. American favorites, Chinese, Mexican, Italian – it's your choice!

Reward #6 - I have more free time.

With foods ready in the freezer, you will suddenly find yourself with more time at the end of the day. Sure, getting them into the freezer will take some time but those last minute trips to the store, unwanted dinners out and sinks full of pots, pans and cookware are time-wasters of the past.

Reward #7 - I have enough to share with others.

Most of us are hospitable at heart and would really love to help others out but our daily busyness keeps us from doing it. When you have extra food in the freezer, it's so easy to pull out a pie or a whole meal to share.

Reward #8 - I actually enjoy cooking now.

For many of us, it's not the cooking that we hate. It's the daily grind of it all. Having food in the freezer gives you the flexibility to decide when (if ever) you want to cook. Some use their creative juices for baking great desserts, some for fresh salads and others for trying out new recipes.

30 Day Gourmet cooks freeze a wide variety of great-tasting foods.

Freezer Cooking Myths

Myth #1 - It takes a whole day to do the cooking.
The great thing about our system is its flexibility. Don't have a whole day? Do a 3-4 hour mini-session. Or triple up on your dinners for a few weeks and build up some reserves. Cook 10 of the same recipe and find 9 friends who will do the same. Then swap 'em out. There are lots of ways to get the job done! And after you try the 30 Day Gourmet plan, you will realize that the time you save in meal preparation and cleanup each evening is well worth the time it takes to shop and cook in large quantities – even a whole day's worth.

Myth #2 - Only gourmet cooks can do this.
Absolutely not! Only the most basic cooking knowledge is needed for most of these recipes. Our 3 Easy Steps are just that – easy. All of our recipes give very detailed instructions so that even the least experienced cook can be successful.

Myth #3 - Owning a large freezer is a must.
Actually, about 30 family size entrées will fit into a standard refrigerator's freezer. But it does help to have some extra space. Chest freezers are an inexpensive option and hold a lot more food than you think! Upright freezers are easy to organize and take up less floor space.

Myth #4 - All those freezer containers and pans will cost a fortune.
Use of freezer bags makes it economical to get started. The foods in them can be thawed and put into your favorite dish for baking. Slowly acquire freezer containers, glass casseroles, and metal baking pans at garage sales and discount stores if you like. Some 30 Day Gourmets use freezer bags almost exclusively, while others opt for a menagerie.

Myth #5 - Freezer foods don't taste fresh.
Our 30 Day Gourmet recipes are made "from scratch" and are designed so that you assemble your foods and freeze them to cook after thawing. All the aromas and flavors of fresh cooking remain. For those extra busy days, you can also choose to pre-bake some of your entrées and side dishes so that you only have a short warm up time.

Myth #6 - Most of the foods my family likes to eat probably can't be frozen.
Actually, most foods freeze really well! Just follow our recommendations and you'll be surprised by how delicious your food will taste.

Myth #7 - Having meals in the freezer means that I can't eat out.
Ha! Don't believe that one for a minute.

Myth #8 - My family will get tired of eating the same meal over and over again.
The easiest way to avoid this is to plan at least a two week rotating menu. Never repeat a meal for at least two weeks. In your plan, include some meals that you generally make fresh such as "breakfast for dinner", quick soup and sandwich night, homemade pizza night, etc. Make freezer cooking fun for your family by letting them help you pick out the recipes to include in your cooking day. This will make the recipe rotation more enjoyable for you and your family!

Myth #9 - My family won't eat casseroles.
Freezer cooking doesn't mean casseroles for every meal! There are so many different foods that freeze great. Try our marinades, soup, sandwich, and breakfast recipes for starters!

Freezer containers and dishes won't cost a fortune if you acquire them over time.

3 Easy Steps to the Plan

EASY STEP 1:

CHOOSE & PLAN

EASY STEP 2:

SHOP & PREP

EASY STEP 3:

ASSEMBLE & FREEZE

Easy Step #1- Choose

Choose the Freezer Cooking method you want to use.

- Cooking by Protein Type
- Cooking by Mini-Sessions
- Cooking BIG!
- Tips for Cooking BIG

Choose whether to cook alone or not.

- Advantages of Going It Alone
- Advantages of Teaming Up
- Ways to Team Up
- Tips for Teaming Up

Easy Step #1- Choose

Choose the freezer cooking method you want to use.

When most people hear about freezer cooking they immediately think "cook all day Saturday once a month and get enough dinners to last until the next month". That's certainly one way to get the job done but there are so many more. Again, find a method that works best for you. If using the "what's on sale" method appeals most to you, then go for it. When life is especially busy, the "mini-session method" might be your best bet. If you like to tackle big projects or have a schedule that fluctuates, the "cook big but not often" method may work great for you.

Here's what our cooks have to say:

Mini-Sessions

I want to first tell you that I LOVE the 30 Day Gourmet. I have done two small sessions to get the hang of before I do the full 30 days. I have learned a lot by starting off small. I think I would have given up starting off doing meals for 30 days.

Brenda

I freezer cook by making 2 to 3 recipes every weekend and making several of each. I will like this way better than doing the whole 30 days. I love that your plan is so flexible and will work for whatever is best for me!

Tammy

The beauty of this system is you can adjust it to fit your needs. It doesn't take much longer to make a double, triple or even quadruple batch of something...you eat one, and freeze the rest. Before you know it, your freezer is full.

Sarah

What's on Sale

I usually do "loss leader plans" meaning I base my freezer cooking on what is on sale. When blade roast was on sale, for .99 lb., I put 3 recipes each of Roast Beef Sandwiches and Delicious Pot Roast in the freezer. When hamburger was on sale, I did a hamburger plan with 4 recipes and made 3 of each. It is so simple.

Teresa

I'm trying to get into the habit of hitting a really good sale at the store and make dishes out of that over a course of a few days or a week, when I have time. Last week my local store had chicken on sale for .49 a pound so I bought six chickens and brought them home and made 4 meals (2 recipes, 2 of each) in no time.

Stephanie

Cook Big

Cooking once a month works great for me. I've been doing it for several years now. In a 6 hour day I can usually get 20 entrées and several sides and desserts in my freezer. It's wonderful.

Vickie

I cook every three months and it's the only way to go! Your software makes my planning easy. The cooking takes 3 days but wow – what a big accomplishment. My friends think I'm some super-cook but it's really not that hard.

Beth

This mini-session yielded 35 individual servings.

Easy Step #1- Choose

Choose the freezer cooking method you want to use.

Three Ways to Freezer Cook

1. Cook by protein-type or the "what's on sale" method

Lots of freezer cooks use this approach. Rather than planning a cooking day once a month, they wait to see what's on sale and buy up a lot of one meat type. Cooks who follow this plan say that they save lots of money and it's much more manageable. If chicken is on a great sale, they might buy 50 pounds of it. 10 pounds can be boiled and diced for use in recipes like Santa Fe Chicken (page 72) or Chicken Florentine Lasagna (page 85). 10 pounds can be used in slow cooker recipes. Another 20 pounds can be put into marinade and frozen to cook on the grill. The last 10 pounds can be made into nuggets, patties or other pre-cooked recipes that will make for quick "last minute" meals.

2. Cook in mini-sessions

Cooking in mini-sessions just means that you aren't trying to put a large amount of food into your freezer in one day. Being a successful freezer cook doesn't mean putting 100+ entrées into your freezer in a day. It means doing what works for you and your family.

Mini-sessions are the way to go for lots of cooks. It could mean cooking every night for a week but making three of each, one to eat that night and two to put into the freezer. It won't take long to build up a nice selection. For some, a mini-session means limiting the recipes to what they can accomplish in 3-4 hours.

Wouldn't it be great to get up early one Saturday morning a month and know that by noon you could have an extra 10-15 meals in the freezer? It's also a good idea to start with mini-sessions until you get comfortable with freezer cooking. There's nothing better than success to keep you motivated!

Using the "what's-on-sale" approach to freezer cooking can save you lots of money!

Easy Step #1- Choose

Choose the freezer cooking method you want to use.

Three Ways to Freezer Cook:

3. Cook Big

Cooking big can mean anything from 30 entrées in one day to 120 entrées over a weekend and anything in between. When Nanci began freezer cooking with a friend in 1993, they set out to put 30 entrées in their freezers by day's end. At first, that was difficult. It took them awhile to get the process down "pat" and choose the right combination of recipes to accomplish their goal. But once they did the 30-meals-in-a-day process for a year or so, it got easier. Nanci and her friend worked their way up to assembling 75-80 entrees every three months. It worked well for several years. Now, Nanci generally does "mini-sessions" and cooks by protein type putting about 10 entrees and several freezer bags of ready-to-go beef and poultry into her freezer.

Again, just do whatever works best for you. Don't feel like you have to cook BIG to *really* be a freezer cook. Anytime you do a little planning ahead and put anything in the freezer you're "doing it".

Tips for Cooking Big

- Planning is the key. Extra trips to the store for milk or freezer bags will chew up precious time.
- Do as much prep work ahead of time as possible. You don't want to be standing around watching turkey breasts boil on Assembly Day. Leave a day or two between the shopping and cooking to do your prep work. This is a lot of work and you will be tired!
- Choose the right combination of recipes. Don't do too many labor and time intensive recipes. Cooking up ground beef and measuring it off into 2-1/2 C. portions counts as a recipe!

- Put your recipes in order ahead of time. Starting your first slow cooker meal at 5 p.m. or putting the chicken in marinade for 5 hours at the end of the day is not a good thing.
- Label your foods before putting them into the freezer. Once entrées are flattened in a freezer bag and frozen, they tend to all look the same. When you cook BIG, it's hard to remember what you put into the freezer. (We call this "brain freeze".)

Cooking BIG means a long day and lots of groceries but it's well worth it!

Easy Step #1- Choose

Choose whether you want to cook alone or not.

There are pros and cons to both. Remember too that you can cook alone one time and with a friend the next. The main question should always be: what will be best for me given my situation right now? We know it sounds selfish but don't cook with a friend just because SHE wants to. Maybe that's best for her but maybe you are faster, more frugal and more efficient when you work alone. On the other hand, maybe you will never get this job done without a "cooking buddy".

What our cooks have to say:

Cooking alone:

When I first read about 30 Day Gourmet I thought that you HAD to cook with a friend. I just knew that wouldn't work for me because of my schedule. I went ahead and tried it alone and it works GREAT! I plan on Wednesday or Thursday, shop on my way home from work Friday and cook on Saturday. My husband takes our daughter "out" for the whole day (dinner included). I turn on the music, wear comfy clothes and shoes and just have a great day to myself. Plus I can put about 50 dinners (there are just 3 of us) into my freezer. What a great feeling!

Missy

I love cooking alone because I can work at my own pace. Sometimes my cooking takes me a few days but that's okay. I'd rather take my time than feel rushed and tied to another person's schedule and tastes. I tried cooking with a friend one time and it drove me nuts. Cooking alone is the way to go!

Sue

Cooking with daughters:

We just had our first cook day yesterday!! What fun!! My two daughters and I rented a local church kitchen with 3 stoves and 3 sinks and tons of counter space. The $50 charge was SO WORTH IT!!! We started at 7 am and ended at 12:30 in the morning. What a day!!

Diane

Cooking with spouse:

Just wanted to tell you all that I am a newbie who just finished my first cooking session. My unexpected cooking partner was my husband who really likes the concept. A whole day spent together talking and cooking really made it fun. My feet hurt, but the freezer looks so great full of yummy food. We are so excited to have our meals ready to go every day and no more wandering around the grocery store at six o'clock wondering what to buy.

Carrie

Friends cooking together:

We cooked for our second time on Friday and made 60 meals in 7 hours with 5 kids "helping". Thanks for all the great ideas.

Michelle and Lisa

Cooking with a friend makes work seem like fun!

Easy Step #1- Choose

Advantages of Going It Alone:

1. You can set your own schedule.
If you have a crazy schedule, it can be difficult to find a mutually compatible day to cook with a friend or family member. Maybe the thought of putting the kids to bed and then pulling an "all-nighter" cooking session appeals to you! Maybe you need to break up your cook-time over two days. Maybe you really don't know until Thursday what Saturday holds. If that's YOU, cooking alone might be best for you.

2. You don't have to pretend to like "her" recipes.
When you cook with a friend, it can be hard sometimes to agree on the recipes. If she has a "family favorite" that she just knows will freeze well how do you say "I'm sure it's great, but I don't think my family will like it?" That's a tough one. When you cook alone, you are solely responsible for choosing the recipes. You're the only one who knows if you are only freezing homemade chicken nuggets, tacos and hot pockets!

3. You don't have to do any complicated math problems.
Cooking with another person means more math to do. It's as simple as that. To keep everything fair, you have to tally the bills, account for the inventory that each cook brings to the pile of groceries, and resist the urge to pick up extra groceries for your family while you are shopping for both freezer cooks.

4. You can cook and package the food any way you want to. It's all yours!
The actual cooking can be easier too. All of the food in the kitchen is yours. That means that you don't have to measure as carefully when you are dividing up the recipes. You can use a "decide-as-you-go" plan for packaging the foods. If a 9x13 dish is too large for your family, you can pull out all of the smaller ones you have and make them work.

5. You can make allowances for special diets and picky eaters.
If you have someone in your family who requires special ingredients or is a "picky eater", it's easier to allow for that if you cook alone. It can be difficult to find a cooking pal whose family is also lactose intolerant or whose husband won't eat anything but meat and potatoes. Many freezer cooks who have one "special eater" in their family create variations of their regular meals and then freeze them separately for that person.

6. You can spend time alone without feeling guilty.
Many women who cook alone choose to because they look forward to being alone in their own kitchen for a whole day. If you've never tried it, give it a whirl sometime. Nanci is a "people person" but she can testify to the thrill of a day alone in the kitchen. She turns on the stereo, stocks up on Diet Mt. Dew and has at it. Because she spends most of her days in the classroom with teenagers, it's actually relaxing for her to be in the kitchen cooking.

Cooking alone means you can package your recipes any way you want!

Easy Step #1- Choose

Advantages of Teaming Up:

1. You can share the planning.

Freezer cooking for the first time can be such a daunting task that some people will NEVER try by themselves. It's often easier to tackle a new project with someone else. Two heads usually are better than one and it's no different with freezer cooking. Choosing recipes, tallying your ingredients and planning your shopping may be a lot easier for you if you do it with a friend or spouse.

2. You can share the work.

It is actually quicker to cook for two families at once. Your time-saving comes in making multiples of recipes. It may take 15 minutes to combine the ingredients for 8 Stuffed Bell Peppers (page 58) but it won't take 90 minutes to assemble 32 of them. One of you may be especially good at planning and shopping while the other is the cooking expert. Great team!

3. You can share the fun!

Okay, let's admit it. This is the same thing as sharing the work. But why is it that work can seem like fun when there's someone else in the room? Many cooks tell us that they look forward to having a whole day with their friend (mom, sis, neighbor, spouse) more than anything else. And because you're working at the same time, it's a win-win situation!

4. You can share the cookware.

One very economical reason for cooking with a partner is that each cook doesn't have to purchase every necessary item. Between the two (or more) of you, you will probably come up with plenty of pans, measuring cups, etc. Only one of you needs a food processor or blender, and a mixer.

5. You can share the commitment.

With the busyness of our schedules these days, you can be certain that something will come up that will tempt you to put off your cooking day. But if you have promised a friend that you would spend this day in the kitchen, you are less likely to give in to outside demands. If you do have to run a child to a practice or take a call from work, your cooking partner can continue on.

6. You can share the bounty.

Many people who cook together find it's easy to agree to each give away a certain amount of their food. They have fun choosing a recipient or two. Maybe one cook has a grandmother who would LOVE to have some individual entrées, soups or desserts. Another may have a neighbor with an upcoming surgery who would appreciate an extra meal or two in the freezer. When you plan for these "giveaways", the money that you spend is minimal and it doesn't seem like nearly as much work as it would if you made that meal separately.

Friends can save money when they team up and share cookware.

Easy Step #1- Choose

Ways to Team Up:

Cook with a friend, sister, mom or spouse.

Our message boards and Facebook group are full of great stories and suggestions from 30 Day Gourmets who cook with a friend or family member. For moms with young children, it can be a great way to have some "adult" time.

Cooking with a family member can be good because you know each other so well and can be more relaxed about dividing the jobs and the food. Mom can watch the grandbaby and work on the "sit down" jobs. You may do most of the cooking but she has been a huge help and won't take home as much of the food. It's a great deal for both!

Cook with a group in the same location.

It can be a lot of fun to cook with a whole group of people. Some cooks have a house large enough to accommodate 3-5 cooks. Remember that you're not limited to using the kitchen. A dining room with a good-sized table is great for assembling recipes. Other cooks have used their church's kitchen or rented a local public building. When you cook in a group, it's fun to work in pairs. One church group paired an older, more experienced cook with a younger, more novice cook. They all had a GREAT day together!

Cook with a group in multiple locations.

We call this "Co-op Cooking". The basic idea is that you put together a group of 10 people and do a planning session where you assign each cook one recipe that he/she will make 10 times. The group sets a date a few weeks away to get back together and "swap out" the frozen entrées. It's much easier and faster to make 10 of the same thing than to make 10 different entrées. And since you didn't have to assemble the other 9 meals, it kind of feels like eating out. Per entrée monies are tallied and bills are "evened up" so that everyone pays the same.

(For more info and recipes, check out our *Co-op Cuisine* eBook at www.30daygourmet.com)

Tips for Teaming Up:

- Don't make a lifelong commitment. Try it once and see how it works. Just because she's nice at playgroup, doesn't mean she will make a perfect cooking partner.

- Consider the sizes of your families. It's just easier if the food can be split down the middle. If you have a family of 6 and she has a family of 2, who's going to run out of food faster?

- See if you can agree on 10 recipes. No two families have the exact same tastes but it's easier if you can assemble the same recipes for both of you. If they are a strictly "meat and potatoes" family and yours is a vegetarian family, your team may not work well.

- Keep careful track of the costs. Consider the cost of the inventory that each person is contributing. Don't shop for groceries that you won't use on cooking day. It's just easier to tally the costs if you limit the ingredients to cooking day only. Of course, mutually agreed-upon snacks and treats are always welcome!

- Split up the recipes by protein type and make enough for everyone. In other words, each cook should be assembling both person's recipes. Your time-saving comes in making multiples.

Co-op Cooking **author Jan Limiero and her cooking group meet to swap out their recipes.**

Easy Step #1- Plan

Planning includes several mini-steps.

They aren't hard to do but these mini-steps are necessary to a successful assembly session.

1. Set the dates for your planning, shopping, and assembling.
2. Choose your recipes and list them on Worksheet A.
3. Take inventory of items you already have and record them on Worksheet A.
4. Tally up your needed ingredients and subtract your inventory using Worksheet A.
5. Make a shopping list by recording those totals on Worksheet C.
6. Choose the type of containers you will use.
7. Plan your prep work using Worksheet D.

Mini-step #1 - Set the dates for your planning, shopping, and assembling.

Whether you are cooking solo or with a friend, you need a little time to plan. The first time you plan, it will seem to take forever. Going through our recipes (those in the book as well as the ones we offer on our website) and deciding which ones your family will most like can be time consuming. Incorporating your own recipes into the system will take a bit of time as well but you WILL get much quicker!

Put your planning time on your calendar and don't let anything keep you from it! At this time, you also need to set your dates for shopping and cooking. Consult your calendar and leave yourself plenty of time to get the work done. It's certainly possible to plan, shop, and cook in a 24 hour time period but it can be very tiring. Planning the day the store ads come out, shopping a day or two later and cooking the next day seems to work well. For example, Nanci plans on Wednesday, shops on Friday after school, and assembles her entrees on Saturday.

Software savvy cooks may want to check out our 30 Day Gourmet Advantage Cooking Software. It comes pre-loaded with all of the recipes in this book and does all of the tally work for you. See page 36 for more information about our unique cooking software.

Mini-step #2 - Choose your recipes and list them on Worksheet A.

- **Decide how many entrées you want to make.**

  We freezer cooks get a bad rap sometimes because once we begin this venture, people expect us to eat an "out-of-the-freezer home-cooked meal" every night. But most of us don't live that way. Be realistic. Freezer cooking is about doing what works for YOU. If you still want to eat out on Sundays and order pizza on Friday nights, that's fine. Plan for it. You're down to 5 dinners a week now. Is there a night when you always clean up the leftovers? Plan for it. Do you eat at Mom's every Monday night? No reason to stop now.

- **Decide how often you want to freezer cook.**

  If you're planning to be a once-a-month cook who needs about 20-25 entrées, we suggest that you choose about 6-8 recipes and make 3 of each. If you cook more often than that, you should still do several recipes but you will be building up a variety over more than one cooking day.

- **Try out new recipes to be sure that you like them.**

  It's always a good idea to try a recipe out on the family before adding it to your Assembly Day list. Sometimes, a recipe might be an "adults only" recipe while others may fall into the "all of us plus guests" category. This is the time to decide whether you want to make any changes to the recipe such as increasing spices or adding/leaving out veggies.

Easy Step #1- Plan

Mini-step #2 - Choose your recipes and list them on Worksheet A.

- **Go through your own favorite recipes to see which ones can be incorporated into your cooking using Worksheet B.**

  All of the recipes in this book and those on our website at www.30daygourmet.com are suitable for freezer cooking but, of course, you have favorite recipes that you might want to assemble as well. Just use the information on the next page to determine whether your recipe can be frozen. Use Worksheet B (page 39) and our Multiplication Chart for Recipes (page 218) to create your own multiplied out recipe. You can also use the online version of the worksheet by accessing the Members' section of our website and clicking on the "worksheets" section. For access info, see page 3.

- **Make multiples.**

  Once you're sure of a recipe, always make more than one. Even if you are doing a "mini-session", make multiples. You can put 15-20 chicken entrées into the freezer on a Saturday morning if you choose 3-4 recipes and make 5 of each. The time you save really adds up. All of our recipes are multiplied out in columns making it very easy to assemble several of each. We've done the hard math problems for you.

- **Choose a variety of "easy" and "hard" recipes.**

  By taking a look at the recipe's directions, you can decide whether it will be an "easy" or "hard" recipe to assemble. For example, meats in marinades like the Orange Marmalade Pork Chops (page 91) or the Rosemary Sage London Broil (page 61) go together very quickly. On the other hand, recipes like the Crab and Portobello Stuffed Chicken (page 80) or the Shrimp and Pork Pot Stickers (page 178) are a bit more time intensive but well worth the extra effort.

- **Always assemble at least one slow cooker meal.**

  Slow cookers are great. You're not limited to using them for wintertime soups and stews. Sandwich fillings, Macaroni and Cheese, and all sorts of other foods can be done in the slow cooker. You can start a recipe the night before cooking day and when you wake up you already have one meal done. See the index for a list of recipes from this book that can be assembled using the slow cooker.

- **Be sure that your recipe can be frozen.**

  Food in your freezer, as long as it is at 0 degrees F. or below, does not spoil or become harmful to you. More foods freeze well than not. All of the recipes in this book and on our website freeze fine. It would be impossible to list every particular food or food ingredient here. The internet provides a wealth of information about freezing at your fingertips. If you have a question about a particular food that we haven't covered, do a quick search and an answer is bound to pop up in a moment. You can also check the information that came with your freezer (you do keep that stuff, right?)

Crab and Portobello Stuffed Chicken takes a little longer to assemble but it is definitely worth it.

Easy Step #1- Plan

Mini-step #2 - Choose your recipes and list them on Worksheet A.

When incorporating your own recipes into the system, be sure to use the following guidelines:

- Although the USDA says that it is safe to refreeze meat that has thawed in the refrigerator without cooking it first, the quality of the meat will suffer. Therefore, we recommend that you do not thaw frozen raw meat and then re-freeze it without cooking it thoroughly first.

  For example, we purchase ground beef when we see it on sale and keep it frozen until our next cooking day. We thaw and cook it to use in recipes like Lazy Day Lasagna (page 47), Make-ahead Chimichangas (page 54), or Spaghetti Pie (page 62) before we refreeze it. If we want to make meatloaf but not pre-cook it before we freeze it, we will plan to use fresh ground beef. Frozen poultry can be thawed, simmered or baked and used for recipes like Country Chicken Pot Pie (page 70) or Chicken Quesadillas (page 180).

- Hard-boiled eggs tend to get rubbery after thawing. If you chop them up in very fine pieces, they are okay.

- Cornstarch-thickened sauces, cheese sauces and gravies made with milk tend to separate when being reheated after freezing. These sauces are fine when they are mixed with other ingredients like the White Sauce recipe (page 161) we use for our Chicken Florentine Lasagna (page 85).

- Don't freeze raw vegetables unless they have been blanched. Blanching is a short period of cooking that seals in color, texture, vitamins and flavor. (See chart on page 223.) Purchased frozen vegetables have already been blanched and can be used "as is". Using these can save you LOTS of prep time. We often use frozen potatoes, broccoli, beans and corn. It's best to stir these into your recipe after it has cooled and is ready to go into the freezer. The quality will be better if the veggies don't thaw and then re-freeze.

- Cured meats, like ham or bacon, should be eaten within a month of freezing. They will lose color and flavor after that.

- Exceptions to the veggie blanching rule are diced onions, green pepper and celery. Chop and use! Just a tip, though. Onions and green peppers can be purchased pre-diced in the frozen foods section for only a few cents more than the "whole" versions.

- Some seasonings change in intensity and flavor. Salt loses some of its flavor in freezing and may cause an off-flavor in high fat items. You can salt after thawing if you wish. Celery and green pepper also lose a little flavor. Black pepper, cloves, bay leaves, onions, sage, and artificial vanilla become stronger in flavor.

- Deep fried foods will not stay crispy after thawing and re-heating. The high fat content may also alter the flavor with time.

- Egg and milk substitutes freeze well in most recipes.

- Fully cooked pasta, dry beans and rice tend to turn mushy when frozen in liquids or sauces. Under cook them by half the recommended time if you plan to stir them into a sauce or broth before freezing. You can also freeze them separately and stir them into your recipe before serving.

- Salad vegetables like lettuce, cucumbers, tomatoes and radishes don't freeze well. Actually they freeze fine – it's the thawing and eating that is a problem!

Thaw and cook previously frozen meat to use in your recipes.

Easy Step #1- Plan

Mini-step #2 - Choose your recipes and list them on Worksheet A.

Reading Our Recipes.

One of the unique features of the 30 Day Gourmet system is in the formatting of our recipes. We learned early on that multiplying endless ingredients on cooking day wasn't a good idea. 1/3 x 5? 4 1/2 x 3? These are not easy math problems to do while assembling 30 entrées. Lots of mistakes are made using the "math in your head" method and you end up doing the same process over and over each time you cook. There's a better way. All of the recipes in this book as well as the ones on our website and in our eBooks are already multiplied out in 6 columns. This makes it easy for you to try out a recipe (follow the "1" column), double a recipe ("2" column) or to cook with a friend and make 6 of a recipe so that you can each take home 3. Each of our recipes has some consistent features.

- **Title:** The recipes in our books and on our website all fall into 11 categories. This makes it easy for cooks who copy/print their recipes and put them into a binder to keep them organized. Beef - Poultry - Pork & Fish - Meatless - Breads & Breakfast - Soups & Sandwiches - Sides & Salads - Sauces & Marinades - Appetizers - Snacks - Desserts

- **Recipes**: Our columns are arranged by the number of recipes not servings. The "1" column is one recipe, the "6" column is 6 recipes.

- **Servings:** To help you plan and because of the nutritional information given, we tell you how many servings there are in each recipe. For example our Shrimp Carbonara (page 92) recipe yields 6 servings per recipe. As a general rule, we try to make the "1" column equal 4-6 servings. An exception to this are the snacks and appetizers which may be listed by total yield.

- **Makes:** For most recipes, we tell you how much each recipe makes or yields. This information is useful when you stir up ingredients in one big bowl and then need to portion them down to separate entrées. If a recipe doesn't include this information, you can usually figure it out by using a large measuring cup when combining ingredients and then doing some simple division.

- **Ingredients**: Our ingredients are listed down the left side of each recipe. We have given you the ingredient in the form that it goes into the recipe. For example, in the Lazy Day Lasagna (page 47) recipe we list "Cooked Ground Beef" rather than "Uncooked Ground Beef". It's much easier to tally up your ingredients this way. If any

equivalents are needed for the recipe, they are listed in the Notes section. This saves you the trouble of turning to the equivalency charts in the Appendix.

- **Assembly Directions**: Each recipe gives you directions for assembling the recipe. Whenever possible, assemble as many recipes as you can in one large mixing container. If the recipe doesn't indicate how many cups per recipe, make a note of that for dividing things up evenly later.

- **Freezing and Cooking Directions**: A few recipes are intentionally designed to be pre-cooked before freezing but most can just be assembled, frozen and then cooked on the day that you want to eat it. Cooking your entrées from the frozen state is fine. Just increase the cook time by half. In other words, the Lazy Day Lasagna (page 47) that takes 1 hour from the thawed state will take about 1-1/2 hours from the frozen state.

- **Notes:** This is where we try to help you out with possible ingredient substitutions, timesavers, or tips. This section will also include page numbers for any additional recipes that are referred to in the Ingredient List or Assembly Directions.

- **Nutritional Information**: These are per serving and are based on the ingredients in the printed list.

Easy Step #1- Plan

Mini-step #3 - Take inventory of ingredients you already have and record them on Worksheet A.

- When taking inventory, actually look inside your spice cans and canisters to determine how much you have. Don't make the mistake of assuming that you have plenty just to end up short on Assembly Day!
- Whether you are cooking alone or with others, take the "Pantry Challenge". You will save money and space if you use up what you have first rather than re-buying things you already have.
- Make sure to take inventory of non-food items that you will need too. Freezer bags, rigid containers, trash bags, dish soap, and disinfectants are all things you may find that you need to purchase for Cooking Day.

Mini-step #4 - Tally up your needed ingredients and subtract your inventory using Worksheet A.

Mini-step #5 - Make a shopping list by recording those totals on Worksheet C.

Tips to Plan Your Shopping:

- Write in the total pounds, ounces, cups, etc. of each item. For example, canned whole tomatoes are sold by the ounce. Rather than writing "6/28 ounce cans", write "whole canned tomatoes/168 oz." By doing this, you might see that you can buy one food service size can, meaning less time with the can opener. Take a hand-held calculator with you when you shop for making on-the-spot conversions.
- Use the Equivalency Charts on pages 219-221 to assist you in figuring totals.
- In the "other" column, include such things as freezer bags, foil, freezer labels, rubber gloves, trash bags, permanent markers, dish soap, and snacks and lunch for Assembly Day.
- Check your grocery advertisements and decide where to get what. Most grocery stores post their ads online which is an easy way to get the best price. It really pays to shop around, especially when buying large quantities. In our area, at least one of the chain stores is usually running chicken and beef on sale. Some stores have a price-matching policy which could save you time also.
- When you know what quantities you need, call the supermarket meat counter in advance and ask about quantity discounts, limits, and bulk packaging.
- The meat department will also grind special meats for you, mix different ground meats together thoroughly, slice large cuts, cube steaks and do many other helpful things. Just ask early enough to give them adequate time to fill your order.
- You can buy jars of chopped, minced, or pureed garlic in the produce section of your grocery store. This will save you a lot of "clove crushing".
- Buy frozen diced onions in the frozen vegetable case in the supermarket. This will spare you a lot of tears!

Ingredients	Purchase Measurement	Beef Stew	Wet Tacos	Meatball Pepper Penne	Roast Beef Sandwich	Total Needed	(-) On Hand	(=) To Buy
Meals for Cook #1		1	1	1	1			
Meals for Cook #2		1	1	1	1			
Ground Beef, Fresh	lb.		4	2		6		6
Cooked Ground Beef								
Stew Beef	lb.	2				2		2
Chuck Roast	lb.				4	4		4
Eggs	ea.			2		2	12	0
Margarine/Butter								
Sour Cream	oz.							
Mozzarella Cheese	c.			2		2		2
Cheddar Cheese	c.		6			6	2	4

Easy Step #1- Plan

Mini-step #6 - Choose the type of containers you will use.

Freezer bags.

If you don't have a lot of freezer space, bags can be a very efficient choice. Here are some freezer bag tips:

- Make sure that you purchase freezer bags and not food storage bags. The freezer bags really are designed for the job.
- Use a permanent marker to label the bags with the contents and date before putting food in the bag. Write simple cooking instructions on the bag. It will save you (or someone else if you're lucky) the hassle of searching for this book to make dinner.
- Bags should not be re-used unless they contain only breadcrumbs or other dry ingredients. Washing the bags in hot water doesn't ensure that you have killed all harmful bacteria. Seams and seals can also be weakened by washing. Who wants to take that chance?
- Don't put hot foods into freezer bags. Wait until they cool down.
- Foods with sharp bones like pork chops or steaks that might puncture a bag should be double bagged or frozen in rigid containers. Leaking bags make a big mess!
- A nine or ten inch pie or quiche dish will fit into most 1-gallon freezer bags. A 9x13x2 baking pan without handles will fit into a 2-gallon freezer bag as will many other shapes of baking dishes.
- Freeze your bags in thin, flat layers. Remove all possible air and then seal the bag. The air can be removed by a couple of methods.

The Squeegee Method:

Seal the bag from one corner to the other, leaving just a small opening at one end. Use the palm of your hand to work the air from the bottom of the bag to the top. Flatten the bag as you go. When all possible air is out, finish sealing the bag. This method works best for soft, formless foods like Mango Salsa (page 179), Broccoli Pesto Pasta (page 156), or Homestyle Macaroni & Cheese (page 151).

The Straw Method:

Place cooled food or a pan containing food in a freezer bag. Insert an ordinary drinking straw in one corner of the bag opening. Seal the bag from one corner all the way to the straw in the other corner. Pinch the straw and corner of the bag tightly together to keep air from escaping, then suck out the excess air. When the air is removed, quickly pull out the straw and finish sealing the bag. This method works with lumpy foods like chicken parts, fish fillets, steaks and chops. It also works well for foods frozen in the serving dish like lasagna, or baked quiche. It is very important that you do not touch the straw to raw meats, into marinades or sauces or into crumbs.

The Vacuum Sealer Method:

Vacuum sealers are great inventions. The lower priced sealers are only useful when you want to remove all possible air and form a vacuum (like a bag of chicken parts). To vacuum seal liquids (like soup or stew) you need to use the sealer that allows you to stop the suction and seal the bag.

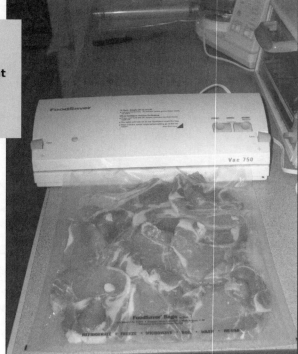

Vacuum sealers are a great option for freezer cooks!

Easy Step #1- Plan

Mini-step #6 - Choose the type of containers you will use.

Rigid plastic freezer containers

These are very common now and can be found at your local grocery or discount store. Rigid containers are great if you have a freezer with plenty of stacking space where they can be easily organized. Plastic containers can be re-used until they crack or the seal no longer fits tightly. Experiment with the different sizes offered. We like to use the individual serving sized containers for lunch items and frozen salads. The goal is to choose the size container that will keep you from thawing, cooking and/or serving and then re-freezing the leftovers.

Do not pour very hot or boiling foods into plastic containers. Cool the foods first and allow adequate space at the top of the container for expansion. About 1/2 inch of air at the top of a quart of liquids is plenty.

Freezer labels should be applied to your containers before freezing them. Good-sized labels can be hard to find. For that reason, we sell customized 30 Day Gourmet labels that can be ordered from our website. Our labels are 2"x3" – large enough for a title, date, quantity and directions. These labels become stronger in the freezer and revert to removable adhesive at room temperature. Don't even think of NOT labeling your foods. You do know that everything looks the same once it's frozen, don't you?

Glass and ceramic dishes

Combined or layered foods such as Spinach Lasagna (page 105) or Farmer's Breakfast Casserole (page 120) may be frozen in the dishes they will be cooked in and served from. When the food in the dish has cooled, it can be wrapped with freezer-weight foil or freezer paper or slid into a large freezer bag. The advantage of freezing in glass and ceramic is that you can freeze, defrost, bake and refrigerate all in the same container. This is convenient and cost effective. The one disadvantage is that dishes will take up more space in your freezer because they usually aren't uniform sizes. The other disadvantage, of course, is in not having enough dishes. Try garage sales, estate auctions and dollar stores. It won't take long to build up a supply.

Find the freezer container combination that works best for you.

Caution: Do not put a frozen glass or ceramic dish in a hot oven. You risk shattering your container but even worse losing your dinner! Thaw these foods in the refrigerator or microwave first.

Disposable or re-usable metal or foil pans

The disadvantage of foil pans is that they are generally fairly flimsy and may not stack well until completely and firmly frozen. They are great for one-time use and can come in handy for meals that you plan to freeze and give as a gift. Aluminum pans will also react chemically to highly acidic foods like tomato sauce and vinegar. You may not want to freeze lasagna or Italian casseroles in aluminum – the flavor may be affected and the pan may even be damaged.

Another option if you don't have many metal, glass or ceramic dishes is to use the "frozen block" trick. Line your baking dish with good quality plastic wrap or foil and leave a few inches extra on the edges. Assemble your cooled recipe ingredients on top of the wrap. Place the assembled recipe on a level surface in the freezer and allow it to freeze until firm. Remove the dish from the freezer and set it on the counter. Grasp the wrap with your hands and pop the firm block of food out of the dish. Either finish wrapping the food with more plastic wrap or foil, or place it inside a freezer bag.

There are as many freezer container options as there are foods that will freeze. Experiment a little and find the combination of containers that works best for you.

Easy Step #1- Plan

Mini-step #7 - Plan your prep work using Worksheet D.

Use the sample page below to help you decide what you want to try to accomplish before the Big Day arrives. If you are cooking with a partner, it helps to divide up the chores ahead of time. Writing down what each cook needs to bring is so helpful. Otherwise, the traveling cook will be standing in her kitchen trying to remember that last item that she said she would bring. Of course, she won't remember until 4 hours later when she is knee-deep in meatball mixture and remembers that she forgot her cookie scoop!

Worksheet D Sample

What To Do Before Assembly Day

Cook # 1	Cook # 2
Brown 5 lbs. of ground beef	Make 24 cups of white sauce
Dice all and celery	Cook 2 lbs. pasta
Dice 3 lbs. of ham	Brown 2 lbs. of ground pork and 2 lbs. sausage
Shred 1 lb. carrots	Cook and dice 10 lbs. of chicken breast
Cook all dry beans	Shred 1 lb. Swiss cheese
Steam all celery	Cook 24 oz. brown rice
Start one slow cooker meal the night before	Start one slow cooker meal the night before

What To Bring On Assembly Day

Cook # 1	Cook # 2
Large cookware	Large measuring cups
Long handled utensils	Cutting boards
Inventory and prep work foods	Inventory and prep work foods
Freezer bags	Freezer bags
Foil	Food processor
Slow cooker	Slow cooker
Cookie scoop	Coolers and cardboard boxes

Chopping green pepper and onion is one example of prep work that can be done the day before. All kinds of work can be done ahead of time!

Easy Step #2 - Shop

Before you go shopping

- Clean out your refrigerator and freezer. You will need as much room as possible for the many groceries you will be bringing home. You should not leave perishable ingredients at room temperature for more than two hours.
- Be sure you allow yourself enough time to get the job done. It's much easier to do it all at once than to go out 4 different times.

When to go shopping

- Although you can stock up on non-perishable items all month long as you watch for sales, the perishable groceries and meats that you want to start with fresh should be purchased no more than 2 or 3 days before Assembly Day.
- Be sure to leave yourself enough time to get your prep work done. If you decide to shop the evening before Assembly Day, then just know that you may end up being on your feet for what seems like 3 days straight!

More Shopping Day Tips:

- Buying your food items in large quantities may save you some money and the time it takes opening, using, and throwing away many small cans or jars. We look for items like Worcestershire sauce, vinegar, soy sauce, and cooking oil in 1-gallon containers.
- If you are cooking with a partner, organize your groceries as you put them on the belt and separate them by "what goes where". Each cook has her own "to do" list before Assembly Day (Worksheet D). Having each cook's ingredients in separated bags or boxes is very helpful.
- Grocers will sometimes waive the limits on advertised specials if you order large quantities and call 3-4 days in advance of when you need to pick them up.
- Try to put refrigerated and frozen items in your cart last, so they stay cold longer.
- Be sure to check expiration dates.
- Don't purchase dented canned goods.

What to take when you shop

Wear comfortable clothing and take the following:

- Tally Sheet (*Worksheet A*)
- Shopping List (*Worksheet C*)
- Prep Work List (*Worksheet D*)
- Coolers during warm weather
- Adequate cash, checks or credit cards
- Calculator
- Store advertisements
- Extra bags and boxes
- Sense of humor

Planning ahead is the key to saving time and money on Assembly Day.

Easy Step #2 - Prep

The more prep work you get done before Assembly Day, the better!

Divide these pre-Assembly Day chores among all of the cooks. If you are cooking solo, enlist some help from the family.

- Skin chicken parts
- Cook and drain pasta
- Make coatings for chicken parts
- Start slow cooker meals
- Chop and steam vegetables
- Brown ground meats
- Dice or grind ham
- Make sauces
- Cook and dice poultry
- Soak and cook dry beans

As you go, try to separate the items for each recipe into its own bag. For example, all the boneless skinless chicken breasts for the chicken fingers go into one bag, and all the boneless skinless chicken breasts for marinades go into another bag. This will keep you from using up too much chicken breast in the first recipe and not having enough for the next one.

To be honest, there will be some Assembly Days when you will start with very few of these things done. It will make for a much longer Assembly Day, but it was better than not cooking at all. Don't be too hard on yourself.

It also helps to explain what you are about to embark on to your family and friends. They need to know that this will require a big time commitment from you, but that the results will be worth it. Go over your cooking week schedule with them and ask them to help you with tasks like carrying in groceries, caring for small children, and helping with simple meal preparations while you do other important tasks to get ready for Assembly Day (it is okay to send them out to eat).

If you are traveling to a cooking partner's house:

- Put as much "stuff" in your vehicle the night before as possible.
- Gather your worksheets and cookbook and put them in a prominent place.
- Turn your freezer to its coldest temperature in readiness for the foods you will bring home.
- Arrange your freezer to accommodate the new foods.

If you are hosting the Assembly Day:

- Remove all unneeded items from your kitchen counters and work spaces.
- Empty your trash and have a large empty trash container for each cook on hand.
- Set out your mixing bowls, pans, utensils, etc.
- Turn your freezer to its coldest temperature.
- Arrange your freezer to accommodate the new foods you will put into it.
- Line all work spaces with several layers of clean newsprint. This is a big help with clean-up tasks.
- As you drip or spill on it, just roll up that layer and discard it.

Clean out your refrigerator (and freezer) BEFORE you go shopping!

Easy Step #2 - Prep

Your Assembly Day will go better if you take the time to get these items out the night before. The following are the kitchen items that we consider to be the "essentials".

Long handled utensils:
Forks
Slotted spoons
Ladles
Wire whisks
Tongs
Metal/Rubber spatulas

Large containers for mixing:
Dish pans with flat bottoms
Mixing bowls
Water bath canners

Cookware and bakeware:
Two large rimmed baking sheets
Two 9"x13"x2" baking pans
One or two 2-quart glass dishes
One paring knife
One chopping knife
One slicing knife
Two sets of standard measuring cups
Two sets of standard measuring spoons
One deep, covered pan or one stockpot
One cutting board
One large 12" skillet with a lid
One 2-quart covered saucepan
One colander (large strainer)
Two oven mitts
Two pot holders
One kitchen timer
One 2-cup glass measure

Items that are great to have:
Microwaveable containers
Mixing bowls with handles and spouts
Extra kitchen timers
Electric hand mixer
Large, lidded containers for marinating
Electric stand mixer
Large-sized sets of measuring cups
Electric can opener
Electric skillets/hot plates
Food processor or blender
Spring mechanism cookie scoops
Slow cooker
Large electric roasting pans
Large pastry brush
4-cup glass measure
Bulb baster
Plastic whisk for non-stick pans
Grilling utensils
Zester
Kitchen scale

Assembly Day "must haves"

Easy Step #3 - Assemble

Assembly Day Procedures

Cooks attempting to assemble 30 entrées should plan on an 8-10 hour day although we have heard from several people using our system who work much faster. On the IDEAL Assembly Day, you will have no kids to watch, no lunch to fix, and nowhere to be that night. On REAL Assembly Days, you may have a sick child, nothing for lunch, and three evening meetings you are expected to attend. Don't get frustrated striving for perfection. No one has the perfect cooking partner, mate, kids, or schedule. Be flexible. You'll live longer!

- **Post your Tally Sheet (Worksheet A) in a prominent place.**
  A kitchen desktop or hanging clip is ideal. You will refer to it throughout the day. It's the only place where you have written down the recipe titles and how many you intend to assemble of each.

- **Organize your recipes.**
  Take a few minutes to organize your recipes. Group them by type. Chicken, Beef, Side Dishes, etc. Then sort them by which one needs to be started first. If you are making Pork Wellington, the recipe calls for you to allow the meat to rest for 15 minutes and then to refrigerate it for an hour. Best to do that first! Then get that slow cooker recipe started. We like to start with a few "quick" recipes. It gives us an early feeling of accomplishment and some extra storage space in our refrigerators.

- **Finish your prep work.**
  If you didn't finish all of your prep work (or do anything ahead of time), get out Worksheet D and see if there are things that you should do now. If the White Sauce that you will use in 3 recipes hasn't been made, you'll want to do that now rather than in the middle of the first recipe that calls for it. Same with chopping veggies or boiling and dicing poultry or browning ground beef. Get it done first thing.

- **Begin assembling entrées.**
  Our method is simple. Work one type at a time, one recipe at a time. Start with the chicken, then do the beef, then do the rest. If you are cooking with a partner, one cook does the chicken, the other does the beef, and then share the remaining recipes. The chance of cross-contamination from meats is greatly reduced this way because you are not switching back and forth between raw meats. Take your first recipe and check the Tally Sheet (Worksheet A) to see how many of that recipe needs to be made. Follow the appropriate column on the recipe and begins assembling the ingredients. If you are cooking with a partner, assemble enough of the recipe for your own AND the other cook's entrées. Time is saved by stirring it all up at once! Obviously, there may be times when you will start a new recipe before finishing the last one. If you are waiting for something to bake, don't use that time to watch a 30-minute television show because the rules say "one recipe at a time". The point is – don't have 8 recipes going at once. You'll drive yourself nuts.

- **Cool and package the recipe.**
  Attempt to get your entrées assembled, cooled, packaged, and frozen *as quickly as possible*. Besides the sense of accomplishment, the quality of the food is better because you have gotten it into the freezer as *quickly as possible*.

Save time by piping your cheese filling. Clip the corner of a freezer bag and forget the spoon.

Choose the right size container for your family. Plan for company meals too!

Easy Step #3 - Assemble

Assembly Day Tips

Start time consuming, slow cooking, or marinating foods early.

- Remember to assemble in large quantities. For example, do not assemble each Breakfast Quiche (page 119) individually. Combine the ingredients for all of the quiche at the same time and distribute the ingredients equally. This will save lots of time!
- Think about which days are your busiest and pre-cook a few items for those days. They will only need a quick warm-up.

Line baking sheets with foil between each batch of a recipe like Meatballs and Pepper Penne (page 49) for easier clean up.

- Use as few pots, pans, and utensils as possible and wash well between recipes. This makes clean up easier and forces you to wash your hands several times during the day.
- Leave perishable ingredients in the refrigerator until they are needed. This can be difficult when making large quantities. In the winter, you may be able to use your porch or garage. Coolers with ice packs might do the trick.

- Look at what's taking up the most space and try to use up those items first.
- Choose your freezer container sizes wisely. Portion your recipes down into what will be eaten at one time. This will cut down on leftovers and food waste.
- Wear good supportive shoes.
- Tall kitchen stools allow you to sit and work at the same time.
- Use a LARGE trashcan! If you are cooking with a partner, use two. None of this cute, little trashcan under the sink stuff.
- Let your voice mail do its job. Answering the phone chews up too much time!
- Hire a babysitter for the children, or better yet, trade childcare with another 30 Day Gourmet!
- If children must be on the premises, keep them happy! Check out some new books and DVDs. Set up a self-serve snack table.
- Wear an apron. Having a couple of pockets for your marking pen and labels is very handy.

Cover all of your work surfaces with several sheets of clean newsprint to catch spills and drips.

- Take a lunch break and enjoy a couple of snacks throughout the day to keep your energy level up.
- Remember to stop and admire your work occasionally. You are accomplishing great things!

Easy Step #3 - Freeze

Freezing Info

- Fill out your Recipe Inventory Checklist (Worksheet E) as you put your foods into the freezer. Don't think that you will fill it out later. Sometimes what's on the Tally Sheet (Worksheet A) doesn't exactly match what you actually have because you might portion one recipe down into 3 containers.

- Use bags and containers designed for the freezer. If the bag or container isn't labeled as being suitable for freezer use, then it probably isn't.

Label bags and containers before filling them. Some markers and labels won't adhere to warm or cold surfaces.

- Label all foods clearly. Many foods look the same when frozen. When cooking with a partner, initial each container of food or designate separate shelves so they are easy to divide later.

- Packaging foods in thin, flat freezer bags or in small, flatter rigid containers will help them freeze faster and will help to protect the flavor, color, moisture content, and nutritional value of your foods.

- Keep your freezer temperature at 0 degrees F. or colder and keep the door shut as much as possible to maintain top quality. Do not attempt to save energy by raising the temperature of frozen food storage above 0 degrees F.

- Temperatures that fluctuate up and down cause the ice in foods to thaw slightly and then refreeze. Each time this happens, small ice crystals become larger and you lose quality. The food is still safe to eat; it may just lose some texture and/or taste.

- If your family opens your freezer often for ice cream, popsicles, or convenience foods, consider storing those foods in your refrigerator's freezer and saving your extra freezer for your 30 Day Gourmet foods. The opposite plan will work too.

- Don't try to freeze hot or warm foods. It will make your freezer work less efficiently and cause ice crystals to form all over your food. Cool foods before packaging them.

- If you have trouble getting your food to freeze quickly, you may be trying to put too much in at one time. Leave some of your foods in the refrigerator overnight and add them when the other food is frozen.

Spread your freezer foods out as much as possible so that the air can circulate freely. This will freeze the foods more quickly. Once the food is frozen, packages can be restacked closer together.

Easy Step #3 - Freeze

Freezing Q & A's

What foods can I freeze?

Almost all foods can be frozen. Some, though, won't taste as good after they have been defrosted. Foods that you should never try to freeze are: food in cans, eggs in shells, lettuce, tomatoes, potatoes, radishes, cucumbers, green onion (See page 21 for more specific information). Foods that freeze fine mixed into a recipe, but not alone are: sour cream, mayonnaise, cream cheese and cottage cheese.

How long can I keep food in the freezer?

Food stored constantly at 0 degrees F. will always be safe. Only the quality suffers with lengthy freezer storage. Freezing preserves food for extended periods because it prevents the growth of microorganisms that cause both food spoilage and food borne illness. Refer to the Freezing Time Chart on page 222 for a specific list of foods and their freezer life.

Can frozen food taste as "fresh" as food cooked without freezing?

Yes, definitely. Freshness and quality at the time of freezing can affect the taste after defrosting. Freeze foods at their peak quality. Freezing foods at 0 degrees F. or lower retains vitamin content, color, flavor and texture. More than anything, proper packaging affects the long term quality of frozen foods.

What's the safest and easiest way to defrost foods?

The three safe ways to defrost foods are in the refrigerator, in cold water or in the microwave. Don't thaw foods on the kitchen counter or outdoors. These methods can leave your foods unsafe to eat.

What is freezer burn and how can I avoid it?

Freezer burn appears as grayish-brown leathery spots on your foods and is caused by air reaching the surface of the food. It doesn't make your food unsafe to eat. Cut freezer-burned portions away. Heavily freezer-burned foods should be discarded for quality reasons.

If my meat changes color in the freezer, it is "bad"?

Color changes occur in frozen foods. The bright red color of meat as purchased usually turns dark or pale brown depending on its variety. Freezing doesn't usually cause color changes in poultry although the bones and the meat near them can become dark. The dulling of color in frozen vegetables and cooked foods is usually the result of excessive drying due to improper packaging or lengthy storage. None of these color changes means that the food is "bad". Food doesn't become unsafe in the freezer.

Is it okay to freeze meats in their grocery store wrapping?

Yes, but this type of wrap is permeable to air. If you won't be using the meat within a month, it's best to over wrap or re-package the meat using heavy duty foil, rigid freezer containers or freezer bags. It isn't necessary to rinse meat and poultry before freezing. Freeze unopened vacuum packages "as is".

What is flash freezing?

Flash freezing or open freezing is when you need to get the food "firmed up" before you package it for long term storage. It usually involves fragile foods that might crush or casseroles that you want to freeze and then "pop out" of their pan and transfer to freezer bags. When you flash freeze or open freeze you can just stick the pan, etc. in the freezer without covering the food. Once it's firm then you pull it out and package it.

Can I re-freeze foods once they have thawed?

According to the USDA, if food has been thawed in the refrigerator, it is safe to refreeze it without cooking although there may be a loss of quality due to the moisture lost during defrosting. This rule only applies if the thawed food has constantly been kept cold.

Can I take my meals straight from the freezer to the oven?

Yes, just increase the cooking time by half. Be careful about putting frozen glass dishes into a hot oven!

Easy Step #3 - Freeze

Fill out the Recipe Inventory Checklist

(Worksheet E) as you put your labeled entrées into the freezer. If you make more than 18 recipes, use two inventory checklists. As you prepare your entrées for the freezer, fill in one of these checklists (sometimes you end up with more than you planned). Put your list on the freezer door (or some equally conspicuous place).

Directions:

Place a slash mark in one box for each recipe as it goes into the freezer (this way you can always know how many total recipes you have.) Fill in any ingredients that you will need to purchase or have on hand to serve with each recipe. You may also make a note of an recipe you need to save for a special occasion. As you remove a recipe from the freezer to serve it, cross it off the list.

Worksheet E Sample

RECIPE INVENTORY CHECKLIST							
Date_____							
# Of Recipes Stored					Recipe	Needed on hand for serving	
/	/	X			Taco Chili	Shredded cheese, sour cream, rolls or bread	
/	X	X			Italian Roast Beef Sandwiches	Sandwich buns, condiments	
/	X	X			Chicken Snack Wraps	Lettuce, shredded cheddar cheese, Ranch dressing	
/	/				Oven Crisp Chicken Fingers	Dips	
/	/	X			Mediterranean Gourmet Burgers	Spinach leaves, provolone or mozzarella cheese, portobello mushrooms, hamburger buns	
/	X				Tuscan White Bean Soup	Zucchini, fresh spinach, canned diced tomatoes, shredded Parmesan cheese	
X	X				Pork Wellington	Egg	
/	X				Cheese-Filled Shells	Spaghetti or marinara sauce, grated parmesan cheese	

Easy Step #3 - Freeze

Clean Up and Evaluate

Leaving yourself some time for cleanup is a good idea. It may take longer than you think, especially if you have not lined your work surfaces with newsprint or limited yourself on the amount of cookware you used. Depending upon the length of your cooking session, your feet may be aching and might be a bit slap-happy, but knowing that you have so much food prepared and stashed in your freezer will feel great! Don't be surprised if you do not want to eat them for a few days and keep opening up your freezer door just to marvel and smile!

Try to do a quick evaluation of what went right and wrong. How did it go? What will you do differently next time? Writing your observations on paper will really help you for your next Assembly Day. Be sure to write changes you would like to make on the recipes also. Save your worksheets from each of your cooking adventures. You'll be surprised at how handy this information will be later on.

Read through the planning section occasionally to remind yourself of procedures and tips. You may discover some information that you missed the first time through! Be sure to check out the Appendix section of this book for helpful information on food safety, safe thawing practices, and much, much more.

Worksheet F Sample

This Monthly Menu Planner can be a great help in planning out your daily meals. Use your Recipe Inventory Sheet and your family calendar to help you plan. Remember, being a successful 30 Day Gourmet doesn't mean eating out of the freezer every single night. If you always eat out on Friday nights and have dinner with your parents on Sundays, write it in. Fill in the dates and make notes of what you want to serve on the especially busy days. Also make note of company meals and what you plan to serve. Some cooks like to assign a meal category to each day of the week. **Sunday** – slow cooker, **Monday** – Beef, **Tuesday** – Chicken, **Wednesday** – Soup & Sandwiches, **Thursday** – Fish or Pork, **Saturday** – leftovers. Thinking ahead a bit will keep you from using up all of your "fast foods" early in the month or spending the last 5 days before your next Assembly Day eating the same two entrees. Again, do whatever works for you!

Give yourself a hand! You just planned, shopped, prepared, assembled, packaged, labeled and froze a bunch of great foods for your family. Whew! Take a deep breath and relax. Tomorrow you will begin to enjoy all the benefits of being a 30 Day Gourmet.

Sunday	Monday	Tuesday	Wednesday	Thursday	Friday	Saturday
	Ballet at 4:30 Chicken Fingers Garlic Smashed Red Potatoes Jell-O & carrots	**Soccer at 4:30** Taco Chili Salad Peaches	**Choir at 7:00** Beef Sandwiches Buns Oven Fries Green Beans	**Soccer at 4:00** Parmesan Crusted Tilapia Rice Carrot Salad Mixed Fruit	Pecan Crusted Chicken Baked Potatoes Broccoli Canned Pears	Lasagna Spinach Salad Breadsticks Fruit Salad
Church 7:00 Oriental Sesame Chicken Strips Stir Fry Veggies Yogurt Fruit Snack Cups Cookies	**Ballet at 4:30** Smoky Boneless Ribs Home Fries Slaw Apple Salad	**Soccer at 4:30** Pizza Dinner W/team in town	**Choir at 7:00** Swiss Steak Noodles	**Soccer at 4:00** Chicken Broccoli Fettuccine Broccoli Salad Orange Salad	Grilled Chicken Corn Casserole Grilled Veggies	**Soccer game** Dinner with Mom & Dad

That's it! You're done! Congratulations and welcome to 30 Day Gourmet cooking!

Planning Worksheets

Ingredients	Purchase Measurement	Meatball Penne Pasta	Master Meat Mix	Parsley Parm. Chicken	Chicken Noodle Soup	Chicken Cordon Bleu	Oriental Chicken	Farmer's Breakfast	Parmesan Tilapia	Easy Marinade	Cheese-Filled Shells			Total Needed	(-) On Hand	(=) To Buy
Meals for Cook #1		2	3	2	2	2	2	2	2	2	1			20		
Meals for Cook #2																
Beef — Ground Beef, Fresh	lb.	2	4.5											6.5	0	6.5
Cooked Ground Beef	C.															
Chicken — Boneless Chicken Breast	ea.			8	6	8	8							30	8	22
Cooked, Diced Chicken	C.															
Pork — Ground Pork	lb.															
Ham	lb.															
Sausage	lb.							1						1	0	1
Bacon	slice															
Pork Loin Chops	ea.									8				8	0	8
Fish — Frozen Fillets	lb.								2					2	0	2
Fresh Fillets																

Your 30 Day Gourmet worksheets will make the job a breeze!

- These worksheets can also be downloaded and printed from the Members' section of our website. Access info is available on page 3.

- This manual uses a special layflat binding which allows for easy copying.

- You will use these worksheets each time you cook so keep this set as a master copy.

- Make 5-10 copies at once. You know how quickly time flies by!

- Please ONLY make copies for yourself. When your friends start begging for your organizational secrets, give them our website address. Thanks!

- If you're thinking - there must be a software program that will do all of this "figuring" – you're right! Our 30 Day Gourmet Advantage Software has the functionality to replace most of these worksheets. You can use the included recipes, import recipes from the 30 Day Gourmet web site, or easily add your own recipes. Group them together based on how you cook. Once you've selected which recipes you want to make, the 30 Day Gourmet Advantage Software quickly gives you a detailed shopping list. Use the variety of reports offered. Check the Container Report to make sure you have the freezer bags and containers you need. Run a Recipe Report for a list of everything you plan to make. Print an Action Report so you know what to chop, dice, fry, grate, bake, etc. The Appliance Report tells you which recipes need the slow cooker, the oven or the microwave to help you work efficiently. Don't be without the best software for freezer cooking! Check it out at www.30daygourmet.com

Worksheet A - Tally Sheet

Ingredients	Purchase Measurement	Recipes														Total Needed	(-) On Hand	(=) To Buy
Meals for Cook #1																		
Meals for Cook #2																		
Beef — Ground Beef, Fresh																		
Cooked Ground Beef																		
Chicken — Boneless Chicken Breast																		
Cooked, Diced Chicken																		
Turkey — Ground Turkey																		
Turkey Breast																		
Pork — Ground Pork																		
Ham																		
Sausage																		
Bacon																		
Fish — Frozen Fillets																		
Fresh Fillets																		
Frozen — Frozen Broccoli																		
Frozen Corn																		
Frozen Peas																		
Dairy — Eggs																		
Margarine/Butter																		
Sour Cream																		

Worksheet A - Tally Sheet

Ingredients	Purchase Measurement	Recipes											Total Needed	(-) On Hand	(=) To Buy
Meals for Cook #1															
Meals for Cook #2															
Canned Goods															
Canned, Diced Tomatoes															
Spaghetti Sauce															
Pasta															
Onions															
Green Peppers															
Flour															
Oil															
Ketchup															

(Row groups, top to bottom: Canned Goods; Grains, Pasta, Beans, Bread; Fresh Produce; Staples - Spices)

Planning Worksheets

WORKSHEET B
Recipe Worksheet

CATEGORY:_____

Recipe:_____

Recipes:	1	2	3	4	5	6
Servings/Makes						
Ingredients:						

Assembly Directions:

Freezing Directions:

Serving Directions:

Notes:

Planning Worksheets

WORKSHEET C – SHOPPING LIST

BEEF	CANNED GOODS	FROZEN FOODS	OILS
CHICKEN			**MIXES**
TURKEY		**FRESH PRODUCE**	**STAPLES**
PORK	**GRAINS**		
FISH	**PASTA**		
DAIRY	**BREADS**	**SPICES**	**MISCELLANEOUS**

Planning Worksheets

What To Do Before Assembly Day

Cook #1	Cook #2

What To Bring On Assembly Day

Cook # 1	Cook #2

Planning Worksheets

Recipe Inventory Checklist		
Date_____		
# Of Recipes Stored	Recipe	Needed On-Hand For Serving

Be sure to place a slash in a box as a recipe goes into the freezer, then cross one off as it comes out to be served. You can use this list for foods other than your **30 Day Gourmet** recipes to help you keep track of what might be lurking in the back corner!

Planning Worksheets

MONTHLY MENU PLANNER – WORKSHEET F   **MONTH**

Saturday					
Friday					
Thursday					
Wednesday					
Tuesday					
Monday					
Sunday					

Beef Recipes

Beef Recipes

TIPS FOR BEEF RECIPES

Yields

- One pound of fresh ground beef will yield approximately 2-1/2 cups of browned beef.
- 1/4 pound of fresh beef is considered to be a standard serving.
- 2 ounces of lean red meat is considered to be a standard serving.

Shopping & Cooking Tips

- When shopping, pick up beef just before checking out. Only put refrigerated beef in your cart if it's very cold. Frozen beef should be solid. If it will take longer than 30 minutes to get your purchase home, keep your beef in a cooler.
- According to the USDA, you may refreeze raw beef as long as it has been thawed in the refrigerator. This means that it's okay to purchase beef on sale, freeze it, thaw it, use it in a recipe in the raw form, and refreeze it. Just be sure not to leave it at room temperature for more than 2 hours.
- If you purchase meats on sale to save up for your next Assembly Day, you may want to re-package them in freezer bags. Grocery store packaging is permeable to air and isn't designed for long term storage.
- Purchase beef that is as fresh as possible. The quality will not improve in the freezer, so start with the best quality you can afford.
- Do you have problems choosing what meat to buy? Here are some general guidelines:
  Uncooked ground beef recipes: buy the best you can afford.
  Cooked ground beef recipes: Cheaper is okay. Drain and rinse if you want to lower the fat content.
  Stew beef recipes: Buy pre-cut and packaged for a faster prep time. If stew beef isn't on sale, you can check prices on any beef chuck or round cut (except top round) and cut it yourself or ask the butcher to cut it into chunks for you.
  Steaks: The more tender the cut, the better they will taste when cooked by dry-heat (grill, broil, stir-fry). The best tender steaks include top loin, T-Bone, Porterhouse, rib-eye and tenderloin. Less expensive but still tender steaks include shoulder center, top sirloin, top blade, chuck eye and round tip.
- Use a cookie scoop with a spring mechanism to form meatballs. Much quicker!
- Ground beef should be heated to a temperature of at least 160 degrees F to be considered safe to eat, no matter what kind of dish it is in or how it is prepared. Thoroughly cooked ground beef will have no pink left in the middle or in juices.
- Check out www.beefitswhatsfordinner.com for lots of great info on beef.

Healthy Tips

- Nutritional information for our ground beef recipes are based on using ground round which is 15% fat. For less fat in your recipes, you may choose ground sirloin (10% fat) or lean ground beef (8% fat).
- If you want to pay the cheaper prices for ground beef but have the benefits of less fat, try rinsing the fat off your cooked ground beef. Drain and discard the fat from your cooked ground beef. Then pour the beef into a colander and run hot water over it, until it is thoroughly rinsed. Continue running the hot water for awhile to keep the fat from clogging your pipes. Allow the water to drain well from the beef before using it in a recipe or packaging it for the freezer.
- Using the Drain and Rinse method will give you the same fat and caloric content as the leanest ground beef. Contrary to popular opinion, you don't lose so much weight with the fat that the cheaper beef isn't as "cost efficient".

Website Recipes & Tips

- For more great 30 Day Gourmet Beef recipes, check out the recipes section of our website at: www.30daygourmet.com
- For more Beef freezing tips and recipes from our cooks, check out our message boards at www.30daygourmet.com

Freeze your food in thin, flat layers for efficient stacking and thawing.

Lazy Day Lasagna

Recipes:	1	2	3	4	5	6
Servings:	12	24	36	48	60	72
Makes: 9x13 pan	1	2	3	4	5	6
Ingredients:						
Lowfat cottage cheese	12 oz.	24 oz.	36 oz.	48 oz.	60 oz.	72 oz.
Shredded mozzarella cheese[1]	2 C.	4 C.	6 C.	8 C.	10 C.	12 C.
Eggs	2	4	6	8	10	12
Chopped parsley	1/3 C.	2/3 C.	1 C.	1-1/3 C.	1-2/3 C.	2 C.
Onion powder	1 t.	2 t.	1 T.	1 T. + 1 t.	1 T. + 2 t.	2 T.
Dried basil leaves	1/2 t.	1 t.	1-1/2 t.	2 t.	2-1/2 t.	1 T.
Black pepper	1/8 t.	1/4 t.	3/8 t.	1/2 t.	1/2 t. + 1/8 t.	3/4 t.
Meatless spaghetti sauce	32 oz.	64 oz.	96 oz.	128 oz.	160 oz.	192 oz.
Cooked ground beef[2]	3/4 C.	1-1/2 C.	2-1/4 C.	3 C.	3-3/4 C.	4-1/2 C.
Uncooked lasagna noodles	9	18	27	36	45	54
Water[3]	3/4 C.	1-1/2 C.	2-1/4 C.	3 C.	3-3/4 C.	4-1/2 C.
On Hand:						
Grated Parmesan cheese						

Assembly Directions:

In a large bowl, mix cottage cheese, mozzarella cheese, eggs, parsley, onion powder, basil and pepper until well blended. Set aside. In a medium bowl, mix together spaghetti sauce and cooked ground beef. In a 9x13 glass baking dish, spread 3/4 C. meat sauce on the bottom. Layer 3 uncooked noodles on top of the meat sauce. Next spread 1/2 of cheese mixture and 1-1/2 C. meat sauce. Layer 3 more uncooked noodles on top of the meat sauce. Spread with remaining cheese mixture. Top with remaining 3 noodles and remaining meat sauce. Pour water around the outside edges.

Freezing Directions:

Place dish in a 2-gallon freezer bag. Or, if you want to wrap it in foil, cover the top of the lasagna with waxed paper or plastic wrap and then the foil, because the acid in the tomato sauce will leave small holes in the foil. Label, seal and freeze.

Serving Directions:

Remove pan from freezer and thaw at least overnight in the refrigerator. If the lasagna is wrapped in waxed paper or plastic wrap, remove it before baking. Cover with foil and bake at 375 degrees for 45 minutes. Uncover and bake an additional 15 minutes. Let stand 10 minutes. Serve with grated Parmesan cheese, if desired. To bake from the frozen state, add 30 minutes to the total baking time.

Notes:

[1] 8 oz. cheese = 2 C. shredded
[2] 1 lb. ground beef = 2-1/2 C. browned
[3] For firmer pasta, decrease the water to 1/2 C. per recipe.
One recipe can also be made in two 8x8 pans.

Nutritional Info:

Per Serving: 228 Calories; 8g Fat (31.3% calories from fat); 16g Protein; 23g Carbohydrate; 2g Dietary Fiber; 51mg Cholesterol; 574mg Sodium.
Exchanges: 1-1/2 Grain (Starch); 1-1/2 Lean Meat; 1/2 Fat.

Italian Roast Beef Sandwiches

Recipes:	1	2	3	4	5	6
Servings:	12	24	36	48	60	72
Makes:	4 C.	8 C.	12 C.	16 C.	20 C.	24 C.
Ingredients:						
Chuck roast, fat trimmed	2-1/2 lbs.	5 lbs.	7-1/2 lbs.	10 lbs.	12-1/2 lbs.	15 lbs.
Dry Italian salad dressing packets	2	4	6	8	10	12
Beef broth	1 C.	2 C.	3 C.	4 C.	5 C.	6 C.
Chopped onion[1]	2 C.	4 C.	6 C.	8 C.	10 C.	12 C.
Banana peppers, sliced in rings	4	8	12	16	20	24
On Hand:						
Hamburger buns	12	24	36	48	60	72

Assembly Directions:
In a cold slow cooker, place the thawed or fresh roast. Pour the contents of the salad dressing packets over the meat. Pour the beef broth over all. Add the chopped onion and sliced banana peppers. Cover slow cooker with lid. Can be cooked overnight on low heat or 6 hours on high heat until meat shreds easily with a fork. When done, turn off slow cooker and uncover it to cool quickly. If you wish, the filling is now ready to eat.

Freezing Directions:
When cooled, place meat and juice in a freezer bag or container. Seal, label, and freeze.

Serving Directions:
Thaw and heat in a microwave or saucepan over medium heat until warmed through. Serve over rolls or in buns.

Notes:
[1] 1 medium onion = 1 C. chopped

Roasts over 7-1/2 lbs. may not fit well in a slow cooker. Try to borrow an extra slow cooker if you choose to make more than 7-1/2 lbs. This is a large recipe and we divide each recipe in half for freezing purposes. About 1/4-1/3 C. of cooked meat is a serving.

For a different flavor, try using ranch dressing mix or onion soup mix packets instead of the Italian dressing mix. Each will give the recipe its own distinctive flavor.

BBQ Option: Substitute water for the beef broth and reduce the amount by half. Add 1 C. of barbecue sauce per recipe. Cook as directed. More barbecue can be added later to taste.

Nutritional Info: including bun
Per Serving: 343 Calories; 17g Fat (45.7% calories from fat); 20g Protein; 26g Carbohydrate; 2g Dietary Fiber; 55mg Cholesterol; 824mg Sodium.
Exchanges: 1-1/2 Grain (Starch); 2-1/2 Lean Meat; 1/2 Vegetable; 2 Fat.

Meatballs and Pepper Penne

Recipes:	1	2	3	4	5	6
Servings:	**6**	**12**	**18**	**24**	**30**	**36**
Ingredients:						
Ground beef	1 lb.	2 lbs.	3 lbs.	4 lbs.	5 lbs.	6 lbs.
Ketchup	2 T.	1/4 C.	1/4 C. + 2 T.	1/2 C.	1/2 C. + 2 T.	3/4 C.
Dry bread crumbs	2 T.	1/4 C.	1/4 C. + 2 T.	1/2 C.	1/2 C. + 2 T.	3/4 C.
Egg	1	2	3	4	5	6
Minced onion	1 T.	2 T.	3 T.	1/4 C.	1/4 C. + 1 T.	1/4 C. + 2 T.
Garlic powder	1/4 t.	1/2 t.	3/4 t.	1 t.	1-1/4 t.	1-1/2 t.
Black pepper	1/4 t.	1/2 t.	3/4 t.	1 t.	1-1/4 t.	1-1/2 t.
Penne pasta	8 oz.	16 oz.	24 oz.	32 oz.	40 oz.	48 oz.
Chopped onion[1]	1 C.	2 C.	3 C.	4 C.	5 C.	6 C.
Chopped green pepper[2]	1 C.	2 C.	3 C.	4 C.	5 C.	6 C.
Zucchini, chopped	1	2	3	4	5	6
Canola oil	2 t.	1 T. + 1 t.	2 T.	2 T. + 2 t.	3 T. + 1 t.	4 T.
Canned diced tomatoes, low sodium	14.5 oz.	29 oz.	43.5 oz.	58 oz.	72.5 oz.	87 oz.
Tomato sauce	16 oz.	32 oz.	48 oz.	64 oz.	80 oz.	96 oz.
Italian seasoning	1 t.	2 t.	1 T.	1 T. + 1 t.	1 T. + 2 t.	2 T.
Minced garlic	1 t.	2 t.	1 T.	1 T. + 1 t.	1 T. + 2 t.	2 T.
On Hand:						
Shredded mozzarella cheese[3]	1 C.	2 C.	3 C.	4 C.	5 C.	6 C.

Assembly Directions:

Preheat oven to 350 degrees. In a large bowl, mix ground beef, ketchup, bread crumbs, egg, onion, garlic powder and black pepper until thoroughly combined. Shape into 1 to 1-1/2 inch meatballs. Line a baking sheet with aluminum foil. Place meatballs on lined sheet and bake for 25 minutes. While meatballs are baking, boil the pasta about 10-12 minutes. The pasta should be firm. Drain pasta and allow to dry and cool. Sauté onion, pepper and zucchini in oil until onions are translucent. Add tomatoes, tomato sauce, Italian seasoning, and garlic. Bring to a boil and cook for 10 minutes. Remove from heat and add meatballs.

Freezing Directions:

When the meatball mixture is cool, portion it into gallon freezer bags or containers. Divide the pasta evenly between gallon freezer bags. Seal, label, and freeze.

Serving Directions:

Thaw the meatball mixture and pasta. Preheat the oven to 350 degrees. Spray a 9x13 pan with cooking spray. Add pasta, meatball mixture and cheese. Stir to combine. Cover with foil and bake for 25 to 30 minutes or until bubbly.

Notes:

[1] 1 medium onion = 1 C. chopped   [2] 1 large green pepper = 1 C. chopped
[3] 8 oz. cheese = 2 C. shredded

Nutritional Info:

Per Serving: 442 Calories; 16g Fat (33.1% calories from fat); 30g Protein; 44g Carbohydrate; 4g Dietary Fiber; 94mg Cholesterol; 698mg Sodium.
Exchanges: 2 Grain (Starch); 3 Lean Meat; 2 Vegetable; 1-1/2 Fat.

Spanish Flank Steak

Recipes:	1	2	3	4	5	6
Servings:	4	8	12	16	20	24
Ingredients:						
Flank steak	1-1/4 lbs.	2-1/2 lbs.	3-3/4 lbs.	5 lbs.	6-1/4 lbs.	7-1/2 lbs.
Spicy brown mustard	1-1/2 t.	1 T.	1 T. + 1-1/2 t.	2 T.	2 T. + 1-1/2 t.	3 T.
Red wine vinegar	3 T.	1/4 C. + 2 T.	1/2 C. + 1 T.	3/4 C.	3/4 C. + 3 T.	1 C. + 2 T.
Sugar	1/2 t.	1 t.	1-1/2 t.	2 t.	2-1/2 t.	1 T.
Canola oil	1/4 C.	1/2 C.	3/4 C.	1 C.	1-1/4 C.	1-1/2 C.
Minced garlic	1/2 t.	1 t.	1-1/2 t.	2 t.	2-1/2 t.	1 T.
Dried parsley	1 t.	2 t.	1 t.	1 T. + 1 t.	1 T. + 2 t.	2 T.
Paprika	1 T.	2 T.	3 T.	1/4 C.	1/4 C. + 1 T.	1/4 C. + 2 T.
Ground coriander	1 t.	2 t.	1 t.	1 T. + 1 t.	1 T. + 2 t.	2 T.
Salt	1 t.	2 t.	1 t.	1 T. + 1 t.	1 T. + 2 t.	2 T.
Black pepper	1 t.	2 t.	1 t.	1 T. + 1 t.	1 T. + 2 t.	2 T.
Lime juice (optional)	2 T.	1/4 C.	1/4 C. + 2 T.	1/2 C.	1/2 C. + 2 T.	3/4 C.

Assembly Directions:

Place flank steak into one gallon freezer bags.

In a mixing bowl, combine mustard, vinegar, sugar, oil, spices and lime juice. Whisk until thoroughly combined.

Pour marinade over steak. One recipe will yield a little over 1/2 cup of marinade.

Freezing Directions:

Seal, label, and freeze.

Serving Directions:

Thaw at least overnight in the refrigerator.

Cook on grill: Coat grill rack with cooking spray. Preheat grill to medium high (about 400 degrees). Remove steak from marinade. Discard marinade. Grill steak 4 to 5 minutes on each side or until an instant-read thermometer reads at least 145 degrees for a medium rare steak. Remove from heat and allow to stand for 10 minutes. Slice steak thinly across the grain.

To broil: Boil the marinade for 10 minutes in a small saucepan prior to using. Move oven rack three to four inches from the broiler unit. Set the oven to broil. Set the marinated meat on a sturdy broiling pan with drip pan underneath. Baste meat with boiled marinade. Place pan in the oven. Crack the oven door. Broil 5 to 7 minutes. Use a fork to flip the meat. Baste meat with marinade. Broil other side 5 to 7 minutes. Remove from heat and allow to stand for 10 minutes. Slice steak thinly across the grain.

Notes:

This marinade has lots of flavor!

Nutritional Info:

Oil was not included in the nutritional analysis.
Per Serving: 267 Calories; 15g Fat (51.9% calories from fat); 28g Protein; 4g Carbohydrate; 1g Dietary Fiber; 72mg Cholesterol; 659mg Sodium.
Exchanges: 4 Lean Meat; 1 Fat.

Slow Smoky Brisket

Recipes:	1	2	3	4	5	6
Servings:	8	16	24	32	40	48
Ingredients:						
Beef brisket	3 lb.	6 lbs.	9 lbs.	12 lbs.	15 lbs.	18 lbs.
Liquid smoke	2 T.	1/4 C.	1/4 C. + 2 T.	1/2 C.	1/2 C. + 2 T.	3/4 C.
Reduced sodium soy sauce	2 T.	1/4 C.	1/4 C. + 2 T.	1/2 C.	1/2 C. + 2 T.	3/4 C.
Garlic powder	1 t.	2 t.	1 T.	1 T. + 1 t.	1 T. + 2 t.	2 T.
Finely minced celery[1]	1/4 C.	1/2 C.	3/4 C.	1 C.	1-1/4 C.	1-1/2 C.
Black pepper	1/2 t.	1 t.	1-1/2 t.	2 t.	2-1/2 t.	1 T.
Worcestershire sauce	1 T.	2 T.	3 T.	1/4 C.	1/4 C. + 1 T.	1/4 C. + 2 T.
Lemon juice	1 T.	2 T.	3 T.	1/4 C.	1/4 C. + 1 T.	1/4 C. + 2 T.
Onion powder	1 t.	2 t.	1 T.	1 T. + 1 t.	1 T. + 2 t.	2 T.

Assembly Directions:
Trim fat from brisket and place in a labeled gallon freezer bag. Add liquid smoke, soy sauce, garlic powder, celery, pepper, Worcestershire sauce, lemon juice, and onion powder to bag.

Freezing Directions:
Seal the freezer bag. Shake or press on the bag to mix the contents. Freeze.

Serving Directions:
Thaw at least overnight in the refrigerator.

Cook in a slow cooker: Place meat and sauce in a slow cooker. Cook on low for 8 to 10 hours or on high for 4 to 5 hours. Remove from cooker and slice meat across the grain.

Cook in oven: Preheat oven to 300 degrees. Place the meat and sauce in a roaster pan spooning some of the sauce over the top. Cover and bake for 4 hours, basting every hour until tender when pierced with a fork. If the sauce in the pan begins to boil rapidly while baking, reduce the oven temperature to 275 degrees.

Notes:
[1] 1 rib celery = 1/2 C. diced

This recipes smells wonderful as it cooks in the slow cooker. For a different flavor, serve it with your favorite barbecue sauce.

Nutritional Info:
Per Serving: 220 Calories; 11g Fat (46.0% calories from fat); 26g Protein; 3g Carbohydrate; trace Dietary Fiber; 78mg Cholesterol; 432mg Sodium.
Exchanges: 3-1/2 Lean Meat.

Wet Tacos

Recipes:	1	2	3	4	5	6
Servings:	**20**	**40**	**60**	**80**	**100**	**120**
Ingredients:						
Lean ground beef	2 lbs.	4 lbs.	6 lbs.	8 lbs.	10 lbs.	12 lbs.
Diced onion[1]	1 C.	2 C.	3 C.	4 C.	5 C.	6 C.
Ground cumin or chili powder	1 t.	2 t.	1 T.	1 T. + 1 t.	1 T. + 2 t.	2 T.
Salt and pepper, to taste						
Gringo Enchilada Sauce[2]	1 recipe	2 recipes	3 recipes	4 recipes	5 recipes	6 recipes
Chicken flavored Fat Free White Sauce[3]	1-1/2 C.	3 C.	4-1/2 C.	6 C.	7-1/2 C.	9 C.
Shredded sharp cheddar cheese[4]	1 C.	2 C.	3 C.	4 C.	5 C.	6 C.
6-inch flour tortillas	20	40	60	80	100	120
Shredded cheddar cheese[4]	2 C.	4 C.	6 C.	8 C.	10 C.	12 C.

Assembly Directions:

Brown meat and onions over medium heat. Drain fat from meat and discard. In a saucepan, whisk together the cumin, salt and pepper, Enchilada Sauce, White Sauce and sharp cheddar cheese. Heat over medium heat until cheese has melted. Do not boil. Warm the tortillas in the microwave or oven to soften. Add about 1 cup of sauce per recipe to the meat and onion mixture and thoroughly mix. Place about 1/4 cup of the meat mixture in the center of a tortilla and wrap burrito style.

Freezing Directions:

Place the burritos on a cookie sheet and flash freeze. Once the burritos are frozen, place them in gallon freezer bags in meal sized portions. Divide the sauce into meal sized portions, and place in a quart freezer bag. Place the cheese in a zippered sandwich or snack bag (depending on the size of the meal). Place the sealed sauce and cheese bags inside the burrito bag. Seal, label, and freeze.

Serving Directions:

Completely thaw the burritos, sauce and cheese. Spray a baking dish with cooking spray. Place burritos in the bottom of the dish. Cover with sauce and then cheese. Cover dish with aluminum foil and bake at 350 degrees for 30 minutes. Uncover the dish and bake for another 10 minutes.

Notes:

[1] 1 medium onion = 1 C. chopped
[2] The recipe for Gringo Enchilada Sauce can be found on page 167. Purchased enchilada sauce may be used instead.
[3] The recipe for Fat Free White Sauce can be found on page 161.
[4] 8 oz. cheese = 2 C. shredded

Nutritional Info:

Per Serving: 296 Calories; 15g Fat (45.8% calories from fat); 18g Protein; 22g Carbohydrate; 2g Dietary Fiber; 50mg Cholesterol; 405mg Sodium.
Exchanges: 1-1/2 Grain (Starch); 2 Lean Meat; 1/2 Vegetable; 1-1/2 Fat.

30 Day Gourmet © 2012

Italian Meatball Subs

Recipes:	1	2	3	4	5	6
Servings:	8	16	24	32	40	48
Ingredients:						
Lean ground beef	1 lb.	2 lbs.	3 lbs.	4 lbs.	5 lbs.	6 lbs.
Dry bread crumbs	1 C.	2 C.	3 C.	4 C.	5 C.	6 C.
Grated Parmesan cheese	1/2 C.	1 C.	1-1/2 C.	2 C.	2-1/2 C.	3 C.
Italian seasoning	1 t.	2 t.	1 T.	1 T. + 1 t.	1 T. + 2 t.	2 T.
Dried parsley	1 t.	2 t.	1 T.	1 T. + 1 t.	1 T. + 2 t.	2 T.
Minced garlic	1/2 t.	1 t.	1-1/2 t.	2 t.	2-1/2 t.	1 T.
Skim milk	1 C.	2 C.	3 C.	4 C.	5 C.	6 C.
Egg	1	2	3	4	5	6
Black pepper	1/2 t.	1 t.	1-1/2 t.	2 t.	2-1/2 t.	1 T.
Tomato puree	29 oz.	58 oz.	87 oz.	116 oz.	145 oz.	174 oz.
Crushed tomatoes	29 oz.	58 oz.	87 oz.	116 oz.	145 oz.	174 oz.
Sugar	1-1/2 t.	1 T.	1 T. + 1-1/2 t.	2 T.	2 T. + 1-1/2 t.	3 T.
Minced onion	2 T.	1/4 C.	1/4 C. + 2 T.	1/2 C.	1/2 C. + 2 T.	3/4 C.
Dried parsley	2 T.	1/4 C.	1/4 C. + 2 T.	1/2 C.	1/2 C. + 2 T.	3/4 C.
Italian seasoning	1-1/2 t.	1 T.	1 T. + 1-1/2 t.	2 T.	2 T. + 1-1/2 t.	3 T.
Garlic powder	1/4 t.	1/2 t.	3/4 t.	1 t.	1-1/4 t.	1-1/2 t.
On Hand Ingredients:						
Sub buns	8	16	24	32	40	48
Mozzarella cheese						

Assembly Directions:

Put the ground beef in a large bowl. Add the bread crumbs, Parmesan cheese, Italian seasoning, parsley, garlic, milk, egg, and pepper to the bowl. Use your hands or a large spoon to evenly combine. Set aside. In another large bowl, combine the tomato puree, crushed tomatoes, sugar, and remaining seasonings. Add salt and pepper as desired. Stir until well mixed. Put about 1/3 of the sauce mixture in the bottom of a 5 or 6 quart slow cooker. Form the meatballs from the raw meat mixture into the size you prefer. Put them in a layer in the sauce in the slow cooker. Add some sauce to cover the tops and sides of the meatballs. Add another layer of meatballs, and cover with more sauce. When all the meatballs are in the slow cooker, pour the rest of the sauce on, and cover. Cook on low for 8 hours or high for 4 hours. Turn slow cooker off and set aside to cool.

Freezing Directions:

Divide the meatballs and sauce into appropriate serving sizes for your family in freezer bags or rigid containers. Seal, label, and freeze.

Serving Directions:

Thaw meatballs and sauce. Put them in a saucepan and reheat on the stove-top. Put 3 to 4 meatballs and some sauce on a sub bun. Serve with optional shredded mozzarella cheese or provolone cheese on top, if desired.

Nutritional Info: including bun

Per Serving: 491 Calories; 15g Fat (28.2% calories from fat); 25g Protein; 62g Carbohydrate; 6g Dietary Fiber; 67mg Cholesterol; 894mg Sodium.
Exchanges: 3 Grain (Starch); 2 Lean Meat; 3 Vegetable; 2 Fat.

Make-Ahead Beef Chimichangas

Recipes:	1	2	3	4	5	6
Servings:	20	40	60	80	100	120
Ingredients:						
Cooked ground beef[1]	2-1/2 C.	5 C.	7-1/2 C.	10 C.	12-1/2 C.	15 C.
Salsa, as spicy as you like	16 oz.	32 oz.	48 oz.	64 oz.	80 oz.	96 oz.
Refried beans	16 oz.	32 oz.	48 oz.	64 oz.	80 oz.	96 oz.
Taco seasoning envelope	1	2	3	4	5	6
8" flour tortillas	20	40	60	80	100	120
Shredded cheddar cheese[2]	2 C.	4 C.	6 C.	8 C.	10 C.	12 C.

Assembly Directions:

In a pan, combine beef, salsa, beans and seasoning envelope. Cook and stir over medium heat until heated through. Heat a non-stick skillet on medium-low and spray with cooking spray. One at a time, put the tortillas in the skillet, heating for about 30 seconds on each side. Put 1/2 C. meat mixture on each heated tortilla and top with some cheese. Fold in the sides and then roll it up.

Freezing Directions:

Wrap each rolled tortilla in foil, plastic wrap or a sandwich bag. Put the individually wrapped Chimichangas in a freezer bag or rigid container. Seal, label, and freeze.

Serving Directions:

Remove the needed amount of Chimichangas from the freezer. If they're wrapped in plastic wrap or a bag, remove and discard the wrap/bag. If they're wrapped in foil, you can leave the foil on to reheat. Bake at 350 degrees for 30-40 minutes. Serve with sour cream, if desired.

Notes:

[1] 1 pound of ground beef = 2-1/2 C. browned
[2] 8 oz. cheese = 2 C. shredded

Vary this recipe based on your family's preference. Cooked, shredded chicken and Monterey Jack cheese taste great too. If you prefer a crispier shell, you can fry the Chimichangas instead of baking them.

Nutritional Info: baked not fried

Per Serving (excluding unknown items): 290 Calories; 11g Fat (33.2% calories from fat); 14g Protein; 34g Carbohydrate; 3g Dietary Fiber; 28mg Cholesterol; 643mg Sodium. Exchanges: 2 Grain(Starch); 1 Lean Meat; 1/2 Vegetable; 1-1/2 Fat; 0 Other Carbohydrates.

Mexican Egg Rolls

Recipes:	1	2	3	4	5	6
Makes:	21	42	63	84	105	126
Ingredients:						
Lean ground beef	1 lb.	2 lbs.	3 lbs.	4 lbs.	5 lbs.	6 lbs.
Onion, chopped[1]	1	2	3	4	5	6
Taco seasoning mix	1 packet	2 packets	3 packets	4 packets	5 packets	6 packets
Water	3/4 C.	1-1/2 C.	2-1/4 C.	3 C.	3-3/4 C.	4-1/2 C.
Shredded mozzarella cheese[2]	1-1/2 C.	3 C.	4-1/2 C.	6 C.	7-1/2 C.	9 C.
Shredded cheddar cheese[2]	1-1/2 C.	3 C.	4-1/2 C.	6 C.	7-1/2 C.	9 C.
Reduced fat sour cream	8 oz.	16 oz.	24 oz.	32 oz.	40 oz.	48 oz.
Canned chopped green chilies, drained	4 oz.	8 oz.	12 oz.	16 oz.	20 oz.	24 oz.
Egg roll wrappers	21	42	63	84	105	126
Egg white	1	2	3	4	5	6
Vegetable oil for frying						
Salsa and additional sour cream						

Assembly Directions:

In a skillet, cook beef and onion over medium heat until meat is no longer pink; drain. Stir in taco seasoning and water. Bring to a boil. Reduce heat. Simmer, uncovered, for 5 minutes, stirring occasionally. Remove from the heat. Cool slightly.

In a bowl, combine the cheeses, sour cream and chilies. Stir in beef mixture. Place an egg roll wrapper on work surface with one point facing you. Place 1/3 cup filling in center. Fold bottom third of wrapper over filling; fold in sides. Brush top point with egg white; roll up to seal. Repeat with remaining wrappers and filling. (Keep remaining egg roll wrappers covered with waxed paper to avoid drying out.)

In a large saucepan, heat 1 inch of oil to 375 degrees. Fry egg rolls for 1-1/2 minutes on each side or until golden brown. Drain on paper towels.

Freezing Directions:

Place frozen egg rolls on a baking sheet and place it in the freezer, uncovered, until firm. Remove and put them into freezer bags. Seal, label, and freeze.

Serving Directions:

Place egg rolls on a baking sheet. Bake at 425 degrees for 5 to 10 minutes or until hot inside.

Notes:

[1] 1 medium onion = 1 C. chopped
[2] 8 oz. cheese = 2 C. shredded

Try making a smaller version of these using wonton wrappers instead of egg roll wrappers. These make wonderful hors d'oeuvres that are great to have on hand for parties. If you want fresh egg rolls, another option is to freeze just the filling. Thaw the filling in time to fry the egg rolls on the day you are serving them.

Nutritional Info:

The oil for frying and the additional salsa and sour cream are not included in the nutritional analysis.
Per Serving: 207 Calories; 8g Fat (34.0% calories from fat); 13g Protein; 21g Carbohydrate; trace Dietary Fiber; 32mg Cholesterol; 405mg Sodium.
Exchanges: 1 Grain (Starch); 1-1/2 Lean Meat; 1 Fat.

Swiss Steak

Recipes:	1	2	3	4	5	6
Servings:	**6**	**12**	**18**	**24**	**30**	**36**
Ingredients:						
Flour	3 T.	1/4 C. + 2 T.	1/2 C. + 1 T.	3/4 C.	3/4 C. + 3 T.	1 C. + 2 T.
Salt	1/2 t.	1 t.	1-1/2 t.	2 t.	2-1/2 t.	1 T.
Dry mustard	1 t.	2 t.	1 T.	1 T. + 1 t.	1 T. + 2 t.	2 T.
Black pepper	1/4 t.	1/2 t.	3/4 t.	1 t.	1-1/4 t.	1-1/2 t.
Garlic powder	1 t.	2 t.	1 T.	1 T. + 1 t.	1 T. + 2 t.	2 T.
Cubed steak	1-1/2 lbs.	3 lbs.	4-1/2 lbs.	6 lbs.	7-1/2 lbs.	9 lbs.
Sliced mushrooms (optional)	8 oz.	16 oz.	24 oz.	32 oz.	40 oz.	48 oz.
Sliced onion[1]	1 C.	2 C.	3 C.	4 C.	5 C.	6 C.
Sliced celery[2]	1/2 C.	1 C.	1-1/2 C.	2 C.	2-1/2 C.	3 C.
Sliced carrots[3]	1 C.	2 C.	3 C.	4 C.	5 C.	6 C.
Worcestershire sauce	1 T.	2 T.	3 T.	1/4 C.	1/4 C. + 1 T.	1/4 C. + 2 T.
Beef broth	1/2 C.	1 C.	1-1/2 C.	2 C.	2-1/2 C.	3 C.
Canned diced tomatoes	14.5 oz.	29 oz.	43.5 oz.	58 oz.	72.5 oz.	87 oz.

Assembly Directions:

In a shallow bowl, mix the flour, salt, mustard, pepper and garlic powder. Coat the meat on both sides with the flour mixture and place in a gallon freezer bag or rigid container and set aside. Sauté or steam the mushrooms, onion, celery, and carrots until tender. Mix the sautéed vegetables with the Worcestershire sauce, broth and tomatoes. Put the sauce in a quart freezer bag or rigid container.

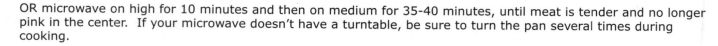

Freezing Directions:

Seal, label, and freeze both freezer bags or containers.

Serving Directions:

Thaw both bags or containers at least overnight in the refrigerator. This recipe can be baked in the oven, microwave or slow cooker. Spray a casserole dish with cooking spray. Put 1/2 C. sauce in the bottom of the dish, and alternate layers of meat and sauce, pouring all the extra sauce over the meat. Cover and bake at 350 degrees for 45-60 minutes, until meat is tender and no longer pink in the center.

OR microwave on high for 10 minutes and then on medium for 35-40 minutes, until meat is tender and no longer pink in the center. If your microwave doesn't have a turntable, be sure to turn the pan several times during cooking.

OR layer sauce and meat as above in the slow cooker and cook on low for 6-8 hours until the meat is tender and no longer pink in the center.

Notes:

[1] 1 medium onion = 1 C. sliced   [2] 1 rib celery = 1/2 C. sliced   [3] 2 carrots = 1 C. sliced

If your kids hate the veggies, either hide them by pureeing them in the blender/food processor or leave them in large, one-inch chunks that can be easily picked out. Serve over hot rice or noodles.

Nutritional Info:

Per Serving: 292 Calories; 16g Fat (50.5% calories from fat); 24g Protein; 11g Carbohydrate; 2g Dietary Fiber; 67mg Cholesterol; 482mg Sodium.
Exchanges: 3 Lean Meat; 1-1/2 Vegetable; 1-/2 Fat.

Adobo Lettuce Wraps

Recipes:	1	2	3	4	5	6
Servings:	**6**	**12**	**18**	**24**	**30**	**36**
Ingredients:						
Lean ground beef	1 lb.	2 lbs.	3 lbs.	4 lbs.	5 lbs.	6 lbs.
Salt	1-1/2 t.	1 T.	1 T. + 1-1/2 t.	2 T.	2 T. + 1-1/2 t.	3 T.
Onion powder	1 t.	2 t.	1 T.	1 T. + 1 t.	1 T. + 2 t.	2 T.
Garlic powder	1 t.	2 t.	1 T.	1 T. + 1 t.	1 T. + 2 t.	2 T.
Black pepper	1 t.	2 t.	1 T.	1 T. + 1 t.	1 T. + 2 t.	2 T.
Dried oregano	1/4 t.	1/2 t.	3/4 t.	1 t.	1-1/4 t.	1-1/2 t.
Chili powder	1/4 t.	1/2 t.	3/4 t.	1 t.	1-1/4 t.	1-1/2 t.
Cumin	1/4 t.	1/2 t.	3/4 t.	1 t.	1-1/4 t.	1-1/2 t.
On Hand:						
Bibb lettuce	2 heads	4 heads	6 heads	8 heads	10 heads	12 heads
Lime Rice[1]	2 C.	4 C.	6 C.	8 C.	10 C.	12 C.
Salsa						

Assembly Directions:
Break up beef in a frying pan and season with remaining ingredients. Brown beef and drain. Cool.

Freezing Directions:
When cooled, place meat in a freezer bag or container. Seal, label, and freeze.

Serving Directions:
Thaw meat mixture.

Reheat the meat in a microwave or saucepan over medium heat until warmed through. If using frozen Lime Rice, it will need to be thawed and reheated as well.

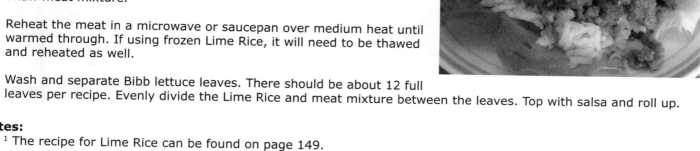

Wash and separate Bibb lettuce leaves. There should be about 12 full leaves per recipe. Evenly divide the Lime Rice and meat mixture between the leaves. Top with salsa and roll up.

Notes:
[1] The recipe for Lime Rice can be found on page 149.

This recipe is a nice change from regular tacos. The Adobo seasoning gives it a different flavor.

Nutritional Info:
Per Serving: 258 Calories; 14g Fat (47.5% calories from fat); 17g Protein; 17g Carbohydrate; 1g Dietary Fiber; 52mg Cholesterol; 602mg Sodium.
Exchanges: 1 Grain (Starch); 2 Lean Meat; 1/2 Vegetable; 1-1/2 Fat.

Stuffed Bell Peppers

Recipes:	1	2	3	4	5	6
Servings:	8	16	24	32	40	48
Ingredients:						
Bell peppers	4 large or 8 small	8 large or 16 small	12 large or 24 small	16 large or 32 small	20 large or 40 small	24 large or 48 small
Uncooked ground beef	1 lb.	2 lbs.	3 lbs.	4 lbs.	5 lbs.	6 lbs.
Chopped onion[1]	1/4 C.	1/2 C.	3/4 C.	1 C.	1-1/4 C.	1-1/2 C.
Minced garlic	1 t.	2 t.	1 T.	1 T. + 1 t.	1 T. + 2 t.	2 T.
Uncooked long-grain rice	1-1/2 C.	3 C.	4-1/2 C.	6 C.	7-1/2 C.	9 C.
Diced tomatoes	15 oz.	30 oz.	45 oz.	60 oz.	75 oz.	90 oz.
Shredded cheddar cheese[2]	1/2 C.	1 C.	1-1/2 C.	2 C.	2-1/2 C.	3 C.
Italian seasoning	1 T.	2 T.	3 T.	1/4 C.	1/4 C. + 1 T.	1/4 C. + 2 T.
Tomato sauce	8 oz.	16 oz.	24 oz.	32 oz.	40 oz.	48 oz.
Italian seasoning	1 T.	2 T.	3 T.	1/4 C.	1/4 C. + 1 T.	1/4 C. + 2 T.

Assembly Directions:

If using large peppers, carefully cut around stem and remove it. Cut pepper lengthwise. Remove the seeds and membrane.

If using small peppers, totally cut the tops from the peppers. Remove the seeds and membrane.

On the stovetop, boil a large pan of water. Place the peppers into the boiling water and allow to cook for about 5 minutes. Remove peppers from the water and drain on a paper towel.

Brown the ground beef with the onions and garlic until meat is no longer pink. Drain.

Cook the long-grain rice half the recommended time.

Drain the diced tomatoes, reserving the liquid for use in the sauce.

In a large bowl, mix together the ground beef mixture, drained tomatoes, partially cooked rice, shredded cheddar cheese, and the first measure of Italian seasonings. Divide stuffing evenly between all the peppers.

To make the sauce, mix together the tomato sauce, reserved liquid from the diced tomatoes, and the second measure of Italian seasoning.

Freezing Directions:

Place the peppers in a gallon-size freezer bag. Place the sauce in a quart-size freezer bag. Seal and label bags. Tape both bags together or place in a larger 2-gallon freezer bag. Freeze.

Serving Directions:

Thaw both bags. Place the bell peppers in the bottom of a 13x9 or 8x8 pan. Pour the sauce over the top of the peppers. Bake uncovered at 350 degrees for 35 minutes.

Notes:

[1] 1 medium onion = 1 C. chopped
[2] 8 oz. cheese = 2 C. shredded

Nutritional Info:

Per Serving: 224 Calories; 10g Fat (38.6% calories from fat); 16g Protein; 19g Carbohydrate; 2g Dietary Fiber; 45mg Cholesterol; 315mg Sodium.
Exchanges: 1/2 Grain (Starch); 2 Lean Meat; 1-1/2 Vegetable; 1/2 Fat.

Meatballs with Sweet and Sour Sauce

Recipes:	1	2	3	4	5	6
Servings:	10	20	30	40	50	60
Makes:	60 meatballs	120 meatballs	180 meatballs	240 meatballs	300 meatballs	360 meatballs
Meatballs:						
Uncooked ground beef	1-1/2 lbs.	3 lbs.	4-1/2 lbs.	6 lbs.	7-1/2 lbs.	9 lbs.
Oats, quick or old fashioned	1 C.	2 C.	3 C.	4 C.	5 C.	6 C.
Water chestnuts, drained and finely diced	8 oz.	16 oz.	24 oz.	32 oz.	40 oz.	48 oz.
Onion powder	1/2 t.	1 t.	1-1/2 t.	2 t.	2-1/2 t.	1 T.
Garlic powder	1/2 t.	1 t.	1-1/2 t.	2 t.	2-1/2 t.	1 T.
Reduced sodium soy sauce	1 T.	2 T.	3 T.	1/4 C.	1/4 C. + 1 T.	1/4 C. + 2 T.
Egg	1	2	3	4	5	6
Skim milk	1/2 C.	1 C.	1-1/2 C.	2 C.	2-1/2 C.	3 C.
Sauce:						
Crushed pineapple; reserve juice	20 oz.	40 oz.	60 oz.	80 oz.	100 oz.	120 oz.
Brown sugar	1 C.	2 C.	3 C.	4 C.	5 C.	6 C.
Cornstarch	2 T.	1/4 C.	1/4 C. + 2 T.	1/2 C.	1/2 C. + 2 T.	3/4 C.
Beef Broth	1 C.	2 C.	3 C.	4 C.	5 C.	6 C.
Vinegar	1/2 C.	1 C.	1-1/2 C.	2 C.	2-1/2 C.	3 C.
Soy sauce	1 T.	2 T.	3 T.	1/4 C.	1/4 C. + 1 T.	1/4 C. + 2 T.
Green pepper, chopped	1 med.	2 med.	3 med.	4 med.	5 med.	6 med.

Assembly Directions:

Meatballs: For each recipe, combine ground beef, oats, diced water chestnuts, onion, garlic, soy sauce, egg and milk. Shape into 40 balls about 1-1 1/4 inch in diameter. (Use a small cookie scoop to make the job go quicker.) Place the meatballs on a sprayed or foil-lined rimmed baking sheet. Bake at 375 degrees for 20-30 minutes until lightly browned and no longer pink in the center. Cool.

Sauce: For each recipe, drain pineapple and reserve juice. Mix brown sugar and cornstarch in medium saucepan. Add drained pineapple juice (about 3/4 C.), beef broth, vinegar and soy sauce. Bring mixture to a boil stirring constantly until it clears and thickens. Remove from heat. Cool. Add chopped green pepper and pineapple.

Freezing Directions:

Freeze meatballs in freezer bags or rigid containers. Pour sauce into quart-sized freezer bags. Keep the meatballs and the sauce together!

Serving Directions:

Thaw and reheat in microwave, on stovetop or in slow cooker. Serve as an appetizer or with rice as a main dish.

Nutritional Info:

Per Serving: 321 Calories; 13g Fat (35.2% calories from fat); 17g Protein; 36g Carbohydrate; 2g Dietary Fiber; 66mg Cholesterol; 410mg Sodium.
Exchanges: 1/2 Grain (Starch); 2 Lean Meat; 1/2 Vegetable; 1/2 Fruit; 1-1/2 Fat; 1 Other Carbohydrates.

Ginger Orange Stir-Fry

Recipes:	1	2	3	4	5	6
Servings:	4	8	12	16	20	24
Ingredients:						
Orange juice	1 C.	2 C.	3 C.	4 C.	5 C.	6 C.
Reduced sodium soy sauce	1/2 C.	1 C.	1-1/2 C.	2 C.	2-1/2 C.	3 C.
Worcestershire sauce	2 T.	1/4 C.	1/4 C. + 2 T.	1/2 C.	1/2 C. + 2 T.	3/4 C.
Minced garlic	1 t.	2 t.	1 T.	1 T. + 1 t.	1 T. + 2 t.	2 T.
Ground ginger	1/2 t.	1 t.	1-1/2 t.	2 t.	2-1/2 t.	1 T.
Round steak, trimmed and cut in strips	1 lb.	2 lbs.	3 lbs.	4 lbs.	5 lbs.	6 lbs.
Onion, cut in wedges	1	2	3	4	5	6
Green pepper, sliced	1	2	3	4	5	6
On Hand:						
Canola oil	2 T.	1/4 C.	1/4 C. + 2 T.	1/2 C.	1/2 C. + 2 T.	3/4 C.
Cornstarch	2 T.	1/4 C.	1/4 C. + 2 T.	1/2 C.	1/2 C. + 2 T.	3/4 C.
Frozen stir-fry vegetables	4 C.	8 C.	12 C.	16 C.	20 C.	24 C.
Cooked rice	2 C.	4 C.	6 C.	8 C.	10 C.	12 C.

Assembly Directions:
In a large bowl, combine the orange juice, soy sauce, Worcestershire sauce, garlic and ginger. For each recipe, place one-half of the sauce in a quart freezer bag (about 3/4 C.). Add the meat, onions and peppers. Place the other half of the sauce in a small container or small freezer bag.

Freezing Directions:
Place the smaller freezer bags inside a gallon freezer bag. Seal, label, and freeze.

Serving Directions:
Thaw overnight in the refrigerator. Heat oil in a large skillet on medium high. Remove meat, onions and peppers from the sauce and place in skillet. Discard marinade. Stir-fry until meat is no longer pink.
Add the frozen vegetables. Cook until heated through. Mix cornstarch with remaining sauce. Add to skillet. Bring to a boil. Cook for about 2 minutes or until thickened. Serve over rice.

Nutritional Info: including rice
Per Serving: 376 Calories; 8g Fat (18.8% calories from fat); 31g Protein; 43g Carbohydrate; 3g Dietary Fiber; 66mg Cholesterol; 724mg Sodium.
Exchanges: 2 Grain (Starch); 3-1/2 Lean Meat; 2 Vegetable; 1/2 Fruit; 1/2 Fat.

Rosemary Sage London Broil

Recipes:	1	2	3	4	5	6
Servings:	6	12	18	24	30	36
Ingredients:						
London broil	1-1/2 lbs.	3 lbs.	4-1/2 lbs.	6 lbs.	7-1/2 lbs.	9 lbs.
Finely chopped fresh rosemary	2 T.	1/4 C.	1/4 C. + 2 T.	1/2 C.	1/2 C. + 2 T.	3/4 C.
Finely chopped fresh sage	3 T.	1/4 C. + 2 T.	1/2 C. + 1 T.	3/4 C.	3/4 C. + 3 T.	1 C. + 2 T.
Canola oil	1/4 C.	1/2 C.	3/4 C.	1 C.	1-1/4 C.	1-1/2 C.
Seasoned salt	1/2 t.	1 t.	1-1/2 t.	2 t.	2-1/2 t.	1 T.
Worcestershire sauce	1 t.	2 t.	1 T.	1 T. + 1 t.	1 T. + 2 t.	2 T.
Lemon juice	2 T.	1/4 C.	1/4 C. + 2 T.	1/2 C.	1/2 C. + 2 T.	3/4 C.
Black pepper	1/2 t.	1 t.	1-1/2 t.	2 t.	2-1/2 t.	1 T.
Minced garlic	1 t.	2 t.	1 T.	1 T. + 1 t.	1 T. + 2 t.	2 T.

Assembly Directions:

Place London broil into one gallon freezer bags. Add rest of ingredients to the freezer bags assembly line style.

Freezing Directions:

Seal, label, and freeze.

Serving Directions:

Thaw in refrigerator overnight.

Cook on grill: Coat grill rack with cooking spray. Preheat grill to medium high (about 400 degrees). Remove steak from marinade. Discard marinade. Grill steak 4 to 5 minutes on each side or until an instant-read thermometer reads at least 145 degrees for a medium rare steak. Remove from heat and allow to stand for 10 minutes. Slice steak thinly across the grain.

To broil: Move oven rack three to four inches from the broiler unit. Set the oven to broil. Set the marinated meat on a sturdy broiling pan with drip pan underneath. Place pan in the oven. Crack the oven door. Broil 5 to 7 minutes. Use a fork or tongs to flip the meat. Broil other side 5 to 7 minutes. Remove from heat and allow to stand for 10 minutes. Slice steak thinly across the grain.

Nutritional Info:

Oil was not included in the nutritional analysis.
Per Serving: 206 Calories; 12g Fat (53.4% calories from fat); 22g Protein; 1g Carbohydrate; trace Dietary Fiber; 58mg Cholesterol; 202mg Sodium.
Exchanges: 3 Lean Meat; 1/2 Fat.

Spaghetti Pie

Recipes:	1	2	3	4	5	6
Servings:	8	16	24	32	40	48
Ingredients:						
Uncooked spaghetti	8 oz.	16 oz.	24 oz.	32 oz.	40 oz.	48 oz.
Egg	1	2	3	4	5	6
Grated Parmesan cheese	3 T.	1/4 C. + 2 T.	1/2 C. + 1 T.	3/4 C.	3/4 C. + 3 T.	1 C. + 2 T.
Frozen chopped spinach	5 oz.	10 oz.	15 oz.	20 oz.	25 oz.	30 oz.
Nonfat cottage cheese	16 oz.	32 oz.	48 oz.	64 oz.	80 oz.	96 oz.
Ground beef[1]	1 lb.	2 lbs.	3 lbs.	4 lbs.	5 lbs.	6 lbs.
Diced onion[2]	1/2 C.	1 C.	1-1/2 C.	2 C.	2-1/2 C.	3 C.
Diced green pepper[3]	1/4 C.	1/2 C.	3/4 C.	1 C.	1-1/4 C.	1-1/2 C.
Minced garlic	1/2 t.	1 t.	1-1/2 t.	2 t.	2-1/2 t.	1 T.
Canned diced tomatoes	15 oz.	30 oz.	45 oz.	60 oz.	75 oz.	90 oz.
Spaghetti sauce	1-1/2 C.	3 C.	4-1/2 C.	6 C.	7-1/2 C.	9 C.
Shredded mozzarella cheese[4]	1 C.	2 C.	3 C.	4 C.	5 C.	6 C.

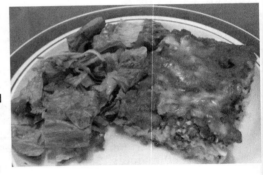

Assembly Directions:

Cook spaghetti as directed on package. Drain. Add eggs and Parmesan cheese. Mix well.

For each recipe, spray a 9x13 pan with cooking spray. Press spaghetti mixture into the bottom of the pan.

Defrost and drain spinach. Process cottage cheese and spinach in a food processor. Spread cottage cheese mixture over spaghetti.

Brown ground beef; add onion, green peppers, and garlic. Drain off excess fat. Add diced tomatoes and spaghetti sauce. Spread meat sauce over spaghetti and cottage cheese. Top with shredded mozzarella cheese.

Freezing Directions:

Place dish in a 2-gallon freezer bag. Or, if you want to wrap it in foil, cover the top of the lasagna with waxed paper or plastic wrap and then the foil, because the acid in the tomato sauce will leave small holes in the foil. Label, seal and freeze.

Serving Directions:

Thaw in refrigerator overnight. If the pie is wrapped in waxed paper or plastic wrap, remove it before baking. Bake covered at 350 degrees for 35-40 minutes.
Frozen pie may be baked for 55-60 minutes at 350 degrees.

Notes:

[1] 1 lb. ground = 2-1/2 C. browned
[2] 1 medium onion = 1 C. diced
[3] 1 large pepper = 1 C. diced
[4] 8 oz. cheese = 2 C. shredded

One recipe can also be made in two 8x8 pans.

Nutritional Info:

Per Serving: 363 Calories; 13g Fat (31.9% calories from fat); 30g Protein; 31g Carbohydrate; 3g Dietary Fiber; 75mg Cholesterol; 513mg Sodium.
Exchanges: 1-1/2 Grain (Starch); 3-1/2 Lean Meat; 1 Vegetable; 1 Fat.

Pepper Steak

Recipes:	1	2	3	4	5	6
Servings:	6	12	18	24	30	36
Ingredients:						
Boneless round steak	1-1/2 lbs.	3 lbs.	4-1/2 lbs.	6 lbs.	7-1/2 lbs.	9 lbs.
Onion, chopped in large chunks	1 C.	2 C.	3 C.	4 C.	5 C.	6 C.
Minced garlic	1 t.	2 t.	1 T.	1 T. + 1 t.	1 T. + 2 t.	2 T.
Ground ginger	1/4 t.	1/2 t.	3/4 t.	1 t.	1-1/4 t.	1-1/2 t.
Low sodium beef broth	1 C.	2 C.	3 C.	4 C.	5 C.	6 C.
Reduced sodium soy sauce	1/4 C.	1/2 C.	3/4 C.	1 C.	1-1/4 C.	1-1/2 C.
On Hand Ingredients:						
Cornstarch	2 T.	1/4 C.	1/4 C. + 2 T.	1/2 C.	1/2 C. + 2 T.	3/4 C.
Water	1/4 C.	1/2 C.	3/4 C.	1 C.	1-1/4 C.	1-1/2 C.
Green peppers, cut into strips	1	2	3	4	5	6
Red peppers, cut into strips	1	2	3	4	5	6
Tomatoes, cut into large chunks	2	4	6	8	10	12
Hot cooked rice	6 C.	12 C.	18 C.	24 C.	30 C.	36 C.

Assembly Directions:

Trim and slice round steak into strips. Spray a skillet with cooking spray. Lightly brown meat over medium heat. Cool. Place steak in freezer container or freezer bag. Add onion, garlic, ginger, beef broth and soy sauce.

Freezing Directions:

Remove excess air from bag. Seal, label, and freeze.

Serving Directions:

Completely thaw beef mixture in the refrigerator. Spray slow cooker with cooking spray. Place mixture in slow cooker. Cook on low for 6 to 8 hours or on high for 3 to 4 hours or until beef is tender.

Turn slow cooker temperature to high. Mix the cornstarch and water in a small mixing bowl. Pour the mixture into the slow cooker stirring as you add the mixture. Add green and red pepper strips and tomatoes. Cook for 30 minutes to 1 hour or until peppers are tender. Serve over rice.

Nutritional Info:

Per Serving: 336 Calories; 5g Fat (12.4% calories from fat); 31g Protein; 40g Carbohydrate; 2g Dietary Fiber; 66mg Cholesterol; 478mg Sodium.
Exchanges: 2 Grain (Starch); 3-1/2 Lean Meat; 1-1/2 Vegetable.

Beef Kabobs

Recipes:	1	2	3	4	5	6
Servings:	8	16	24	32	40	48
Makes: skewers	16	32	48	64	80	96
Ingredients:						
Beef sirloin, cut in cubes	2 lbs.	4 lbs.	6 lbs.	8 lbs.	10 lbs.	12 lbs.
Canola oil	1/4 C.	1/2 C.	3/4 C.	1 C.	1-1/4 C.	1-1/2 C.
Reduced sodium soy sauce	1/4 C.	1/2 C.	3/4 C.	1 C.	1-1/4 C.	1-1/2 C.
Worcestershire sauce	1/4 C.	1/2 C.	3/4 C.	1 C.	1-1/4 C.	1-1/2 C.
Yellow, dijon or spicy brown mustard	3 T.	1/4 C. + 2 T.	1/2 C. + 1 T.	3/4 C.	3/4 C. + 3 T.	1 C. + 2 T.
Coarse black pepper	1 t.	2 t.	1 T.	1 T. + 1 t.	1 T. + 2 t.	2 T.
Red wine vinegar	1/2 C.	1 C.	1-1/2 C.	2 C.	2-1/2 C.	3 C.
Dried parsley	1-1/2 t.	1 T.	1 T. + 1-1/2 t.	2 T.	2 T. + 1-1/2 t.	3 T.
Minced garlic	1 t.	2 t.	1 T.	1 T. + 1 t.	1 T. + 2 t.	2 T.
Lemon juice	1/3 C.	2/3 C.	1 C.	1-1/3 C.	1-2/3 C.	2 C.
On Hand:						
Green peppers, cut in chunks	2	4	6	8	10	12
Large onions, cut in chunks	2	4	6	8	10	12
Zucchini, sliced	2	4	6	8	10	12

Assembly Directions:

Place beef cubes into one gallon freezer bags. In a mixing bowl, combine oil, soy sauce, Worcestershire sauce, mustard, pepper, red wine vinegar, parsley, garlic, and lemon juice. Whisk until thoroughly combined. Pour marinade over beef cubes. One recipe will yield a little over 1-3/4 cup of marinade.

Freezing Directions:

Seal, label, and freeze.

Serving Directions:

Thaw in refrigerator overnight. Soak bamboo skewers in water for at least 30 minutes before using. Heat grill to medium high heat. Alternate meat and on hand vegetables on skewers until all skewers are loaded. Place on grill and cook to desired doneness. Discard marinade.

Nutritional Info: 2 skewers per serving

Oil was not included in the nutritional analysis.
Per Serving: 303 Calories; 16g Fat (47.9% calories from fat); 28g Protein; 12g Carbohydrate; 2g Dietary Fiber; 84mg Cholesterol; 512mg Sodium.
Exchanges: 3-1/2 Lean Meat; 1 Vegetable; 1 Fat; 1/2 Other Carbohydrates.

Lasagna Rollups

Recipes:	1	2	3	4	5	6
Servings:	8	16	24	32	40	48
Ingredients:						
Lean ground beef	1 lb.	2 lbs.	3 lbs.	4 lbs.	5 lbs.	6 lbs.
Minced onion[1]	2 T.	1/4 C.	1/4 C. + 2 T.	1/2 C.	1/2 C. + 2 T.	3/4 C.
Minced green pepper[2]	2 T.	1/4 C.	1/4 C. + 2 T.	1/2 C.	1/2 C. + 2 T.	3/4 C.
Minced garlic	1/2 t.	1 t.	1-1/2 t.	2 t.	2-1/2 t.	1 T.
Lasagna noodles	8	16	24	32	40	48
Lowfat cottage cheese	1 C.	2 C.	3 C.	4 C.	5 C.	6 C.
Shredded mozzarella cheese[3]	2/3 C.	1-1/3 C.	2 C.	2-2/3 C.	3-1/3 C.	4 C.
Italian seasoning	1 t.	2 t.	1 T.	1 T. + 1 t.	1 T. + 2 t.	2 T.
Grated Parmesan cheese	1/3 C.	2/3 C.	1 C.	1-1/3 C.	1-2/3 C.	2 C.
On Hand:						
Spaghetti sauce	2 C.	4 C.	6 C.	8 C.	10 C.	12 C.
Shredded mozzarella cheese[3]	1 C.	2 C.	3 C.	4 C.	5 C.	6 C.

Assembly Directions:

Brown hamburger and add the onion, green pepper and garlic while it is cooking. Drain fat and discard. Cool. Cook noodles 2 minutes short of the recommended time. Drain and lay flat on waxed paper. Meanwhile, in a mixing bowl, combine the cottage cheese, mozzarella, Italian seasoning, Parmesan cheese, and the meat mixture. Spread the meat mixture evenly down each noodle staying away from the edges. Roll up each noodle lengthwise and place on a baking sheet seam side down.

Freezing Directions:

Flash freeze the lasagna rolls until firm. Remove from baking sheet and place in gallon freezer bags or freezer containers. Seal, label, and freeze.

Serving Directions:

Preheat oven to 350 degrees. Spray an appropriate sized baking dish with cooking spray. Place frozen rolls in dish. Cover with spaghetti sauce and mozzarella cheese. Cover with aluminum foil. Bake for 45 minutes or until heated through and bubbly.

Notes:

[1] 1 medium onion = 1 C. diced
[2] 1 large green pepper = 1 C. diced
[3] 8 oz. cheese = 2 C. shredded

Nutritional Info:

Per Serving: 355 Calories; 15g Fat (38.1% calories from fat); 28g Protein; 26g Carbohydrate; 2g Dietary Fiber; 56mg Cholesterol; 591mg Sodium.
Exchanges: 1-1/2 Grain (Starch); 3-1/2 Lean Meat; 1 Fat.

Cranberry Chuck Roast on the Grill

Recipes:	1	2	3	4	5	6
Servings:	6	12	18	24	30	36
Ingredients:						
Chuck roast, trimmed	2 lbs.	4 lbs.	6 lbs.	8 lbs.	10 lbs.	12 lbs.
Cranberry juice	1/2 C.	1 C.	1-1/2 C.	2 C.	2-1/2 C.	3 C.
Reduced sodium soy sauce	1/3 C.	2/3 C.	1 C.	1-1/3 C.	1-2/3 C.	2 C.
Dried oregano	1/2 t.	1 t.	1-1/2 t.	2 t.	2-1/2 t.	1 T.
Garlic powder	1/2 t.	1 t.	1-1/2 t.	2 t.	2-1/2 t.	1 T.
Seasoned meat tenderizer	1/2 t.	1 t.	1-1/2 t.	2 t.	2-1/2 t.	1 T.

Assembly Directions:
Place chuck roast into one gallon freezer bags. In a mixing bowl, combine cranberry juice, soy sauce, oregano, garlic powder, and meat tenderizer. Whisk until thoroughly combined. Pour marinade over chuck roast. One recipe will yield a little over 1 cup of marinade.

Freezing Directions:
Seal, label, and freeze.

Serving Directions:
Thaw in refrigerator overnight.

Cook on grill: Coat grill rack with cooking spray. Preheat grill to medium high (about 400 degrees). Remove steak from marinade. Grill until meat is browned and an instant read thermometer registers between 140 and 150 degrees. This may take up to 30 minutes depending on the thickness of the roast. Discard marinade.

Cook in oven: Preheat oven to 350 degrees. Place the meat and sauce in a roaster pan spooning some of the sauce over the top. Cover and bake for 2 hours, basting every hour until tender when pierced with a fork.

Nutritional Info:
Per Serving: 337 Calories; 24g Fat (64.4% calories from fat); 25g Protein; 5g Carbohydrate; trace Dietary Fiber; 87mg Cholesterol; 724mg Sodium.
Exchanges: 3-1/2 Lean Meat; 1/2 Vegetable; 2-1/2 Fat.

Poultry Recipes

Poultry Recipes

TIPS FOR POULTRY RECIPES

Yields

- 2 ounces of chicken or turkey (one breast or two smaller pieces) is considered a standard serving.
- When figuring how much cooked meat will be yielded from a whole bird, you can usually figure that one cup of meat will come from each pound of bird. A 4 pound chicken equals 4 pounds of meat.

Shopping & Cooking Tips

- You can substitute diced turkey breast for diced chicken. It is often less expensive too.
- Don't buy leaking packages. Don't let raw meat juices run onto any other foods. Always clean surfaces, mixing bowls, utensils, and hands well after working with raw poultry.
- Poultry is often labeled as "previously frozen" which can be confusing. That means that at some point the poultry was kept below 26 degrees. According to the USDA, if you thaw the poultry in the refrigerator and use it uncooked in a recipe, you can put it back into the freezer in the raw form. This is good to know for assembling chicken in marinade as well as for other recipes.
- A large enameled or aluminum water bath canner is very useful. It will hold 2-3 turkey breasts or whole chickens. Placing a trivet or wire rack in the bottom will keep the meat from sticking.
- Heavy duty latex gloves or "chicken gloves" as we like to call them, are great for boning and handling hot meat. The meat will come off much quicker when it's hot.
- When cooking, insert a meat thermometer into the poultry to check the temperature. Poultry has completed cooking when the inserted thermometer reaches 185 degrees F internal temperature. Or insert a fork into the thigh or breast and check the juices that flow. It is done when the juices run clear. When chicken is completely cooked, Salmonella germs are killed and will not cause food-borne illness. It's often the raw chicken juice that gets into other foods that can cause food poisoning.

Healthy Tips

- Plan for extra diced, cooked poultry to use in salads and sandwiches. Freeze in 2-cup portions.
- Use fat-free broth whenever possible. Wouldn't you rather consume your fat in hot fudge sundaes than in chicken broth? To remove the fat from your homemade broth, chill it in the refrigerator until the fat that collects at the top is hard. Use a slotted spatula to lift it out and discard it.
- Try our Fat Free White Sauce recipe to replace creamed soups in your own recipes. It tastes great!
- Bake or broil your chicken instead of frying it. Remove the skin or start with skinless meat. You can greatly reduce the fat just by following these two rules of thumb.

Website Recipes & Tips

- For more great 30 Day Gourmet poultry recipes, check out the recipes section of our website at: www.30daygourmet.com
- For more poultry freezing tips and recipes from our cooks, check out the Cooking-Poultry section of our message boards at www.30daygourmet.com

Which fettuccine would you rather eat - theirs or yours?

Elegant Chicken in Marinade

Recipes:	1	2	3	4	5	6
Servings:	6	12	18	24	30	36
Makes:	3 C.	6 C.	9 C.	12 C.	15 C.	18 C.
Ingredients:						
Salt	2 t.	1 T. + 1 t.	2 T.	2 T. + 2 t.	3 T. + 1 t.	4 T.
Worcestershire sauce	1/4 C.	1/2 C.	3/4 C.	1 C.	1-1/4 C.	1-1/2 C.
Dry mustard	2 T.	1/4 C.	1/4 C. + 2 T.	1/2 C.	1/2 C. + 2 T.	3/4 C.
Oil (any kind)	1 C.	2 C.	3 C.	4 C.	5 C.	6 C.
Red wine vinegar	1/2 C.	1 C.	1-1/2 C.	2 C.	2-1/2 C.	3 C.
Soy sauce	3/4 C.	1-1/2 C.	2-1/4 C.	3 C.	3-3/4 C.	4-1/2 C.
Pepper	1 t.	2 t.	1 T.	1 T. + 1 t.	1 T. + 2 t.	2 T.
Minced garlic	1 t.	2 t.	1 T.	1 T. + 1 t.	1 T. + 2 t.	2 T.
Parsley flakes	1-1/2 t.	1 T.	1 T. + 1-1/2 t.	2 T.	2 T. + 1-1/2 t.	3 T.
Boneless, skinless chicken breasts	6	12	18	24	30	36

Assembly Directions:

Combine all marinade ingredients. Place the chicken pieces in a one gallon freezer bag or rigid container. Pour marinade over the meat.

Freezing Directions:

Seal, label, and freeze.

Serving Directions:

Thaw in refrigerator or in microwave. Grill or cook chicken until the meat is no longer pink inside and the juices run clear. Discard marinade.

Notes:

Great to have on hand for grilling season or anytime! (We make our husbands clean snow off the grill to serve this in the winter!)

Buy Worcestershire sauce, red wine vinegar, and soy sauce in bulk from a buying club like Sam's or Costco or from a store such as GFS Marketplace. It is incredibly cheaper and easier to use than the little bottles.

For Chicken Strips: Cut chicken breasts into strips and marinade to use for stir fry, fajitas, or hot off the grill.

Nutritional Info:

Oil, soy sauce and Worcestershire sauce has been removed from the nutritional analysis.
Per Serving: 142 Calories; 2g Fat (12.6% calories from fat); 28g Protein; 2g Carbohydrate; trace Dietary Fiber; 68mg Cholesterol; 788mg Sodium.
Exchanges: 4 Lean Meat.

Country Chicken Pot Pie

Recipes:	1	2	3	4	5	6
Servings:	12	24	36	48	60	72
Makes: pies	2	4	6	8	10	12
Ingredients:						
Chopped onions[1]	1 C.	2 C.	3 C.	4 C.	5 C.	6 C.
Chopped carrots[2]	1 C.	2 C.	3 C.	4 C.	5 C.	6 C.
Chopped celery[3]	1 C.	2 C.	3 C.	4 C.	5 C.	2 C.
Butter/margarine, melted	1/3 C.	2/3 C.	1 C.	1-1/3 C.	1-2/3 C.	2 C.
Flour	1/2 C.	1 C.	1-1/2 C.	2 C.	2-1/2 C.	3 C.
Chicken broth	2 C.	4 C.	6 C.	8 C.	10 C.	12 C.
Evaporated milk	1 C.	2 C.	3 C.	4 C.	5 C.	6 C.
Chicken; cooked & chopped[4]	4 C.	8 C.	12 C.	16 C.	20 C.	24 C.
Frozen peas, thawed	1 C.	2 C.	3 C.	4 C.	5 C.	6 C.
Salt	1-1/2 t.	1 T.	1 T. + 1-1/2 t.	2 T.	2 T. + 1-1/2 t.	3 T.
Pepper	1/4 t.	1/2 t.	3/4 t.	1 t.	1-1/4 t.	1-1/2 t.
Puff pastry sheets	2	4	6	8	10	12

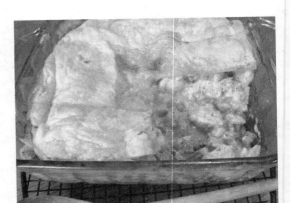

Assembly Directions:
Sauté onions, carrots, and celery in butter in a large skillet over medium heat until tender. Add flour and stir until smooth. Cook one minute, stirring constantly. Add chicken broth and evaporated milk. Cook, stirring constantly until thickened and bubbly. Stir in chicken, peas, salt and pepper.

Freezing Directions:
Cool and divide filling in half. Place in one gallon freezer bags. Seal, label, and freeze. Keep frozen puff pastry on hand in its original packaging.

Serving Directions:
Thaw filling. Bring puff pastry to room temperature. Preheat oven to 350 degrees. Spray dish with cooking spray.

Add filling. Unfold pastry sheet and place over chicken mixture. Fold under edges of pastry and press onto top of baking dish to seal. An 8x8 baking dish works well. Make a few slits in the top crust for the steam to escape. Bake uncovered for 30 minutes or until pastry is golden brown. Let stand 10 minutes before serving.

Notes:
[1] 1 medium onion = 1 C. chopped
[2] 3 carrots = 1 C. chopped
[3] 1 rib celery = 1/2 C. chopped
[4] 1 large chicken breast = 3/4 C. cooked and chopped

For a quicker meal, prebake the pot pie on cooking day. Cool and freeze pie whole in gallon freezer bags. On serving day, thaw the pot pie. Individual pieces may be reheated in a microwave for 3 minutes on high. Or a whole thawed pie can be reheated at 350 degrees for 20 to 30 minutes in a regular oven.

Pie crusts may be substituted for puff pastry sheets.

Nutritional Info:
Per Serving: 371 Calories; 20g Fat (49.6% calories from fat); 21g Protein; 25g Carbohydrate; 2g Dietary Fiber; 46mg Cholesterol; 678mg Sodium.
Exchanges: 1-1/2 Grain (Starch); 2 Lean Meat; 1/2 Vegetable; 4-1/2 Fat.

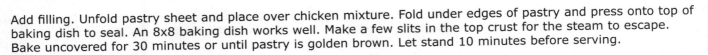

BBQ Chicken Pizza

Recipes:	1	2	3	4	5	6
Servings:	**8**	**16**	**24**	**32**	**40**	**48**
Ingredients:						
Boneless, skinless chicken breasts	1/2 lb.	1 lb.	1-1/2 lbs.	2 lbs.	2-1/2 lbs.	3 lbs.
Garlic powder	1/8 t.	1/4 t.	3/8 t.	1/2 t.	1/2 t. + 1/8 t.	3/4 t.
Black pepper	1/8 t.	1/4 t.	3/8 t.	1/2 t.	1/2 t. + 1/8 t.	3/4 t.
Ketchup	1/2 C.	1 C.	1-1/2 C.	2 C.	2-1/2 C.	3 C.
Brown sugar	1/4 C.	1/2 C.	3/4 C.	1 C.	1-1/4 C.	1-1/2 C.
Chili sauce	1/4 C.	1/2 C.	3/4 C.	1 C.	1-1/4 C.	1-1/2 C.
Cider vinegar	1 T.	2 T.	3 T.	1/4 C.	1/4 C. + 1 T.	1/4 C. + 2 T.
Liquid smoke	1 T.	2 T.	3 T.	1/4 C.	1/4 C. + 1 T.	1/4 C. + 2 T.
Lemon juice	1-1/2 t.	1 T.	1 T. + 1-1/2 t.	2 T.	2 T. + 1-1/2 t.	3 T.
On Hand:						
Chopped onion[1]	1/4 C.	1/2 C.	3/4 C.	1 C.	1-1/4 C.	1-1/2 C.
Cooked bacon, crumbled	2 slices	4 slices	6 slices	8 slices	10 slices	12 slices
Roma tomato, sliced	2	4	6	8	10	12
Shredded cheddar cheese[2]	1/2 C.	1 C.	1-1/2 C.	2 C.	2-1/2 C.	3 C.
Shredded mozzarella cheese[2]	1/2 C.	1 C.	1-1/2 C.	2 C.	2-1/2 C.	3 C.
Pizza Crust[3]	1	2	3	4	5	6

Assembly Directions:

Cut chicken into bite sized pieces. Spray a frying pan with cooking spray. Place chicken in pan. Sprinkle with garlic powder and black pepper. Cook over medium high heat until chicken is no longer pink in the center. Combine the remaining ingredients in a saucepan. Bring to a boil. Cook over medium heat for 10 minutes, stirring occasionally. Allow to cool.

Freezing Directions:

Place chicken in gallon freezer bag. Pour barbecue sauce over chicken. Seal, label, and freeze bags.

Serving Directions:

Thaw chicken mixture overnight in the refrigerator. Preheat oven to 425 degrees. Spread chicken and barbecue sauce mixture over a 12-inch pizza crust. Top with chopped onion, cooked bacon, sliced tomatoes, and cheeses. Bake for 15 to 20 minutes or until crust is golden brown and cheese is melted.

Notes:

[1] 1 medium onion = 1 C. chopped
[2] 8 oz. cheese = 2 C. shredded
[3] A recipe for Pizza Crust can be found on page 116.

For a quicker meal, par bake the crust for 5 to 10 minutes, top with toppings, flash freeze, and store in large freezer bags. On serving day, bake the pizza at 375 for 15 minutes to finish cooking the pizza.

Nutritional Info: per slice

Per Serving: 197 Calories; 6g Fat (26.4% calories from fat); 13g Protein; 24g Carbohydrate; 1g Dietary Fiber; 30mg Cholesterol; 346mg Sodium.
Exchanges: 1 Grain (Starch); 1-1/2 Lean Meat; 1/2 Vegetable; 1/2 Fat; 1/2 Other Carbohydrates.

Santa Fe Chicken

Recipes:	1	2	3	4	5	6
Servings:	10	20	30	40	50	60
Ingredients:						
Cooked & chopped chicken[1]	3 C.	6 C.	9 C.	12 C.	15 C.	18 C.
Canned corn, drained	15 oz.	30 oz.	45 oz.	60 oz.	75 oz.	90 oz.
Black beans, drained/rinsed	15 oz.	30 oz.	45 oz.	60 oz.	75 oz.	90 oz.
Black-eyed peas, drained	15 oz.	30 oz.	45 oz.	60 oz.	75 oz.	90 oz.
Pinto beans, drained	15 oz.	30 oz.	45 oz.	60 oz.	75 oz.	90 oz.
Ro-Tel tomatoes[2]	12 oz.	24 oz.	36 oz.	48 oz.	60 oz.	72 oz.
Picante sauce	15 oz.	30 oz.	45 oz.	60 oz.	75 oz.	90 oz.
Chili powder	1 T.	2 T.	3 T.	1/4 C.	1/4 C. + 1 T.	1/4 C. + 2 T.
Cumin	2 t.	1 T. + 1 t.	2 T.	2 T. + 2 t.	3 T. + 1 t.	1/4 C.
Shredded cheddar cheese[3]	1 C.	2 C.	3 C.	4 C.	5 C.	6 C.

Assembly Directions:
In a large bowl, mix together the chicken, corn, black beans, black-eyed peas, pinto beans, tomatoes and picante sauce. Add the chili powder and cumin, stirring until evenly mixed.

Freezing Directions:
Put mixture in a one-gallon freezer bag. Put the shredded cheddar in a quart freezer bag. Seal, label, and freeze both bags.

Serving Directions:
Thaw both bags. Preheat oven to 350 degrees. Spray a 9x13 pan with cooking spray. Pour the bag of chicken mixture into the pan. Cover with foil and bake for 30 minutes, or until heated through. Remove foil. Top with shredded cheese. Bake an additional 10 minutes, or until the cheese is melted.

Notes:
[1] 1 large chicken breast = 3/4 C. cooked and chopped
[2] Ro-Tel is a brand of canned tomatoes with chopped chili peppers added.
[3] 8 oz. cheese = 2 C. shredded

This dish is very healthy, with lots of fiber, and lower in fat than many other casseroles. It tastes great served over brown rice.

One recipe can be made in two 8x8 pans.

Nutritional Info:
Per Serving: 382 Calories; 7g Fat (16.7% calories from fat); 32g Protein; 49g Carbohydrate; 10g Dietary Fiber; 48mg Cholesterol; 923mg Sodium.
Exchanges: 3 Grain (Starch); 3 Lean Meat; 1 Vegetable; 1/2 Fat.

Caesar Chicken Marinade

Recipes:	1	2	3	4	5	6
Servings:	6	12	18	24	30	36
Ingredients:						
Yogurt	1/4 C.	1/2 C.	3/4 C.	1 C.	1-1/4 C.	1-1/2 C.
Shredded Parmesan cheese	2 T.	1/4 C.	1/4 C. + 2 T.	1/2 C.	1/2 C. + 2 T.	3/4 C.
Lemon juice	2 T.	1/4 C.	1/4 C. + 2 T.	1/2 C.	1/2 C. + 2 T.	3/4 C.
Buttermilk[1]	2 T.	1/4 C.	1/4 C. + 2 T.	1/2 C.	1/2 C. + 2 T.	3/4 C.
Dijon mustard	1 T.	2 T.	3 T.	1/4 C.	1/4 C. + 1 T.	1/4 C. + 2 T.
Worcestershire sauce	2 t.	1 T. + 1 t.	2 T.	2 T. + 2 t.	3 T. + 1 t.	1/4 C.
Anchovy paste[2]	2 t.	1 T. + 1 t.	2 T.	2 T. + 2 t.	3 T. + 1 t.	1/4 C.
Pepper	1/4 t.	1/2 t.	3/4 t.	1 t.	1-1/4 t.	1-1/2 t.
Minced garlic	1 T.	2 T.	3 T.	1/4 C.	1/4 C. + 1 T.	1/4 C. + 2 T.
Boneless, skinless chicken breasts	1-1/2 lbs.	3 lbs.	4-1/2 lbs.	6 lbs.	7-1/2 lbs.	9 lbs.

Assembly Directions:

Add the yogurt, Parmesan cheese, lemon juice, buttermilk, Dijon mustard, Worcestershire sauce, anchovy paste, pepper and garlic to a one gallon freezer bag. Seal and shake or squish together to mix the ingredients.

Freezing Directions:

Add the chicken to the bag. Seal, label, and freeze.

Serving Directions:

Thaw overnight in the refrigerator. Remove meat from marinade and discard marinade. Broil 4" from heat, or grill over medium coals 8-10 minutes or until cooked through, turning frequently. You can also cook the chicken in a non-stick skillet on the stovetop.

Notes:

[1] Make your own buttermilk substitute by adding 1 t. of lemon juice to 1/3 C. of milk. Allow to sit for 5 minutes. Stir and use the appropriate amount in the recipe.
[2] 2 oz. tube anchovy paste = 4 T.

For easier assembly:
1. Use a one gallon freezer bag for each recipe you make.
2. Put the freezer bag in a drinking glass, small bowl or measuring cup.
3. Add the ingredients assembly-line style to each bag.

Anchovy paste is generally found in the canned seafood area of the grocery store.

Nutritional Info:

Per Serving: 147 Calories; 4g Fat (22.6% calories from fat); 26g Protein; 1g Carbohydrate; trace Dietary Fiber; 71mg Cholesterol; 103mg Sodium.
Exchanges: 3-1/2 Lean Meat.

Chicken Taquitos

Recipes:	1	2	3	4	5	6
Servings:	8	16	24	32	40	48
Makes:	16	32	48	64	80	96
Ingredients:						
Boneless, skinless chicken breasts	2 lbs.	4 lbs.	6 lbs.	8 lbs.	10 lbs.	12 lbs.
Salsa	3/4 C.	1-1/2 C.	2-1/4 C.	3 C.	3-3/4 C.	4-1/2 C.
Tomato paste	3 oz.	6 oz.	9 oz.	12 oz.	15 oz.	18 oz.
Chicken broth	1 C.	2 C.	3 C.	4 C.	5 C.	6 C.
Chopped onion[1]	1/2 C.	1 C.	1-1/2 C.	2 C.	2-1/2 C.	3 C.
Chopped cilantro	1-1/2 t.	1 T.	1 T. + 1-1/2 t.	2 T.	2 T. + 1-1/2 t.	3 T.
Cumin	1-1/2 t.	1 T.	1 T. + 1-1/2 t.	2 T.	2 T. + 1-1/2 t.	3 T.
Salt	1/2 t.	1 t.	1-1/2 t.	2 t.	2-1/2 t.	1 T.
Black pepper	1/4 t.	1/2 t.	3/4 t.	1 t.	1-1/4 t.	1-1/2 t.
Minced garlic	1-1/2 t.	1 T.	1 T. + 1-1/2 t.	2 T.	2 T. + 1-1/2 t.	3 T.
Corn tortillas	16	32	48	64	80	96
Shredded cheddar cheese[2]	1 C.	2 C.	3 C.	4 C.	5 C.	6 C.
On Hand:						
Oil for frying						

Assembly Directions:

Place chicken and salsa into a slow cooker. Cook at high for 3 to 4 hours or until the chicken shreds easily. Remove chicken from slow cooker and shred. Place chicken back into the slow cooker. Add the next 8 ingredients to the slow cooker and cook another 10 minutes. Warm the tortillas in the microwave for 2 to 3 minutes.

Begin filling the enchiladas with about 1/4 cup of filling and 1 tablespoon of shredded cheese along the center of each tortilla. Use a toothpick to close up taquito, if desired.

Freezing Directions:

Place taquitos on baking sheet seam side down. Flash freeze taquitos. Remove from baking sheet and place into a freezer container. Seal, label, and freeze.

Serving Directions:

Heat oil in saucepan to 350 degrees. Deep fry taquitos until lightly browned. Drain on paper towel.
Or coat a baking sheet with oil or cooking spray. Bake at 375 degrees for 20 minutes or until lightly browned.

Notes:

[1] 1 medium onion = 1 C. chopped
[2] 8 oz. cheese = 2 C. shredded

Nutritional Info: two taquitos per serving

Nutritional analysis does not include oil for frying.
Per Serving: 330 Calories; 9g Fat (25.1% calories from fat); 33g Protein; 29g Carbohydrate; 4g Dietary Fiber; 84mg Cholesterol; 652mg Sodium.
Exchanges: 1-1/2 Grain (Starch); 4 Lean Meat; 1 Vegetable; 1 Fat.

South Sea Pineapple Chicken

Recipes:	1	2	3	4	5	6
Servings:	6	12	18	24	30	36
Ingredients:						
Boneless, skinless chicken breasts	6	12	18	24	30	36
Pineapple juice; reserved from canned tidbits	3/4 C.	1-1/2 C.	2-1/4 C.	3 C.	3-3/4 C.	4-1/2 C.
Chicken broth	1/2 C.	1 C.	1-1/2 C.	2 C.	2-1/2 C.	3 C.
Reduced sodium soy sauce	2 T.	1/4 C.	1/4 C. + 2 T.	1/2 C.	1/2 C. + 2 T.	3/4 C.
Lemon juice	3 T.	1/4 C. + 2 T.	1/2 C. + 1 T.	3/4 C.	3/4 C. + 3 T.	1 C. + 2 T.
Cornstarch	1 T.	2 T.	3 T.	1/4 C.	1/4 C. + 1 T.	1/4 C. + 2 T.
Pineapple tidbits; drained and reserved	20 oz.	40 oz.	60 oz.	80 oz.	100 oz.	120 oz.
Sliced green onion[1]	1/2 C.	1 C.	1-1/2 C.	2 C.	2-1/2 C.	3 C.
Frozen pea pods	8 oz.	16 oz.	24 oz.	32 oz.	40 oz.	48 oz.

Assembly Directions:
Spray a skillet with cooking spray. Brown chicken in skillet. Cool chicken pieces. In medium saucepan, heat reserved pineapple juice, chicken broth, soy sauce, lemon juice and cornstarch. Stir constantly until mixture is smooth and thick. Cool sauce. Add pineapple tidbits, green onions, and pea pods.

Freezing Directions:
Freeze chicken separately in a one gallon freezer bag or rigid container. Freeze sauce with fruit and vegetables in second freezer bag. Label and freeze with chicken.

Serving Directions:
Thaw. Spray a 9x13 baking dish with cooking spray. Arrange chicken in the baking dish. Pour sauce, fruit, vegetable mix over all. Bake at 350 degrees for 35-40 minutes.

Notes:
[1] 7 medium green onions = 1/2 C. sliced

This meal is great served over wild rice.

Nutritional Info:
Per Serving: 203 Calories; 2g Fat (8.7% calories from fat); 29g Protein; 16g Carbohydrate; 2g Dietary Fiber; 68mg Cholesterol; 487mg Sodium.
Exchanges: 4 Lean Meat; 1 Vegetable; 1/2 Fruit.

Chicken and Broccoli Lo Mein

Recipes:	1	2	3	4	5	6
Servings:	4	8	12	16	20	24
Ingredients:						
Boneless, skinless chicken breasts	2	4	6	8	10	12
Mushrooms	8 oz.	16 oz.	24 oz.	32 oz.	40 oz.	48 oz.
Canola oil	1 T.	2 T.	3 T.	1/4 C.	1/4 C. + 1 T.	1/4 C. + 2 T.
Chopped onion[1]	1 C.	2 C.	3 C.	4 C.	5 C.	6 C.
Broccoli florets[2]	3 C.	6 C.	9 C.	12 C.	15 C.	18 C.
Minced garlic	2 t.	1 T. + 1 t.	2 T.	2 T. + 2 t.	3 T. + 1 t.	1/4 C.
Reduced sodium soy sauce	3 T.	1/4 C. + 2 T.	1/2 C. + 1 T.	3/4 C.	3/4 C. + 3 T.	1 C. + 2 T.
White vinegar	1 T.	2 T.	3 T.	1/4 C.	1/4 C. + 1 T.	1/4 C. + 2 T.
Ketchup	1 T.	2 T.	3 T.	1/4 C.	1/4 C. + 1 T.	1/4 C. + 2 T.
Sesame oil	1 t.	2 t.	1 T.	1 T. + 1 t.	1 T. + 2 t.	2 T.
Ground ginger	1 t.	2 t.	1 T.	1 T. + 1 t.	1 T. + 2 t.	2 T.
On Hand:						
Linguine	8 oz.	16 oz.	24 oz.	32 oz.	40 oz.	48 oz.

Assembly Directions:

Chop chicken into bite-sized pieces. Slice mushrooms. Heat oil in a large skillet over medium heat. Add chicken, mushrooms, onions, and broccoli to the skillet. Cook, stirring frequently, until the chicken is no longer pink in the center. Mix the remaining ingredients in a small bowl. Add to the chicken and vegetable mixture. Stir to blend. Remove from heat and allow to cool.

Freezing Directions:

Place the chicken mixture in a freezer bag or container. Seal, label, and freeze.

Serving Directions:

Thaw chicken mixture. Reheat chicken mixture either in the microwave on 50 percent power for about 5 minutes or in a saucepan on low until mixture is hot but not boiling. Cook linguine until aldente (slightly chewy). Drain and place it back in the pot. Add chicken and vegetable mixture and stir until combined. Serve immediately.

Notes:

[1] 1 medium onion = 1 C. chopped
[2] 1 lb. fresh or frozen broccoli = 2 C. florets

Nutritional Info:

Per Serving: 371 Calories; 7g Fat (16.1% calories from fat); 25g Protein; 53g Carbohydrate; 4g Dietary Fiber; 34mg Cholesterol; 555mg Sodium.
Exchanges: 3 Grain (Starch); 2 Lean Meat; 2 Vegetable; 1 Fat.

Oven Crisp Chicken Fingers

Recipes:	1	2	3	4	5	6
Servings:	4	8	12	16	20	24
Ingredients:						
Boneless, skinless chicken breasts	4	8	12	16	20	24
Seasoned bread crumbs	1 C.	2 C.	3 C.	4 C.	5 C.	6 C.
Garlic powder	1/2 t.	1 t.	1-1/2 t.	2 t.	2-1/2 t.	1 T.
Paprika	1/2 t.	1 t.	1-1/2 t.	2 t.	2-1/2 t.	1 T.
Onion powder	1/4 t.	1/2 t.	3/4 t.	1 t.	1-1/4 t.	1-1/2 t.
Black pepper	1/4 t.	1/2 t.	3/4 t.	1 t.	1-1/4 t.	1-1/2 t.
Egg	1	2	3	4	5	6

Assembly Directions:

Cut chicken breast into tender size pieces.

Mix bread crumbs, garlic powder, paprika, onion powder, and pepper in a shallow dish.

Beat egg in a separate bowl.

Dip chicken into beaten egg. Allow excess egg to drip off. Dip chicken into bread crumb mixture coating all sides of the chicken.

Freezing Directions:

Place chicken on lined baking sheets. Flash freeze until chicken is solid. Place in freezer bags or containers. Seal, label, and freeze.

Serving Directions:

Preheat oven to 350 degrees. Place chicken on a lined baking sheet. Bake for 30 to 40 minutes or until an instant read thermometer inserted into the thickest piece of chicken reads 170 degrees.

Notes:

These are great dipped in warm marinara sauce or a mustard sauce.

Nutritional Info:

Per Serving: 259 Calories; 3g Fat (12.2% calories from fat); 33g Protein; 22g Carbohydrate; 1g Dietary Fiber; 116mg Cholesterol; 886mg Sodium.
Exchanges: 1-1/2 Grain (Starch); 4 Lean Meat; 1/2 Fat.

Pecan Crusted Chicken

Recipes:	1	2	3	4	5	6
Servings:	4	8	12	16	20	24
Ingredients:						
Boneless, skinless chicken breasts	4	8	12	16	20	24
Poultry seasoning	1/2 t.	1 t.	1-1/2 t.	2 t.	2-1/2 t.	1 T.
Paprika	1/2 t.	1 t.	1-1/2 t.	2 t.	2-1/2 t.	1 T.
Chopped pecans[1]	1/2 C.	1 C.	1-1/2 C.	2 C.	2-1/2 C.	3 C.
Cornflake crumbs[2]	1/2 C.	1 C.	1-1/2 C.	2 C.	2-1/2 C.	3 C.
Skim milk	1 C.	2 C.	3 C.	4 C.	5 C.	6 C.
Egg	1	2	3	4	5	6
Flour	1 C.	2 C.	3 C.	4 C.	5 C.	6 C.

Assembly Directions:

Pound chicken to an even thickness of 1/2 inch.

In a shallow bowl, combine poultry seasoning, paprika, chopped pecans and cornflake crumbs.

In a second shallow bowl, beat egg with the milk.

Place flour in a third shallow bowl.

Crust chicken breast by dipping chicken in flour, then the egg mixture and then the pecan mixture.

Freezing Directions:

Place chicken on a baking sheet lined with aluminum foil. Flash freeze. When chicken is solid, place in freezer bags or containers. Seal, label, and freeze.

Serving Directions:

Preheat oven to 350 degrees. Line a baking sheet with aluminum foil. Spray with cooking spray. Place chicken on baking sheet. Bake for 30 minutes or until an instant read thermometer inserted into the thickest piece of chicken reads 170 degrees.

Notes:

[1] 1 lb. pecans = 3-3/4 cups chopped
[2] 2 C. cornflakes = 3/4 C. crumbs

Nutritional Info:

Per Serving: 422 Calories; 13g Fat (28.2% calories from fat); 36g Protein; 39g Carbohydrate; 2g Dietary Fiber; 116mg Cholesterol; 240mg Sodium.
Exchanges: 2-1/2 Grain (Starch); 4 Lean Meat; 1/2 Non-Fat Milk; 2 Fat.

Oriental Sesame Chicken Strips

Recipes:	1	2	3	4	5	6
Servings:	4	8	12	16	20	24
Ingredients:						
Boneless, skinless chicken breasts	4	8	12	16	20	24
Honey	1/2 C.	1 C.	1-1/2 C.	2 C.	2-1/2 C.	3 C.
Orange juice	1/4 C.	1/2 C.	3/4 C.	1 C.	1-1/4 C.	1-1/2 C.
Reduced sodium soy sauce	2 T.	1/4 C.	1/4 C. + 2 T.	1/2 C.	1/2 C. + 2 T.	3/4 C.
Chicken bouillon granules	1 t.	2 t.	1 T.	1 T. + 1 t.	1 T. + 2 t.	2 T.
Red pepper flakes	1/4 t.	1/2 t.	3/4 t.	1 t.	1-1/4 t.	1-1/2 t.
Ground ginger	1/8 t.	1/4 t.	3/8 t.	1/2 t.	1/2 t. + 1/8 t.	3/4 t.
Garlic powder	1/4 t.	1/2 t.	3/4 t.	1 t.	1-1/4 t.	1-1/2 t.
Sesame seeds, optional	1 T.	2 T.	3 T.	1/4 C.	1/4 C. + 1 T.	1/4 C. + 2 T.

Assembly Directions:

Cut chicken into tender sized strips or leave as full breasts, if desired.

Mix honey, juice, soy sauce, bouillon granules, red pepper flakes, ground ginger, garlic powder and sesame seeds in large bowl until well blended. One recipe will make a little more than 3/4 C. of marinade.

Freezing Directions:

Place the chicken strips or breasts in a freezer bag. Pour marinade over chicken in bag. Seal, label, and freeze.

Serving Directions:

Thaw chicken overnight in the refrigerator.

If using chicken strips, soak bamboo skewers in water for 30 minutes prior to grilling. Thread chicken strips onto skewers.

Broil 4" from heat, or grill over medium coals 8-10 minutes or until cooked through, turning frequently. You can also cook the chicken in a non-stick skillet on the stovetop.

Nutritional Info:

Nutritional analysis was done using 1/4 cup of actual marinade per recipe or 1 tablespoon per serving.
Per Serving: 182 Calories; 2g Fat (9.4% calories from fat); 28g Protein; 13g Carbohydrate; trace Dietary Fiber; 68mg Cholesterol; 280mg Sodium.
Exchanges: 4 Lean Meat; 1 Other Carbohydrates.

Crab and Portobello Stuffed Chicken

Recipes:	1	2	3	4	5	6
Servings:	4	8	12	16	20	24
Ingredients:						
Margarine	3 T.	1/4 C. + 2 T.	1/2 C. + 1 T.	3/4 C.	3/4 C. + 3 T.	1 C. + 2 T.
Sliced portobello mushrooms, divided	8 oz.	16 oz.	24 oz.	32 oz.	40 oz.	48 oz.
Flour	1/4 C.	1/2 C.	3/4 C.	1 C.	1-1/4 C.	1-1/2 C.
Skim milk	1-3/4 C.	3-1/2 C.	5-1/4 C.	7 C.	8-3/4 C.	10-1/2 C.
Chicken bouillon granules	1-1/2 t.	1 T.	1 T. + 1-1/2 t.	2 T.	2 T. + 1-1/2 t.	3 T.
Garlic powder	1/2 t.	1 t.	1-1/2 t.	2 t.	2-1/2 t.	1 T.
Boneless, skinless chicken breasts	4	8	12	16	20	24
Canned crabmeat; drained, cartilage removed[1]	6 oz.	12 oz.	18 oz.	24 oz.	30 oz.	36 oz.
Italian seasoning	1 t.	2 t.	1 T.	1 T. + 1 t.	1 T. + 2 t.	2 T.
Salt	1/2 t.	1 t.	1-1/2 t.	2 t.	2-1/2 t.	1 T.
Black pepper	1/8 t.	1/4 t.	3/8 t.	1/2 t.	1/2 t. + 1/8 t.	3/4 t.
On Hand:						
Shredded Swiss cheese[2]	1/2 C.	1 C.	1-1/2 C.	2 C.	2-1/2 C.	3 C.

Assembly Directions:

In a saucepan, melt margarine and add 1/2 cup sliced mushrooms per recipe. Cook for 2 or 3 minutes or just until mushrooms begin to darken. Stir in flour until smooth. Gradually stir in milk. Add chicken bouillon granules. Bring to a boil. Cook and stir for 2 minutes. Remove mushroom sauce from heat and set aside.

Pound chicken breasts between sheets of plastic wrap until 1/4 inch thick.

Place remaining mushrooms, crab, Italian seasoning, salt, pepper, and 2 tablespoons (per recipe) of the mushroom sauce in a food processor. Process with chopping blade until thoroughly combined and a coarse stuffing is formed.

Evenly divide the crab and mushroom stuffing between chicken breasts. Fold in sides and roll up.

Freezing Directions:

Place chicken rolls on a baking sheet. Flash freeze. When chicken rolls are solid, place in a freezer bag or container. Pour mushroom sauce into a separate freezer bag or container. Seal, label, and freeze.

Serving Directions:

Spray an 8x8 baking pan with cooking spray. Place chicken rolls in pan. Cover with aluminum foil. Allow to thaw in the refrigerator overnight. Remove foil covering and pour mushroom sauce over chicken. Recover with aluminum foil. Bake at 350 degrees for 45 minutes. Remove aluminum foil. Sprinkle cheese on top. Bake for 5 or 10 more minutes uncovered or until cheese is melted.

Notes:

[1] Imitation crab can be substituted for the canned crab
[2] 8 oz. cheese = 2 C. shredded

Nutritional Info:

Per Serving: 356 Calories; 12g Fat (30.4% calories from fat); 46g Protein; 15g Carbohydrate; 1g Dietary Fiber; 113mg Cholesterol; 726mg Sodium.
Exchanges: 1/2 Grain (Starch); 5-1/2 Lean Meat; 1/2 Vegetable; 1/2 Non-Fat Milk; 1-1/2 Fat.

Cheesy Chicken and Penne

Recipes:	1	2	3	4	5	6
Servings:	6	12	18	24	30	36
Ingredients:						
Penne pasta	8 oz.	16 oz.	24 oz.	32 oz.	40 oz.	48 oz.
Frozen chopped spinach	10 oz.	20 oz.	30 oz.	40 oz.	50 oz.	60 oz.
Boneless, skinless chicken breasts	2	4	6	8	10	12
Italian seasoning	1 t.	2 t.	1 T.	1 T. + 1 t.	1 T. + 2 t.	2 T.
Minced garlic	1 t.	2 t.	1 T.	1 T. + 1 t.	1 T. + 2 t.	2 T.
Black pepper	1/4 t.	1/2 t.	3/4 t.	1 t.	1-1/4 t.	1-1/2 t.
Spaghetti sauce	2 C.	4 C.	6 C.	8 C.	10 C.	12 C.
Low sodium canned diced tomatoes	15 oz.	30 oz.	45 oz.	60 oz.	75 oz.	90 oz.
Lowfat cream cheese	2 oz.	4 oz.	6 oz.	8 oz.	10 oz.	12 oz.
Shredded mozzarella cheese[1]	1 C.	2 C.	3 C.	4 C.	5 C.	6 C.

Assembly Directions:
Cook penne until aldente (slightly chewy). Drain and set aside. Defrost frozen spinach and squeeze to remove liquid. Set aside. Cut chicken into bite sized pieces. Spray a skillet with cooking spray. Add chicken, Italian seasoning and garlic. Cook over medium heat until chicken is no longer pink in the center. Stir in the spinach and remaining ingredients. Cook until cheeses are melted. Remove from heat and cool.

Freezing Directions:
Place the chicken mixture in a freezer bag or container. Remove excess air and seal. Place the aldente pasta in a freezer bag or container. Remove excess air and seal. If the 2 components of this recipe are in freezer bags, place the 2 bags inside of one larger bag to keep them together and label the outer bag.

Serving Directions:
Thaw both bags. Spray a 9x13 pan with cooking spray. In a large mixing bowl, combine chicken mixture and pasta. Stir to mix. Pour into 9x13 pan. Bake covered for 30 minutes or until bubbly.

Notes:
[1] 8 oz. cheese = 2 C. shredded

One recipe can be made in two 8x8 pans.

Nutritional Info:
Per Serving: 326 Calories; 7g Fat (20.5% calories from fat); 23g Protein; 41g Carbohydrate; 5g Dietary Fiber; 38mg Cholesterol; 563mg Sodium.
Exchanges: 2-1/2 Grain (Starch); 2 Lean Meat; 1 Vegetable; 1 Fat.

Lemonade Chicken

Recipes:	1	2	3	4	5	6
Servings:	**12**	**24**	**36**	**48**	**60**	**72**
Ingredients:						
Boneless, skinless chicken breasts	1-1/2 lbs.	3 lbs.	4-1/2 lbs.	6 lbs.	7-1/2 lbs.	9 lbs.
Worcestershire sauce	1/3 C.	2/3 C.	1 C.	1-1/3 C.	1-2/3 C.	2 C.
Frozen lemonade concentrate	3/4 C.	1-1/2 C.	2-1/4 C.	3 C.	3-3/4 C.	4-1/2 C.
Celery seeds	1 t.	2 t.	1 T.	1 T. + 1 t.	1 T. + 2 t.	2 T.
Seasoned salt	1 t.	2 t.	1 T.	1 T. + 1 t.	1 T. + 2 t.	2 T.
Black pepper	1/2 t.	1 t.	1-1/2 t.	2 t.	2-1/2 t.	1 T.
Minced garlic	1/2 t.	1 t.	1-1/2 t.	2 t.	2-1/2 t.	1 T.

Assembly Directions:

Add the Worcestershire sauce, lemonade, celery seed, seasoned salt, pepper and garlic to a one gallon freezer bag. Seal and shake or squish together to mix the ingredients. Add chicken to bag.

Freezing Directions:

Seal, label, and freeze.

Serving Directions:

Thaw overnight in the refrigerator. Remove meat from marinade and discard marinade. Broil 4" from heat, or grill over medium coals 8-10 minutes or until cooked through, turning frequently. You can also cook the chicken in a non-stick skillet on the stovetop.

Notes:

For easier assembly:
1. Use a one gallon freezer bag for each recipe you make.
2. Put the freezer bag in a drinking glass, small bowl or measuring cup.
3. Add the ingredients assembly-line style to each bag.

Nutritional Info:

Per Serving: 174 Calories; 3g Fat (16.2% calories from fat); 25g Protein; 10g Carbohydrate; trace Dietary Fiber; 69mg Cholesterol; 240mg Sodium.
Exchanges: 3-1/2 Lean Meat.

Chicken Cordon Bleu

Recipes:	1	2	3	4	5	6
Servings:	4	8	12	16	20	24
Ingredients:						
Boneless, skinless chicken breasts	4	8	12	16	20	24
Thin ham slices	4 slices	8 slices	12 slices	16 slices	20 slices	24 slices
Thin Swiss cheese slices	4 slices	8 slices	12 slices	16 slices	20 slices	24 slices
Flour	2/3 C.	1-1/3 C.	2 C.	2-2/3 C.	3-1/3 C.	4 C.
Garlic powder	1/2 t.	1 t.	1-1/2 t.	2 t.	2-1/2 t.	1 T.
Onion powder	1/2 t.	1 t.	1-1/2 t.	2 t.	2-1/2 t.	1 T.
Salt	1/4 t.	1/2 t.	3/4 t.	1 t.	1-1/4 t.	1-1/2 t.
Black pepper	1/4 t.	1/2 t.	3/4 t.	1 t.	1-1/4 t.	1-1/2 t.
Egg	1	2	3	4	5	6
Water	2 t.	1 T. + 1 t.	2 T.	2 T. + 2 t.	3 T. + 1 t.	1/4 C.
Dry bread crumbs	2/3 C.	1-1/3 C.	2 C.	2-2/3 C.	3-1/3 C.	4 C.

Assembly Directions:

Pound chicken breasts between sheets of plastic wrap until 1/4 inch thick. Place a slice of ham on each piece of chicken. Place a slice of cheese on each piece of ham. Roll up chicken and secure with tooth picks.

Combine flour and seasonings in a shallow bowl. In another bowl, lightly beat egg and water. Place the bread crumbs in a third bowl. Dip the chicken into the flour coating all sides. Shake to remove any excess flour. Slide chicken through egg mixture. Allow excess to drip off. Then dip chicken into bread crumbs coating all sides. Place on a baking sheet.

Freezing Directions:

Flash freeze until chicken is solid. Remove chicken from baking sheet and place in a freezer bag or container. Seal, label, and freeze.

Serving Directions:

Spray an 8x8 baking dish with cooking spray. Place chicken in baking dish. Cover and allow to thaw in the refrigerator. Bake chicken at 350 degrees for 45 minutes.

If frozen when baking, add 30 minutes to the cooking time. Bake until an instant-read thermometer inserted into the center of chicken reads 165 degrees.

Nutritional Info:

Per Serving: 347 Calories; 6g Fat (16.1% calories from fat); 40g Protein; 31g Carbohydrate; 1g Dietary Fiber; 128mg Cholesterol; 603mg Sodium.
Exchanges: 2 Grain (Starch); 5 Lean Meat; 1/2 Fat.

Chicken in Cherry Sauce

Recipes:	1	2	3	4	5	6
Servings:	**4**	**8**	**12**	**16**	**20**	**24**
Ingredients:						
Dried cherries	1/3 C.	2/3 C.	1 C.	1-1/3 C.	1-2/3 C.	2 C.
Grape juice	2/3 C.	1-1/3 C.	2 C.	2-2/3 C.	3-1/3 C.	4 C.
Butter or margarine	1 T.	2 T.	3 T.	1/4 C.	1/4 C. + 1 T.	1/4 C. + 2 T.
Minced green onion[1]	1/4 C.	1/2 C.	3/4 C.	1 C.	1-1/4 C.	1-1/2 C.
Ground thyme	1/4 t.	1/2 t.	3/4 t.	1 t.	1-1/4 t.	1-1/2 t.
Chicken broth	1/2 C.	1 C.	1-1/2 C.	2 C.	2-1/2 C.	3 C.
Salt	1/4 t.	1/2 t.	3/4 t.	1 t.	1-1/4 t.	1-1/2 t.
Black pepper	1/8 t.	1/4 t.	3/8 t.	1/2 t.	1/2 t. + 1/8 t.	3/4 t.
Boneless, skinless chicken breasts	4	8	12	16	20	24
Olive oil	1 T.	2 T.	3 T.	1/4 C.	1/4 C. + 1 T.	1/4 C. + 2 T.
Salt	Dash	1/8 t.	1/4 t.	1/4 t. + 1/8 t.	1/2 t.	1/2 t. + 1/8 t.
Black pepper	Dash	1/8 t.	1/4 t.	1/4 t. + 1/8 t.	1/2 t.	1/2 t. + 1/8 t.

Assembly Directions:

Combine cherries and grape juice in a saucepan. Bring to a boil. Boil for about 5 minutes or until the cherries plump to full size. Remove from heat.

In a small skillet, melt butter over medium-high heat. Add onion and cook 2 or 3 minutes or until tender. Add thyme, chicken broth, salt and pepper. Stir to combine.

Add onion mixture to cherry mixture. Stir to combine and allow to cool.

In a skillet, brown the chicken about 4 minutes on each side in olive oil. Season with salt and pepper. Remove from heat and allow to cool.

Freezing Directions:

Place browned chicken and cherry sauce in separate freezer bags or containers. Seal, label, and freeze.

Serving Directions:

Thaw chicken and cherry sauce. Pour sauce into a non-stick skillet. Add chicken. Simmer on medium until sauce is reduced and chicken is no longer pink in the center. Serve sauce over chicken.

Notes:

[1] 7 medium green onions = 1/2 C. sliced

Nutritional Info:

Per Serving: 258 Calories; 8g Fat (28.6% calories from fat); 29g Protein; 17g Carbohydrate; 1g Dietary Fiber; 76mg Cholesterol; 405mg Sodium.
Exchanges: 4 Lean Meat; 1 Fruit; 1-1/2 Fat.

Chicken Florentine Lasagna

Recipes:	1	2	3	4	5	6
Servings:	**12**	**24**	**36**	**48**	**60**	**72**
Ingredients:						
Butter or margarine	2 T.	1/4 C.	1/4 C. + 2 T.	1/2 C.	1/2 C. + 2 T.	3/4 C.
Minced garlic	1 T.	2 T.	3 T.	1/4 C.	1/4 C. + 1 T.	1/4 C. + 2 T.
Chopped onion[1]	1 C.	2 C.	3 C.	4 C.	5 C.	6 C.
Fat free white sauce[2]	4 C.	8 C.	12 C.	16 C.	20 C.	24 C.
Grated Parmesan cheese; divided	1 C.	2 C.	3 C.	4 C.	5 C.	6 C.
Dried basil	1 t.	2 t.	1 T.	1 T. + 1 t.	1 T. + 2 t.	2 T.
Dried oregano	1/2 t.	1 t.	1-1/2 t.	2 t.	2-1/2 t.	1 T.
Black pepper	1/4 t.	1/2 t.	3/4 t.	1 t.	1-1/4 t.	1-1/2 t.
Lasagna noodles, uncooked	12	24	36	48	60	72
Lowfat cottage cheese	2 C.	4 C.	6 C.	8 C.	10 C.	12 C.
Shredded mozzarella cheese[3]	2 C.	4 C.	6 C.	8 C.	10 C.	12 C.
Cooked chicken, cubed[4]	3 C.	6 C.	9 C.	12 C.	15 C.	18 C.
Frozen chopped spinach, defrosted and drained	10 oz.	20 oz.	30 oz.	40 oz.	50 oz.	60 oz.

Assembly Directions:

Melt butter in a skillet. Add garlic and onion and cook until onions are translucent. Add white sauce, 1/2 C. Parmesan cheese (per recipe), basil, oregano and black pepper. Stir to combine.

Spray a 9x13 baking pan with cooking spray. Spread 1/4 of the cheese sauce in the bottom of the pan. Layer with:
4 uncooked lasagna noodles
1 C. cottage cheese
1/4 of the cheese sauce
2/3 C. mozzarella cheese
1-1/2 C. chopped chicken
5 oz. spinach

Repeat this layer again. Finish off with the remaining lasagna noodles, cheese sauce, mozzarella cheese, and Parmesan cheese.

Freezing Directions:

Place baking dish in a 2 gallon freezer bag. Seal, label, and freeze.

Serving Directions:

Thaw lasagna in refrigerator overnight. Preheat oven to 350 degrees. Cover baking dish with aluminum foil. Bake for 1 hour. Remove from oven and allow to rest for 15 minutes before cutting.

Notes:

[1] 1 medium onion = 1 C. chopped
[2] A recipe for Fat Free White Sauce can be found on page 161.
[3] 8 oz. cheese = 2 C. shredded
[4] 1 large chicken breast = 3/4 C. cooked chicken
One recipe can be made in two 8x8 pans.

Nutritional Info:

Per Serving: 349 Calories; 10g Fat (25.9% calories from fat); 31g Protein; 32g Carbohydrate; 2g Dietary Fiber; 48mg Cholesterol; 608mg Sodium.
Exchanges: 1-1/2 Grain (Starch); 3-1/2 Lean Meat; 1/2 Vegetable; 1/2 Non-Fat Milk; 1/2 Fat.

Orange Cinnamon Chicken

Recipes:	1	2	3	4	5	6
Servings:	4	8	12	16	20	24
Ingredients:						
Butter or margarine	1/4 C.	1/2 C.	3/4 C.	1 C.	1-1/4 C.	1-1/2 C.
Cinnamon	1/4 t.	1/2 t.	3/4 t.	1 t.	1-1/4 t.	1-1/2 t.
Brown sugar	2 T.	1/4 C.	1/4 C. + 2 T.	1/2 C.	1/2 C. + 2 T.	3/4 C.
Frozen orange juice concentrate	1 t.	2 t.	1 T.	1 T. + 1 t.	1 T. + 2 t.	2 T.
Grated orange peel	1 T.	2 T.	3 T.	1/4 C.	1/4 C. + 1 T.	1/4 C. + 2 T.
Lime juice	1 t.	2 t.	1 T.	1 T. + 1 t.	1 T. + 2 t.	2 T.
Split chicken breasts	4	8	12	16	20	24

Assembly Directions:

Using a mixer, beat butter, cinnamon and brown sugar until butter is fluffy.

Beat in orange juice concentrate, orange peel and lime juice until combined.

Gently lift the skin from the chicken breasts leaving it attached on 2 to 3 sides forming a pocket.

Spread the butter mixture on top of the chicken breast under the skin. Gently replace the skin to cover the butter.

Freezing Directions:

Place chicken breasts in a freezer bag or container. Seal, label, and freeze.

Serving Directions:

Thaw the chicken overnight in the refrigerator. Preheat the oven to 350 degrees. Line a rimmed baking sheet with aluminum foil. Place chicken on the baking sheet and bake for 1 hour.

Nutritional Info:

Per Serving: 254 Calories; 13g Fat (46.7% calories from fat); 27g Protein; 6g Carbohydrate; trace Dietary Fiber; 99mg Cholesterol; 196mg Sodium.
Exchanges: 4 Lean Meat; 2-1/2 Fat; 1/2 Other Carbohydrates.

Chicken Broccoli Fettuccine

Recipes:	1	2	3	4	5	6
Servings:	6	12	18	24	30	36
Ingredients:						
Boneless, skinless chicken breasts	3	6	9	12	15	18
Canola oil	1 T.	2 T.	3 T.	1/4 C.	1/4 C. + 1 T.	1/4 C. + 2 T.
Poultry seasoning	1/2 t.	1 t.	1-1/2 t.	2 t.	2-1/2 t.	1 T.
Chopped fresh broccoli[1]	4 C.	8 C.	12 C.	16 C.	20 C.	24 C.
Alfredo Sauce[2]	1-1/2 C.	3 C.	4-1/2 C.	6 C.	7-1/2 C.	9 C.
On Hand:						
Fettuccine	12 oz.	24 oz.	36 oz.	48 oz.	60 oz.	72 oz.

Assembly Directions:
Cut chicken breasts into bite-sized pieces or cut crosswise into 1/2 inch wide slices.

Heat oil in a large skillet over medium heat. When the skillet is hot, add the chicken, broccoli, and poultry seasoning to the skillet. Cook and stir until the meat is no longer pink in the center (8-10 minutes per recipe).

Remove the skillet from heat and allow to cool. When cooled, add Alfredo Sauce and mix until thoroughly combined.

Freezing Directions:
Place the chicken mixture in a freezer bag or container. Seal, label, and freeze.

Serving Directions:
Thaw overnight in the refrigerator.

Reheat sauce mixture either in the microwave on 50 percent power for about 5 minutes or in a saucepan on low until mixture is hot but not boiling.

Cook fettuccine until aldente (slightly chewy). Drain.

Plate the pasta and use a large scoop or spoon to ladle the sauce over the top.

Notes:
[1] 1 lb. fresh or frozen broccoli = 2 C. florets
[2] A recipe for Alfredo Sauce can be found on page 170.

Nutritional Info: with Alfredo Sauce
Per Serving: 476 Calories; 18g Fat (35.0% calories from fat); 29g Protein; 48g Carbohydrate; 3g Dietary Fiber; 60mg Cholesterol; 389mg Sodium.
Exchanges: 3 Grain (Starch); 2-1/2 Lean Meat; 1/2 Vegetable; 3 Fat.

Nutritional Info: with Light Alfredo Sauce
Per Serving: 414 Calories; 9g Fat (18.9% calories from fat); 30g Protein; 54g Carbohydrate; 3g Dietary Fiber; 48mg Cholesterol; 433mg Sodium.
Exchanges: 3 Grain (Starch); 2 Lean Meat; 1/2 Vegetable; 1/2 Non-Fat Milk; 1 Fat.

Chicken Tikka

Recipes:	1	2	3	4	5	6
Servings:	4	8	12	16	20	24
Ingredients:						
Plain lowfat yogurt	2/3 C.	1-1/3 C.	2 C.	2-2/3 C.	3-1/3 C.	4 C.
Canola oil	1 T.	2 T.	3 T.	1/4 C.	1/4 C. + 1 T.	1/4 C. + 2 T.
Lime juice	2 T.	1/4 C.	1/4 C. + 2 T.	1/2 C.	1/2 C. + 2 T.	3/4 C.
Minced garlic	1-1/2 t.	1 T.	1 T. + 1-1/2 t.	2 T.	2 T. + 1-1/2 t.	3 T.
Ground ginger	1 t.	2 t.	1 T.	1 T. + 1 t.	1 T. + 2 t.	2 T.
Ground coriander	1 t.	2 t.	1 T.	1 T. + 1 t.	1 T. + 2 t.	2 T.
Cumin	1 t.	2 t.	1 T.	1 T. + 1 t.	1 T. + 2 t.	2 T.
Cayenne pepper	1/4 t.	1/2 t.	3/4 t.	1 t.	1-1/4 t.	1-1/2 t.
Ground turmeric	1/2 t.	1 t.	1-1/2 t.	2 t.	2-1/2 t.	1 T.
Cinnamon	1/2 t.	1 t.	1-1/2 t.	2 t.	2-1/2 t.	1 T.
Ground cloves	1/4 t.	1/2 t.	3/4 t.	1 t.	1-1/4 t.	1-1/2 t.
Black pepper	1/4 t.	1/2 t.	3/4 t.	1 t.	1-1/4 t.	1-1/2 t.
Boneless, skinless chicken breasts or thighs	4	8	12	16	20	24

Assembly Directions:
Combine yogurt, oil, lime juice, garlic, ginger, coriander, cumin, cayenne pepper, turmeric, cinnamon, cloves and pepper in a small mixing bowl.

Freezing Directions:
Place the chicken in a gallon freezer bag. Add the sauce to the bag. Seal and label. Press on the sides of the bag to thoroughly coat the chicken. Freeze.

Serving Directions:
Thaw overnight in the refrigerator. As the chicken is thawing, press on the sides to keep coating the chicken.

Heat grill to medium high heat. Cook on grill until an instant read thermometer registers 170 degrees in the thickest part of the meat.

Chicken can also be baked at 350 degrees for 30 to 40 minutes depending on the thickness of the chicken.

Nutritional Info:
Per Serving: 199 Calories; 6g Fat (26.9% calories from fat); 30g Protein; 6g Carbohydrate; 1g Dietary Fiber; 71mg Cholesterol; 108mg Sodium.
Exchanges: 4 Lean Meat; 1 Fat.

Pork & Fish Recipes

Pork & Fish Recipes

TIPS FOR PORK & FISH RECIPES

Yields

- 2 ounces of lean pork (Canadian bacon, tenderloin, fresh ham) is considered a serving.
- 3 ounces of tuna, crab or broiled fish is considered a standard serving.
- 1/4 lb. of raw fish is an adult serving.
- 1/4 C. of cooked ground pork (as in sausage) is an adult serving.

Shopping & Cooking Tips

- Most fresh fish should not have a strong "fishy" odor and the packages should not be leaking.
- Fresh fish steaks and fillets should be firm. When you lightly press on the fish with your finger, the flesh should spring back into shape.
- When choosing fish for the grill, the firmer the better. Salmon, swordfish, tuna and halibut are perfect for grilling. Steaks that are one to two inches thick work best.
- As a general rule, the lighter the color, the lighter the flavor. Sole, Pacific and Atlantic halibut, cod, flounder, grouper, sea or fresh water bass, haddock, orange roughy, and trout are some of the milder tasting fish varieties. Ling cod, snapper, whiting, perch, rockfish, bluefish, catfish, and salmon are considered to be in the moderate flavored range. Swordfish, mackerel, shad and tuna are some of the stronger flavored fish varieties.
- Generally, ten minutes of cooking time per inch of thickness is a good rule. If a fish variety is translucent (sort of clear) to begin with, it is done as soon as it is opaque (not clear). When you are sautéing fish, the pan is too hot if you can smell the fish.
- Pork roasts, steaks, and chops are considered medium done if the internal temperature reaches 160 degrees F. Well done roasts, steaks and chops will have a temperature of 170 degrees F.
- When choosing ribs for barbecuing, country style ribs have quite a bit more meat on them.
- Make a cut at one-inch intervals through the fat on the edges of steaks and chops to prevent curling during cooking.

- When trying to cut thin slices, it is easier if you put the meat into the freezer for 30 minutes to an hour before slicing to help firm it up or if meat was frozen, slice before it is completely thawed.

Healthy Tips for Pork and Fish

- Broil, bake, or grill fish instead of frying it in fat.
- Sole, Pacific halibut, cod, flounder, grouper, sea bass, haddock, orange roughy, ling cod, red snapper, whiting, perch, pike, and rockfish all have less than 11 grams of fat per pound.
- You can automatically cut out many fat grams by trimming all the visible fat from the outsides of steaks and chops.
- Boneless pork loin chops are a lower fat chop compared to other cuts, but be careful not to over-cook them or they will be very dry and chewy!

Website Recipes & Tips

- For more great 30 Day Gourmet Pork & Fish recipes, check out the recipes section of our website at: www.30daygourmet.com
- For more Pork & Fish freezing tips and recipes from our cooks, check out our message boards at www.30daygourmet.com

Having meals in the freezer makes dinnertime less stressful.

Orange Marmalade Pork Chops

Recipes:	1	2	3	4	5	6
Servings:	4	8	12	16	20	24
Ingredients:						
Pork loin chops	4	8	12	16	20	24
Orange juice	1/2 C.	1 C.	1-1/2 C.	2 C.	2-1/2 C.	3 C.
Minced garlic	1/2 t.	1 t.	1-1/2 t.	2 t.	2-1/2 t.	1 T.
Brown sugar	2 T.	1/4 C.	1/4 C. + 2 T.	1/2 C.	1/2 C. + 2 T.	3/4 C.
Orange marmalade	1/3 C.	2/3 C.	1 C.	1-1/3 C.	1-2/3 C.	2 C.
Reduced sodium soy sauce	2 T.	1/4 C.	1/4 C. + 2 T.	1/2 C.	1/2 C. + 2 T.	3/4 C.
White vinegar	1 T.	2 T.	3 T.	1/4 C.	1/4 C. + 1 T.	1/4 C. + 2 T.
Black pepper	Dash	1/8 t.	1/4 t.	1/4 t. + 1/8 t.	1/2 t.	1/2 t. + 1/8 t.

Assembly Directions:

Place meat in a freezer bag or container.

In a mixing bowl, combine orange juice, garlic, brown sugar, marmalade, soy sauce, vinegar, and pepper. Whisk until thoroughly combined. Each recipe makes a little more than 1 C. of marinade.

Pour the marinade over the meat.

Freezing Directions:

Seal, label, and freeze.

Serving Directions:

Thaw. Grill, broil or pan fry pork chops until browned on both sides and no longer pink in the center. Discard marinade.

Notes:

This a great general purpose marinade recipe. Try it with chicken or even fish, such as cod, white fish or tilapia.

Nutritional Info:

Per Serving: 256 Calories; 8g Fat (28.7% calories from fat); 19g Protein; 26g Carbohydrate; 1g Dietary Fiber; 41mg Cholesterol; 361mg Sodium.
Exchanges: 2-1/2 Lean Meat; 1/2 Fruit; 1-1/2 Other Carbohydrates.

Shrimp Carbonara

Recipes:	1	2	3	4	5	6
Servings:	6	12	18	24	30	36
Ingredients:						
Butter or margarine	1 T.	2 T.	3 T.	1/4 C.	1/4 C. + 1 T.	1/4 C. + 2 T.
Minced garlic	1/2 t.	1 t.	1-1/2 t.	2 t.	2-1/2 t.	1 T.
Sliced mushrooms	4 oz.	8 oz.	12 oz.	16 oz.	20 oz.	24 oz.
Bacon slices, cooked and crumbled[1]	4	8	12	16	20	24
Frozen peas	3/4 C.	1-1/2 C.	2-1/4 C.	3 C.	4-3/4 C.	5-1/2 C.
Alfredo Sauce[2]	1-1/2 C.	3 C.	4-1/2 C.	6 C.	7-1/2 C.	9 C.
Frozen, cooked shrimp	12 oz.	24 oz.	36 oz.	48 oz.	60 oz.	72 oz.
On Hand:						
Linguine	12 oz.	24 oz.	36 oz.	48 oz.	60 oz.	72 oz.
Cherry tomatoes, halved	1 C.	2 C.	3 C.	4 C.	5 C.	6 C.

Assembly Directions:
Melt butter in a skillet over medium heat. Cook garlic and mushrooms until mushrooms begin to darken. Remove from the heat.

Add crumbled bacon slices, frozen peas and the Alfredo Sauce. Stir to mix. Leave the frozen shrimp in its original packaging.

Freezing Directions:
Place the Alfredo Sauce mixture in a freezer bag or container. Seal, label, and freeze. Attach the bag of frozen shrimp to the freezer bag or container.

Serving Directions:
Thaw sauce and the shrimp. Remove the tails from the shrimp.

Pour the Alfredo Sauce mixture into a saucepan or microwave safe bowl. Add the shrimp to the Alfredo Sauce mixture. Reheat sauce mixture either in the microwave on 50 percent power for about 5 minutes or in a saucepan on low until mixture is hot but not boiling. Add the cherry tomatoes. Stir to mix.

Cook linguine until aldente (slightly chewy). Drain.

Plate the pasta. Use a large scoop or spoon to ladle the sauce over the top of the pasta.

Notes:
[1] 4 slices = 1/4 C. cooked and crumbled. Check out the precooked and crumbled bacon in the meat section at the grocery store.
[2] A recipe for Light Alfredo Sauce can be found on page 170.

Nutritional Info: Alfredo Sauce
Per Serving: 505 Calories; 20g Fat (36.0% calories from fat); 29g Protein; 51g Carbohydrate; 3g Dietary Fiber; 139mg Cholesterol; 587mg Sodium.
Exchanges: 3 Grain (Starch); 2-1/2 Lean Meat; 1/2 Vegetable; 3 Fat.

Nutritional Info: Light Alfredo Sauce
Per Serving: 442 Calories; 10g Fat (21.0% calories from fat); 30g Protein; 57g Carbohydrate; 3g Dietary Fiber; 128mg Cholesterol; 630mg Sodium.
Exchanges: 3 Grain (Starch); 2 Lean Meat; 1/2 Vegetable; 1/2 Non-Fat Milk; 1-1/2 Fat.

Bourbon Mustard Pork Tenderloin

Recipes:	1	2	3	4	5	6
Servings:	6	12	18	24	30	36
Ingredients:						
Pork tenderloin	1-1/2 lbs.	3 lbs.	4-1/2 lbs.	6 lbs.	7-1/2 lbs.	9 lbs.
Bourbon	1/4 C.	1/2 C.	3/4 C.	1 C.	1-1/4 C.	1-1/2 C.
Reduced sodium soy sauce	1/4 C.	1/2 C.	3/4 C.	1 C.	1-1/4 C.	1-1/2 C.
Brown sugar	1/4 C.	1/2 C.	3/4 C.	1 C.	1-1/4 C.	1-1/2 C.
Minced garlic	1 t.	2 t.	1 T.	1 T. + 1 t.	1 T. + 2 t.	2 T.
Dijon mustard	1/4 C.	1/2 C.	3/4 C.	1 C.	1-1/4 C.	1-1/2 C.
Ground ginger	1/2 t.	1 t.	1-1/2 t.	2 t.	2-1/2 t.	1 T.
Worcestershire sauce	1 T.	2 T.	3 T.	1/4 C.	1/4 C. + 1 T.	1/4 C. + 2 T.
Canola oil	1/4 C.	1/2 C.	3/4 C.	1 C.	1-1/4 C.	1-1/2 C.
Red pepper flakes	1/4 t.	1/2 t.	3/4 t.	1 t.	1-1/4 t.	1-1/2 t.

Assembly Directions:

Place pork tenderloin in a gallon freezer bag.

In a mixing bowl, combine bourbon, soy sauce, brown sugar, garlic, mustard, ginger, Worcestershire sauce, oil and red pepper. Whisk until thoroughly combined. Each recipe makes a little more than 1-1/4 C. of marinade.

Pour the marinade over the meat.

Freezing Directions:

Seal, label, and freeze.

Serving Directions:

Thaw overnight in the refrigerator.

To Grill: Heat grill to medium high heat. Grill for 15 to 25 minutes or until the pork has reached 165 degrees using an instant-read thermometer.

To Bake: Preheat oven to 325 degrees. Remove pork from marinade and place on the rack of a shallow roasting pan. Bake for 45 minutes or until an instant-read meat thermometer registers 165 degrees.

Slice in 1/2 inch slices.

Notes:

This recipe is great served with Garlic Smashed Potatoes Red Potatoes (page 155) and a leafy, green salad.

Nutritional Info:

Oil was not included in the nutritional analysis.
Per Serving: 206 Calories; 5g Fat (23.1% calories from fat); 26g Protein; 8g Carbohydrate; trace Dietary Fiber; 59mg Cholesterol; 602mg Sodium.
Exchanges: 3-1/2 Lean Meat; 1/2 Vegetable; 1/2 Other Carbohydrates.

Honey Lime Scallops

Recipes:	1	2	3	4	5	6
Servings:	4	8	12	16	20	24
Ingredients:						
Honey	1/4 C. + 2 T.	3/4 C.	1 C. + 2 T.	1-1/2 C.	1-3/4 C. + 2 T.	2-1/4 C.
Lime juice	3 T.	1/4 C. + 2 T.	1/2 C. + 1 T.	3/4 C.	3/4 C. + 3 T.	1 C. + 2 T.
Canola oil	2 T.	1/4 C.	1/4 C. + 2 T.	1/2 C.	1/2 C. + 2 T.	3/4 C.
Grated lime peel	1 t.	2 t.	1 T.	1 T. + 1 t.	1 T. + 2 t.	2 T.
Salt	1 t.	2 t.	1 T.	1 T. + 1 t.	1 T. + 2 t.	2 T.
Red pepper flakes	1/4 t.	1/2 t.	3/4 t.	1 t.	1-1/4 t.	1-1/2 t.
Bay scallops	1-1/2 lbs.	3 lbs.	4-1/2 lbs.	6 lbs.	7-1/2 lbs.	9 lbs.

Assembly Directions:

Combine honey, lime juice, oil, lime peel, salt and red pepper flakes in large bowl. Each recipe makes a little less than 3/4 C. of marinade.

Rinse scallops and pat dry with paper towel.

Freezing Directions:

Pour marinade into a gallon freezer bag or container. Add scallops to marinade. Seal, label, and freeze.

Serving Directions:

Thaw overnight in the refrigerator.

Drain most of the marinade from scallops. Place scallops in a frying pan. Sauté until scallops are opaque. The residual marinade will thicken and begin to caramelize. Remove from heat and serve.

Notes:

Scallops are great served on a bed of long grain and wild rice!

Nutritional Info:

Per Serving: 209 Calories; 6g Fat (24.0% calories from fat); 21g Protein; 20g Carbohydrate; trace Dietary Fiber; 49mg Cholesterol; 597mg Sodium.
Exchanges: 3 Lean Meat; 1 Fat; 1 Other Carbohydrates.

Smoky Boneless Ribs

Recipes:	1	2	3	4	5	6
Servings:	**6**	**12**	**18**	**24**	**30**	**36**
Ingredients:						
Boneless country-style ribs	3 lbs.	6 lbs.	9 lbs.	12 lbs.	15 lbs.	18 lbs.
Garlic powder	1/4 t.	1/2 t.	3/4 t.	1 t.	1-1/4 t.	1-1/2 t.
Black pepper	1/4 t.	1/2 t.	3/4 t.	1 t.	1-1/4 t.	1-1/2 t.
Ketchup	1 C.	2 C.	3 C.	4 C.	5 C.	6 C.
Brown sugar	1/2 C.	1 C.	1-1/2 C.	2 C.	2-1/2 C.	3 C.
Chili sauce	1/2 C.	1 C.	1-1/2 C.	2 C.	2-1/2 C.	3 C.
Cider vinegar	2 T.	1/4 C.	1/4 C. + 2 T.	1/2 C.	1/2 C. + 2 T.	3/4 C.
Liquid smoke	2 T.	1/4 C.	1/4 C. + 2 T.	1/2 C.	1/2 C. + 2 T.	3/4 C.
Lemon juice	1 T.	2 T.	3 T.	1/4 C.	1/4 C. + 1 T.	1/4 C. + 2 T.

Assembly Directions:
Place ribs in a gallon freezer bag or container.

Place garlic powder, pepper, ketchup, brown sugar, chili sauce, cider vinegar, liquid smoke, and lemon juice in a large saucepan. Bring to a boil over medium high heat. Reduce to medium and simmer for 10 minutes.

Remove from heat and allow to cool.

Freezing Directions:
Pour barbecue sauce over ribs. Seal, label, and freeze.

Serving Directions:
Thaw overnight in the refrigerator.

Slow Cooker: Place ribs and sauce in a slow cooker. Cover and cook on high for 3 hours or on low for 6 hours or until the ribs are tender.

Grill: Preheat grill to medium heat. Lightly oil grate. Place ribs on prepared grill. Cook 10 minutes on each side. Continue cooking 20 minutes or until an instant-read meat thermometer reads 165 degrees.

Bake: Preheat oven to 350 degrees. Spray a 9x13 pan with cooking spray. Place ribs in pan and cover with aluminum foil. Bake 1-1/2 hours or until meat begins to fall off the bone.

Notes:
This recipe is great served with Garlic Smashed Potatoes Red Potatoes (page 155) and Garlic Green Beans with Red Peppers (page 153).

Nutritional Info:
Per Serving: 520 Calories; 29g Fat (49.5% calories from fat); 41g Protein; 24g Carbohydrate; 1g Dietary Fiber; 121mg Cholesterol; 586mg Sodium.
Exchanges: 5-1/2 Lean Meat; 2-1/2 Fat; 1-1/2 Other Carbohydrates.

Parmesan Crusted Tilapia

Recipes:	1	2	3	4	5	6
Servings:	4	8	12	16	20	24
Ingredients:						
Dried basil	1/4 t.	1/2 t.	3/4 t.	1 t.	1-1/4 t.	1-1/2 t.
Black pepper	1/4 t.	1/2 t.	3/4 t.	1 t.	1-1/4 t.	1-1/2 t.
Paprika	1/2 t.	1 t.	1-1/2 t.	2 t.	2-1/2 t.	1 T.
Garlic powder	1/2 t.	1 t.	1-1/2 t.	2 t.	2-1/2 t.	1 T.
Grated Parmesan cheese	1/3 C.	2/3 C.	1 C.	1-1/3 C.	1-2/3 C.	2 C.
Italian seasoned bread crumbs	1/3 C.	2/3 C.	1 C.	1-1/3 C.	1-2/3 C.	2 C.
Frozen tilapia fillets	1 lb.	2 lbs.	3 lbs.	4 lbs.	5 lbs.	6 lbs.
On Hand:						
Butter or margarine, melted	2 T.	1/4 C.	1/4 C. + 2 T.	1/2 C.	1/2 C. + 2 T.	3/4 C.
Mayonnaise or salad dressing; regular or reduced fat	3 T.	1/4 C. + 2 T.	1/2 C. + 1 T.	3/4 C.	3/4 C. + 3 T.	1 C. + 2 T.

Assembly Directions:
Combine basil, black pepper, paprika, and garlic powder in snack size bag.

Combine cheese and bread crumbs in a second snack size bag.

Place both bags inside a quart freezer bag.

Freezing Directions:
Seal and label quart freezer bag. Attach freezer bag to bag of frozen fish. Freeze.

Serving Directions:
Thaw overnight in the refrigerator.

Preheat oven to 425 degrees.

Drain any liquid from the fish. Line a baking sheet with aluminum foil.

In a shallow container thoroughly mix butter and mayonnaise until combined. Stir in seasoning mix until combined.
Place crumb mixture in another shallow container.

Coat fish on both sides with butter/mayonnaise mixture then dip one piece at a time in the bread crumb/cheese mixture flipping over to coat both sides.

Place fish on baking sheet. Bake for 10 to 12 minutes or until fish easily flakes when touched with a fork.

Nutritional Info: with Miracle Whip Light®
Per Serving: 246 Calories; 12g Fat (43.4% calories from fat); 25g Protein; 10g Carbohydrate; 1g Dietary Fiber; 58mg Cholesterol; 589mg Sodium.
Exchanges: 1/2 Grain (Starch); 3 Lean Meat; 2 Fat.

Pork Wellington

Recipes:	1	2	3	4	5	6
Servings:	**4**	**8**	**12**	**16**	**20**	**24**
Ingredients:						
Pork tenderloin	1 lb.	2 lbs.	3 lbs.	4 lbs.	5 lbs.	6 lbs.
Salt and pepper to taste						
Canola oil	1 T.	2 T.	3 T.	1/4 C.	1/4 C. + 1 T.	1/4 C. + 2 T.
Sliced baby portobello mushrooms	4 oz.	8 oz.	12 oz.	16 oz.	20 oz.	24 oz.
Thin sliced prosciutto	2 oz.	4 oz.	6 oz.	8 oz.	10 oz.	12 oz.
Frozen chopped spinach	5 oz.	10 oz.	15 oz.	20 oz.	25 oz.	30 oz.
Puff pastry sheet	1	2	3	4	5	6
On Hand:						
Egg, beaten	1	2	3	4	5	6

Assembly Directions:

Rinse tenderloin and dry. Season with salt and pepper. Sear in canola oil for 3 or 4 minutes on all sides until brown. Remove from pan. Allow meat to rest for 15 minutes. Refrigerate for 1 hour.

Sauté mushrooms in remaining oil until they release their water.

Preheat oven to 350 degrees. Place prosciutto on baking sheet and bake for 7 minutes. Remove from oven and place on paper towel to drain.

Thaw spinach. Drain and squeeze out all remaining liquid.

Slice loin in half. Layer prosciutto, spinach and mushrooms inside loin. Close up loin.

Place pastry sheet on a floured surface. Place loin in center of pastry and fold pastry over top of loin. Trim edges to fit.

Freezing Directions:

Place loin on a baking sheet. Flash freeze. When tenderloin is solid, place in a freezer bag or container. Seal, label, and freeze.

Serving Directions:

Thaw. Preheat oven to 350 degrees. Brush the wellington with the beaten egg. Bake seam side down on a baking sheet 35 minutes. Carve into 1/2 inch slices.

Nutritional Info:

Per Serving: 481 Calories; 26g Fat (50.0% calories from fat); 35g Protein; 24g Carbohydrate; 2g Dietary Fiber; 130mg Cholesterol; 690mg Sodium.
Exchanges: 2 Grain (Starch); 4 Lean Meat; 1/2 Vegetable; 5-1/2 Fat.

Tilapia with Mango Salsa

Recipes:	1	2	3	4	5	6
Servings:	4	8	12	16	20	24
Ingredients:						
Frozen tilapia fillets	1 lb.	2 lbs.	3 lbs.	4 lbs.	5 lbs.	6 lbs.
Canola oil	1/4 C.	1/2 C.	3/4 C.	1 C.	1-1/4 C.	1-1/2 C.
Lemon juice	1 T.	2 T.	3 T.	1/4 C.	1/4 C. + 1 T.	1/4 C. + 2 T.
Dried parsley	1 t.	2 t.	1 T.	1 T. + 1 t.	1 T. + 2 t.	2 T.
Minced garlic	1 t.	2 t.	1 T.	1 T. + 1 t.	1 T. + 2 t.	2 T.
Dried basil	1 t.	2 t.	1 T.	1 T. + 1 t.	1 T. + 2 t.	2 T.
Black pepper	1 t.	2 t.	1 T.	1 T. + 1 t.	1 T. + 2 t.	2 T.
Salt	1/2 t.	1 t.	1-1/2 t.	2 t.	2-1/2 t.	1 T.
Frozen diced mango	2 C.	4 C.	6 C.	8 C.	10 C.	12 C.
Red bell pepper, diced[1]	1 C.	2 C.	3 C.	4 C.	5 C.	6 C.
Minced red onion[2]	1/4 C.	1/2 C.	3/4 C.	1 C.	1-1/4 C.	1-1/2 C.
On Hand:						
Chopped fresh cilantro	2 T.	1/4 C.	1/4 C. + 2 T.	1/2 C.	1/2 C. + 2 T.	3/4 C.
Canned green chilies	4 oz.	8 oz.	12 oz.	16 oz.	20 oz.	24 oz.
Lime juice	1/4 C.	1/2 C.	3/4 C.	1 C.	1-1/4 C.	1-1/2 C.
Lemon juice	2 T.	1/4 C.	1/4 C. + 2 T.	1/2 C.	1/2 C. + 2 T.	3/4 C.
Salt and pepper to taste						

Assembly Directions:
Remove frozen tilapia fillets from their package and place in a quart freezer bag. Add oil, lemon juice, parsley, garlic, basil, pepper and salt.

Place mango, red pepper and red onion in a separate quart freezer bag.

Freezing Directions:
Seal both quart freezer bags and place inside a gallon freezer bag. Seal, label, and freeze.

Serving Directions:
Thaw the fish and mango mixture in the refrigerator about 6 to 8 hours before serving.

Place mango mixture in a small serving bowl. Stir in cilantro, green chilies, lime juice and lemon juice. Add salt and pepper to taste.

Preheat oven to 425 degrees. Line a baking sheet with aluminum foil. Place fish on baking sheet and bake for 10 to 12 minutes or until fish flakes easily with a fork. Place the fish on serving plates and spoon the fresh salsa over the top before serving.

Notes:
[1] 1 large red pepper = 1 C. diced
[2] 1 medium onion = 1 C. diced

Nutritional Info:
The oil was not included in the nutritional analysis.
Per Serving: 176 Calories; 1g Fat (5.6% calories from fat); 22g Protein; 21g Carbohydrate; 3g Dietary Fiber; 49mg Cholesterol; 333mg Sodium.
Exchanges: 2-1/2 Lean Meat; 1 Vegetable; 1 Fruit.

Cranberry Curry Pork Tenderloins

Recipes:	1	2	3	4	5	6
Servings:	4	8	12	16	20	24
Ingredients:						
Pork loin chops	4	8	12	16	20	24
Curry powder	1 t.	2 t.	1 T.	1 T. + 1 t.	1 T. + 2 t.	2 T.
Salt	1/4 t.	1/2 t.	3/4 t.	1 t.	1-1/4 t.	1-1/2 t.
Black pepper	1/4 t.	1/2 t.	3/4 t.	1 t.	1-1/4 t.	1-1/2 t.
Canola oil	1 T.	2 T.	3 T.	1/4 C.	1/4 C. + 1 T.	1/4 C. + 2 T.
Grape juice	1 C.	2 C.	3 C.	4 C.	5 C.	6 C.
Dried cranberries	1 C.	2 C.	3 C.	4 C.	5 C.	6 C.
Minced garlic	1-1/2 t.	1 T.	1 T. + 1-1/2 t.	2 T.	2 T. + 1-1/2 t.	3 T.
Chopped green onions	2	4	6	8	10	12
Ground ginger	1 t.	2 t.	1 T.	1 T. + 1 t.	1 T. + 2 t.	2 T.
Chicken broth	2 C.	4 C.	6 C.	8 C.	10 C.	12 C.
Black pepper	1/4 t.	1/2 t.	3/4 t.	1 t.	1-1/4 t.	1-1/2 t.
Salt	1/4 t.	1/2 t.	3/4 t.	1 t.	1-1/4 t.	1-1/2 t.
Brown sugar	1 T.	2 T.	3 T.	1/4 C.	1/4 C. + 1 T.	1/4 C. + 2 T.
Cinnamon	1 t.	2 t.	1 T.	1 T. + 1 t.	1 T. + 2 t.	2 T.

Assembly Directions:
Sprinkle loin chops on both sides with curry powder, salt and pepper. Heat oil in a skillet and lightly brown the chops on both sides. Remove from heat and cool.

Boil grape juice and dried cranberries in a medium saucepan for 5 minutes or until cranberries plump. Add the garlic, green onions, ginger, chicken broth, pepper, salt, brown sugar and cinnamon. Cook for an additional 2 minutes or until onions are tender. Remove from heat and cool.

Freezing Directions:
Place pork chops and sauce in separate freezer bag or containers. Seal, label, and freeze.

Serving Directions:
Thaw pork chops and sauce in the refrigerator overnight.

Preheat oven to 350 degrees. Line a baking sheet with aluminum foil. Spray with cooking spray. Place pork chops on baking sheet. Bake for 30 minutes or until an instant read thermometer inserted into the thickest piece of pork reads 160 to 170 degrees.

While the pork chops are baking, pour the sauce into a medium saucepan. Bring to a boil. Boil for 10 to 15 minutes or until reduced by half. Pour into a blender and blend until smooth. Return to pan and keep warm until chops are done.

Remove chops from oven. Place chops on plates and spoon cranberry sauce over top.

Nutritional Info:
Per Serving: 260 Calories; 12g Fat (43.3% calories from fat); 22g Protein; 15g Carbohydrate; 1g Dietary Fiber; 41mg Cholesterol; 561mg Sodium.
Exchanges: 3 Lean Meat; 1/2 Fruit; 1/2 Fat.

Sweet and Simple Salmon Marinade

Recipes:	1	2	3	4	5	6
Servings:	4	8	12	16	20	24
Ingredients:						
Reduced sodium soy sauce	1/4 C.	1/2 C.	3/4 C.	1 C.	1-1/4 C.	1-1/2 C.
Brown sugar	1/4 C.	1/2 C.	3/4 C.	1 C.	1-1/4 C.	1-1/2 C.
Water	2 T.	1/4 C.	1/4 C. + 2 T.	1/2 C.	1/2 C. + 2 T.	3/4 C.
Canola oil	2 T.	1/4 C.	1/4 C. + 2 T.	1/2 C.	1/2 C. + 2 T.	3/4 C.
Garlic powder	1/4 t.	1/2 t.	3/4 t.	1 t.	1-1/4 t.	1-1/2 t.
Black pepper	1/4 t.	1/2 t.	3/4 t.	1 t.	1-1/4 t.	1-1/2 t.
Lemon juice	2 T.	1/4 C.	1/4 C. + 2 T.	1/2 C.	1/2 C. + 2 T.	3/4 C.
Salmon fillets	1 lb.	2 lbs.	3 lbs.	4 lbs.	5 lbs.	6 lbs.

Assembly Directions:

In a mixing bowl, combine soy sauce, brown sugar, water, oil, garlic powder, pepper, and lemon juice. Whisk until thoroughly combined. Each recipe makes about 3/4 C. of marinade.

Cut salmon into 4 oz. portions. Place on a foil lined baking sheet.

Freezing Directions:

Flash freeze salmon. When salmon is solid, place it in a freezer bag.

Pour marinade into a separate bag. Seal, label, and freeze both bags.

Serving Directions:

Thaw salmon and marinade overnight in the refrigerator.

Once the marinade has thawed, pour marinade into salmon freezer bag. Reseal bag and turn to coat. The salmon should marinate at least 2 hours.

Grill: Heat grill to medium. Oil grill grates and cook salmon for 6 to 8 minutes on each side or until the fish flakes easily with a fork.

Broil: Spray broiler pan with cooking spray. Place salmon fillets on the broiler pan. Broil 5 to 7 minutes or until fish flakes easily with a fork.

Nutritional Info:

Per Serving: 239 Calories; 11g Fat (41.2% calories from fat); 24g Protein; 11g Carbohydrate; trace Dietary Fiber; 59mg Cholesterol; 685mg Sodium.
Exchanges: 3 Lean Meat; 1-1/2 Fat; 1/2 Other Carbohydrates.

Meatless Recipes

Meatless Recipes

TIPS FOR MEATLESS RECIPES

General Tips for Meatless Recipes

- Don't make the mistake of thinking that you can't eat meatless and be a freezer cook. Just follow the freezing tips and rules and apply them to the recipes that you already make. If your recipe depends upon using fresh vegetables, see if there are other parts of the recipe that could be made ahead of time and frozen. You can always add the veggies just before the final cooking time.

- Eating meatless doesn't have to mean searching a vegetarian cookbook or trying "weirdo" foods. It can be as easy as replacing the meat in one of your favorite meals with tofu, legumes, nuts or vegetables.

- Herbs will keep for several months in the freezer. Leaves from larger-leafed herbs like basil and sage should be removed from their stems, while tiny-leafed herbs like thyme and dill may be frozen while still on the stem. Wash and dry the herbs, then store individual varieties in sealed plastic bags or small freezer containers, labeled and dated. Frozen herbs often become limp or rubbery, so use them in dishes that call for some simmering, like soups or pasta sauces.

- When freezing your food, divide it up into portion sizes first so that you do not need to thaw the entire quantity when you want some. Your food will stay fresher, and if you do this with several dishes, you will have a variety of items to choose from in your freezer for a quick meal. If you need more than one portion, simply take out more than one package.

- In many recipes, you can create your own egg substitute by any of the following methods: use one ounce of mashed tofu; use 1/2 mashed banana in sweet recipes; mix one tablespoon of flax meal with two tablespoons water; or use one tablespoon of cornstarch or arrowroot mixed with two tablespoons of water. These techniques will help the recipe to "bind" when eggs are included for that purpose.

- Rice freezes great! Fully cook it and when cooled, package it in various sized freezer bags. Remove all of the air and freeze the bags flat. Rice can be reheated on the stovetop or in the microwave and served with steamed vegetables, bean burritos, tacos, vegetarian chili, or used to fill cabbage rolls, make fried rice or rice pudding.

- Freezing uncooked rice is fine too. Buy it in bulk and store it in the freezer safely for up to 2 years.

- Tofu can be frozen up to 5 months. Defrosted tofu has a pleasant caramel color and a chewy, spongy texture that soaks up marinade sauces and is great for the grill. For freezing, buy firm or extra-firm tofu. (Silken tofu will turn mushy.) Remove the tofu from its packaging and drain the tofu slightly. Pat the tofu dry with a paper towel and cut it into desired shapes (this speeds the thawing process later). Wrap each piece individually in plastic wrap and then put all the wrapped pieces into a freezer bag. Press the excess air out of the freezer bag and seal the bag.

Website Recipes & Tips

- For more great 30 Day Gourmet Meatless recipes, check out the recipes section of our website at: www.30daygourmet.com
- For more Meatless freezing tips and recipes from our cooks, check out our message boards at www.30daygourmet.com
- Check out the *Vegetarian Freezer Cooking* eBook offered on our website for more great Meatless recipes and tips.

There are plenty of vegetarian recipes that freeze well.

Cheese-Filled Shells

Recipes:	1	2	3	4	5	6
Servings:	**8**	**16**	**24**	**32**	**40**	**48**
Ingredients:						
Jumbo pasta shells	40	80	120	160	200	240
Lowfat cottage cheese	32 oz.	64 oz.	96 oz.	128 oz.	160 oz.	192 oz.
Shredded mozzarella cheese[1]	2 C.	4 C.	6 C.	8 C.	10 C.	12 C.
Grated Parmesan cheese	1/2 C.	1 C.	1-1/2 C.	2 C.	2-1/2 C.	3 C.
Eggs	2	4	6	8	10	12
Dried oregano	3/4 t.	1-1/2 t.	2-1/4 t.	1 T.	1 T. + 3/4 t.	1 T. + 1-1/2 t.
Black pepper	1/2 t.	1 t.	1-1/2 t.	2 t.	2-1/2 t.	1 T.
On Hand:						
Meatless spaghetti sauce	26 oz.	52 oz.	78 oz.	104 oz.	130 oz.	156 oz.

Assembly Directions:
Cook jumbo shells 1/2 of recommended time until just limp. Drain. Cool in a single layer on pan or waxed paper.

Combine cheeses, eggs, oregano and pepper. Fill each shell with 2 T. cheese mixture.

Tip: Using an icing bag with a wide tip works well for this or make your own by snipping the corner off a freezer bag.

Freezing Directions:
Freeze quantity of shells for one meal in a rigid container.

Serving Directions:
Thaw cheese-filled shells. Spread 1/2 C. spaghetti sauce in bottom of 9 x 13 baking dish. Arrange shells in dish. Pour remaining sauce over shells. Warm at 350 degrees for 30 minutes.

Notes:
[1] 8 oz. cheese = 2 C. shredded

Most kids really like these. They can be totally fat free depending on your cheese, sauce and egg choices. You could also use manicotti shells and whole wheat pasta works fine.

One recipe can be made in two 8x8 pans.

Nutritional Info: 5 shells per serving
Per Serving: 402 Calories; 11g Fat (25.4% calories from fat); 32g Protein; 42g Carbohydrate; 3g Dietary Fiber; 71mg Cholesterol; 1091mg Sodium.
Exchanges: 2-1/2 Grain(Starch); 3-1/2 Lean Meat; 1 Fat.

Lentils with Rice

Recipes:	1	2	3	4	5	6
Servings:	**4**	**8**	**12**	**16**	**20**	**24**
Ingredients:						
Dry lentils	3/4 C.	1-1/2 C.	2-1/4 C.	3 C.	3-3/4 C.	4-1/2 C.
Uncooked brown rice	1/2 C.	1 C.	1-1/2 C.	2 C.	2-1/2 C.	3 C.
Chopped onion[1]	3/4 C.	1-1/2 C.	2-1/4 C.	3 C.	3-3/4 C.	4-1/2 C.
Grated carrots[2]	1/4 C.	1/2 C.	3/4 C.	1 C.	1-1/4 C.	1-1/2 C.
Dried basil	1/2 t.	1 t.	1-1/2 t.	2 t.	2-1/2 t.	1 T.
Dried oregano	1/4 t.	1/2 t.	3/4 t.	1 t.	1-1/4 t.	1-1/2 t.
Dried thyme	1/4 t.	1/2 t.	3/4 t.	1 t.	1-1/4 t.	1-1/2 t.
Garlic powder	1/4 t.	1/2 t.	3/4 t.	1 t.	1-1/4 t.	1-1/2 t.
On Hand:						
Vegetable broth or chicken broth	3 C.	6 C.	9 C.	12 C.	15 C.	18 C.
Shredded cheddar cheese[3]	1/2 C.	1 C.	1-1/2 C.	2 C.	2-1/2 C.	3 C.

Assembly Directions:
Combine the lentils, brown rice, onions, carrots, basil, oregano, thyme and garlic powder in a quart freezer bag.

Freezing Directions:
Seal, label, and freeze.

Serving Directions:
Slow Cooker: Place contents of bag in slow cooker. Add vegetable broth or chicken broth. Cook on high for 2 to 3 hours or on low for 4 to 6 hours. Sprinkle cheese on top during last 15 minutes before serving to melt it.

Stovetop: Place contents of bag in a medium saucepan. Add vegetable broth or chicken broth. Bring to a boil over medium high heat. When mixture begins to boil, cover with lid and reduce heat to low. Cook for 30 to 40 minutes or until lentils and rice are tender. Remove from heat. Sprinkle cheese on top. Cover the pan and allow the mixture to sit for 5 minutes or until cheese is melted. Serve.

Notes:
[1] 1 medium onion = 1 C. chopped
[2] 1 medium carrot = 1/2 C. grated
[3] 8 oz. cheese = 2 C. shredded

Nutritional Info:
Per Serving: 406 Calories; 9g Fat (18.9% calories from fat); 20g Protein; 63g Carbohydrate; 15g Dietary Fiber; 17mg Cholesterol; 1318mg Sodium.
Exchanges: 4 Grain (Starch); 1-1/2 Lean Meat; 1 Vegetable; 1-1/2 Fat.

Spinach Lasagna

Recipes:	1	2	3	4	5	6
Servings:	**12**	**24**	**36**	**48**	**60**	**72**
Ingredients:						
Frozen, chopped spinach; thawed and drained	20 oz.	40 oz.	60 oz.	80 oz.	100 oz.	120 oz.
Eggs, beaten	2	4	6	8	10	12
Lowfat cottage cheese	12 oz.	24 oz.	36 oz.	48 oz.	60 oz.	72 oz.
Spaghetti sauce	52 oz.	104 oz.	156 oz.	208 oz.	260 oz.	312 oz.
Uncooked lasagna noodles	8	16	24	32	40	48
Shredded mozzarella cheese[1]	2 C.	4 C.	6 C.	8 C.	10 C.	12 C.
Grated Parmesan cheese	1/3 C.	2/3 C.	1 C.	1-1/3 C.	1-2/3 C.	2 C.

Assembly Directions:

Mix drained spinach, eggs, and cottage cheese in a mixing bowl.

Spray a 9x13 pan with cooking spray.

Layer 1/3 of the sauce, four noodles, 1/2 the spinach mixture and 1/2 of the mozzarella cheese in the bottom of the pan. Repeat layers, cover with remaining spaghetti sauce and sprinkle with Parmesan cheese.

Freezing Directions:

Place dish in a 2-gallon freezer bag. Or, if you want to wrap it in foil, cover the top of the lasagna with waxed paper or plastic wrap and then the foil, because the acid in the tomato sauce will leave small holes in the foil. Label, seal and freeze.

Serving Directions:

Thaw completely.

Preheat oven to 350 degrees. If the lasagna is wrapped in waxed paper or plastic wrap, remove it before baking. Cover pan with foil and bake for 30 minutes.

Remove foil and bake for another 30 minutes or until lightly browned. Let lasagna set up 15 minutes before cutting.

Notes:

[1] 8 oz. cheese = 2 C. shredded

One recipe can be made in two 8x8 pans.

Run the spinach through a food processor to chop it finer. This may help with the picky eaters in your household.

Nutritional Info:

Per Serving: 253 Calories; 9g Fat (33.1% calories from fat); 15g Protein; 28g Carbohydrate; 4g Dietary Fiber; 51mg Cholesterol; 784mg Sodium.
Exchanges: 1-1/2 Grain (Starch); 1-1/2 Lean Meat; 1/2 Vegetable; 1 Fat.

Tofu Stir-Fry

Recipes:	1	2	3	4	5	6
Servings:	**4**	**8**	**12**	**16**	**20**	**24**
Ingredients:						
Extra firm or firm tofu	1 lb.	2 lbs.	3 lbs.	4 lbs.	5 lbs.	6 lbs.
Reduced sodium soy sauce	1/2 C.	1 C.	1-1/2 C.	2 C.	2-1/2 C.	3 C.
Minced garlic	1 T.	2 T.	3 T.	1/4 C.	1/4 C. + 1 T.	1/4 C. + 2 T.
White vinegar	2 T.	1/4 C.	1/4 C. + 2 T.	1/2 C.	1/2 C. + 2 T.	3/4 C.
Ketchup	2 T.	1/4 C.	1/4 C. + 2 T.	1/2 C.	1/2 C. + 2 T.	3/4 C.
Ground ginger	2 t.	1 T. + 1 t.	2 T.	2 T. + 2 t.	3 T. + 1 t.	1/4 C.
Sesame oil	2 t.	1 T. + 1 t.	2 T.	2 T. + 2 t.	3 T. + 1 t.	1/4 C.
On Hand:						
Vegetable or olive oil	2 T.	1/4 C.	1/4 C. + 2 T.	1/2 C.	1/2 C. + 2 T.	3/4 C.
Carrots, sliced	2	4	6	8	10	12
Cauliflower florets[1]	1-1/2 C.	3 C.	4-1/2 C.	6 C.	7-1/2 C.	9 C.
Broccoli florets[2]	1-1/2 C.	3 C.	4-1/2 C.	6 C.	7-1/2 C.	9 C.
Onion, chopped[3]	1 C.	2 C.	3 C.	4 C.	5 C.	6 C.
Snow or sugar snap peas	1 C.	2 C.	3 C.	4 C.	5 C.	6 C.
Sliced mushrooms	1 C.	2 C.	3 C.	4 C.	5 C.	6 C.
Cooked long-grain white rice	3 C.	6 C.	9 C.	12 C.	15 C.	18 C.

Assembly Directions:
Press tofu to remove the excess liquid. Cut the tofu into 1-inch squares.

In a mixing bowl, whisk together the soy sauce, garlic, vinegar, ketchup, ginger and sesame oil. One recipe will yield about one cup of stir-fry sauce.

Freezing Directions:
Place tofu in a freezer bag or container. Pour the stir-fry sauce over top. Seal, label, and freeze.

Serving Directions:
Thaw in the refrigerator overnight. In a wok or a large skillet, heat the oil over medium high heat. Remove the tofu from the stir-fry sauce. Reserve the stir-fry sauce. Cook the tofu, carrots, cauliflower, broccoli and onions until the vegetables are crisp tender. Add the snow peas, mushrooms and reserved stir-fry sauce. Cook for a few more minutes. Vegetables should be tender but not soft. Serve over the cooked rice.

Notes:
[1] 1 lb. fresh or frozen cauliflower = 2 C. florets
[2] 1 lb. fresh or frozen broccoli = 2 C. florets
[3] 1 medium onion = 1 C. chopped

To save time, the rice can be cooked and frozen ahead of time. Reheat in a microwave safe dish on high for 6 minutes.

Nutritional Info: including rice
Per Serving: 405 Calories; 14g Fat (28.9% calories from fat); 20g Protein; 54g Carbohydrate; 6g Dietary Fiber; 0mg Cholesterol; 1336mg Sodium.
Exchanges: 2-1/2 Grain (Starch); 1-1/2 Lean Meat; 3 Vegetable; 1-1/2 Fat; 1/2 Other Carbohydrates.

Veggie Pizza

Recipes:	1	2	3	4	5	6
Servings:	32	64	96	128	160	192
Ingredients:						
Crescent roll packages	2	4	6	8	10	12
Reduced fat cream cheese, softened	8 oz.	16 oz.	24 oz.	32 oz.	40 oz.	48 oz.
Lowfat cottage cheese	8 oz.	16 oz.	24 oz.	32 oz.	40 oz.	48 oz.
Reduced fat mayonnaise or salad dressing	1 C.	2 C.	3 C.	4 C.	5 C.	6 C.
Ranch dry dressing mix	1 packet	2 packets	3 packets	4 packets	5 packets	6 packets
On Hand Toppings:						
Finely chopped broccoli[1]	1 C.	2 C.	3 C.	4 C.	5 C.	6 C.
Chopped cauliflower[2]	1 C.	2 C.	3 C.	4 C.	5 C.	6 C.
Chopped carrots[3]	1 C.	2 C.	3 C.	4 C.	5 C.	6 C.
Other optional vegetables: onions, bell peppers, fresh mushrooms, tomatoes						

Assembly Directions:
On a large cookie sheet or two small pizza pans, unroll crescent rolls and press edges together to cover pan. Bake 10-12 minutes at 375 degrees. Cool.

Freezing Directions:
Mix softened cream cheese, cottage cheese, mayonnaise and dry dressing. Spread on cooled dough. Use a pizza cutter to divide the dough into pieces suitable for serving. Seal, label, and freeze in a freezer bag or rigid container.

Serving Directions:
Thaw dough. Top with your choice of on hand toppings and serve.

Notes:
[1] 1 lb. fresh or frozen broccoli = 2 C. florets
[2] 1 lb. fresh or frozen cauliflower = 2 C. florets
[3] 3 medium carrots = 1 C. chopped

Nutritional Info:
Per Serving: 102 Calories; 6g Fat (56.5% calories from fat); 3g Protein; 8g Carbohydrate; trace Dietary Fiber; 7mg Cholesterol; 233mg Sodium.
Exchanges: 1/2 Grain (Starch); 1 Fat.

Baked Ziti

Recipes:	1	2	3	4	5	6
Servings:	**6**	**12**	**18**	**24**	**30**	**36**
Ingredients:						
Ziti pasta	8 oz.	16 oz.	24 oz.	32 oz.	40 oz.	48 oz.
Egg	1	2	3	4	5	6
Nonfat cottage cheese	2 C.	4 C.	6 C.	8 C.	10 C.	12 C.
Frozen chopped spinach	10 oz.	20 oz.	30 oz.	40 oz.	50 oz.	60 oz.
Meatless spaghetti sauce	3-1/2 C.	7 C.	10-1/2 C.	14 C.	17-1/2 C.	21 C.
Shredded mozzarella cheese[1]	2 C.	4 C.	6 C.	8 C.	10 C.	12 C.
On Hand:						
Grated Parmesan cheese	1/4 C.	1/2 C.	3/4 C.	1 C.	1-1/4 C.	1-1/2 C.

Assembly Directions:

Boil the ziti pasta in a large pot of water for about 10-12 minutes. The pasta should be firm. Drain pasta.

In a food processor, combine the egg and cottage cheese.

Defrost and drain spinach.

Transfer the egg and cottage cheese mixture to a large mixing bowl. Add the ziti, spaghetti sauce, spinach and shredded mozzarella cheese. Stir to combine.

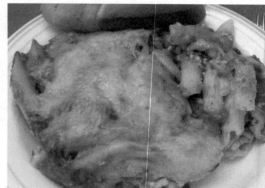

Freezing Directions:

Place the entire mixture into a freezer bag or container. Seal, label, and freeze.

Serving Directions:

Thaw in the refrigerator overnight. Preheat oven to 350 degrees.
Spray a 2-1/2 quart, 3 quart, or a 9x13 baking dish with cooking spray. Add the ziti mixture. Sprinkle with the Parmesan cheese. Cover and bake for 30 minutes or until the dish is hot and bubbly.

Notes:

[1] 8 oz. cheese = 2 C. shredded

One recipe can be made in two 8x8 pans.

Nutritional Info:

Per Serving: 413 Calories; 12g Fat (26.0% calories from fat); 31g Protein; 45g Carbohydrate; 5g Dietary Fiber; 57mg Cholesterol; 1108mg Sodium.
Exchanges: 2-1/2 Grain (Starch); 3 Lean Meat; 1/2 Vegetable; 1 Fat.

Vegetable Frittata

Recipes:	1	2	3	4	5	6
Servings:	**4**	**8**	**12**	**16**	**20**	**24**
Ingredients:						
Chopped onion[1]	2/3 C.	1-1/3 C.	2 C.	2-2/3 C.	3-1/3 C.	4 C.
Chopped zucchini[2]	2/3 C.	1-1/3 C.	2 C.	2-2/3 C.	3-1/3 C.	4 C.
Chopped red pepper[3]	2/3 C.	1-1/3 C.	2 C.	2-2/3 C.	3-1/3 C.	4 C.
Eggs	4	8	12	16	20	24
Egg whites	6	12	18	24	30	36
Water	1 T.	2 T.	3 T.	1/4 C.	1/4 C. + 1 T.	1/4 C. + 2 T.
Dried sweet basil	1/2 t.	1 t.	1-1/2 t.	2 t.	2-1/2 t.	1 T.
Salt	1 t.	2 t.	1 T.	1 T. + 1 t.	1 T. + 2 t.	2 T.
Black pepper	Dash	1/8 t.	1/4 t.	1/4 t. + 1/8 t.	1/2 t.	1/2 t. + 1/8 t.

Assembly Directions:

Spray a skillet with cooking spray. Cook onions, zucchini and red peppers until softened and slightly browned.

In a large mixing bowl, whisk together the eggs, egg whites, water, basil, salt and pepper.

Freezing Directions:

Pour egg mixture into a gallon freezer bag.

Add the vegetable mixture. Seal, label, and freeze.

Serving Directions:

Thaw the mixture overnight in the refrigerator. Preheat oven to 350 degrees. Spray a 9-inch pie pan with cooking spray. Pour the egg mixture into the pie pan. Bake for 30 to 45 minutes or until lightly browned and well set in the center. Cool 5 to 10 minutes before serving.

Notes:

[1] 1 medium onion = 1 C. chopped
[2] 1 small zucchini = 1 C. chopped
[3] 1 large pepper = 1 C. chopped

Nutritional Info:

Per Serving: 111 Calories; 5g Fat (37.0% calories from fat); 12g Protein; 6g Carbohydrate; 1g Dietary Fiber; 187mg Cholesterol; 673mg Sodium.
Exchanges: 1-1/2 Lean Meat; 1 Vegetable; 1/2 Fat.

Vegetarian Chili

Recipes:	1	2	3	4	5	6
Servings:	8	16	24	32	40	48
Ingredients:						
Chopped onion[1]	1 C.	2 C.	3 C.	4 C.	5 C.	6 C.
Chopped bell pepper	1 C.	2 C.	3 C.	4 C.	5 C.	6 C.
Quartered and sliced zucchini [3]	2 C.	4 C.	6 C.	8 C.	10 C.	12 C.
Sliced celery[4]	1 C.	2 C.	3 C.	4 C.	5 C.	6 C.
Canned black beans, undrained	15 oz.	30 oz.	45 oz.	60 oz.	75 oz.	90 oz.
Canned kidney beans, drained and rinsed	15 oz.	30 oz.	45 oz.	60 oz.	75 oz.	90 oz.
Canned garbanzo beans, drained and rinsed	15 oz.	30 oz.	45 oz.	60 oz.	75 oz.	90 oz.
Canned vegetarian baked beans	16 oz.	32 oz.	48 oz.	64 oz.	80 oz.	96 oz.
Crushed tomatoes	29 oz.	58 oz.	87 oz.	116 oz.	145 oz.	174 oz.
Minced garlic	1 t.	2 t.	1 T.	1 T. + 1 t.	1 T. + 2 t.	2 T.
Canned diced green chilies	4 oz.	8 oz.	12 oz.	16 oz.	20 oz.	24 oz.
Chili powder	2 T.	1/4 C.	1/4 C. + 2 T.	1/2 C.	1/2 C. + 2 T.	3/4 C.
Cumin	2 t.	1 T. + 1 t.	2 T.	2 T. + 2 t.	3 T. + 1 t.	1/4 C.
Dried parsley	2 t.	1 T. + 1 t.	2 T.	2 T. + 2 t.	3 T. + 1 t.	1/4 C.
Dried oregano	2 t.	1 T. + 1 t.	2 T.	2 T. + 2 t.	3 T. + 1 t.	1/4 C.
Dried basil	1 t.	2 t.	1 T.	1 T. + 1 t.	1 T. + 2 t.	2 T.
Frozen corn	2 C.	4 C.	6 C.	8 C.	10 C.	12 C.

Assembly Directions:

Spray a skillet with cooking spray. Cook the onions, peppers, zucchini and celery until lightly browned. Add the vegetable mixture, beans, tomatoes, garlic, green chilies, chili powder, cumin, parsley, oregano, and basil to a slow cooker. Stir to combine. Cook on low for 6 hours. Remove the lid and allow to cool. Stir in the frozen corn when cooled.

Freezing Directions:

Pour the chili into meal sized freezer bags or containers. Seal, label, and freeze.

Serving Directions:

Thaw in the refrigerator overnight. Reheat on the stovetop or in the microwave. Serve with tortillas, cornbread, rice or a crusty bread.

Notes:

[1] 1 medium onion = 1 C. chopped
[2] 1 large pepper = 1 C. chopped
[3] 1 small zucchini = 1 C. chopped
[4] 1 rib celery = 1/2 C. sliced

This soup can also be cooked on the stovetop. Bring the soup to a boil and then reduce heat to low. Simmer for 30 minutes.

Nutritional Info:

Per Serving: 306 Calories; 3g Fat (7.2% calories from fat); 15g Protein; 61g Carbohydrate; 15g Dietary Fiber; 0mg Cholesterol; 919mg Sodium.
Exchanges: 3 Grain (Starch); 1/2 Lean Meat; 2-1/2 Vegetable.

Spinach Triangles

Recipes:	1	2	3	4	5	6
Servings:	26	52	78	104	130	156
Ingredients:						
Frozen, chopped spinach; thawed and squeezed dry	10 oz.	20 oz.	30 oz.	40 oz.	50 oz.	60 oz.
Chopped green onions[1]	1/2 C.	1 C.	1-1/2 C.	2 C.	2-1/2 C.	3 C.
Chopped fresh parsley	1/4 C.	1/2 C.	3/4 C.	1 C.	1-1/4 C.	1-1/2 C.
Minced fresh dill	2 T.	1/4 C.	1/4 C. + 2 T.	1/2 C.	1/2 C. + 2 T.	3/4 C.
Crumbled Feta cheese[2]	1/2 C.	1 C.	1-1/2 C.	2 C.	2-1/2 C.	3 C.
Lowfat cream cheese, softened	4 oz.	8 oz.	12 oz.	16 oz.	20 oz.	24 oz.
Lowfat cottage cheese	4 oz.	8 oz.	12 oz.	16 oz.	20 oz.	24 oz.
Grated Parmesan cheese	2 T.	1/4 C.	1/4 C. + 2 T.	1/2 C.	1/2 C. + 2 T.	3/4 C.
Eggs	2	4	6	8	10	12
Salt and pepper to taste						
Phyllo dough, thawed	40 sheets	80 sheets	120 sheets	160 sheets	200 sheets	240 sheets
Cooking spray						

Assembly Directions:

In food processor, combine spinach, green onions, parsley, dill, cheeses, eggs, salt and pepper. Process until smooth.

On a cutting board, spray and layer three sheets of phyllo dough with cooking spray. Cut layered phyllo in half lengthwise.

Place one tablespoon of filling about 1" from corner of each strip. Fold one corner of phyllo diagonally across to opposite edge to form a triangle. Spray lightly. Continue to fold triangle onto itself. Spray the outside of the triangle to produce a golden brown color when baked.

Freezing Directions:

Place the triangles on a baking sheet lined with waxed paper leaving space in between each triangle. Freeze for 45 minutes. Remove from freezer and place in freezer bags. Seal, label, and freeze.

Serving Directions:

Do not thaw the triangles before baking because they will become soggy. Bake without thawing in a 350 degree oven for 30 to 35 minutes or until the triangles are golden brown.

Notes:

[1] 7 medium green onions = 1/2 C. sliced
[2] 8 oz. Feta = 2 C. crumbled

Nutritional Info:

Per Serving: 118 Calories; 4g Fat (55.8% calories from fat); 4g Protein; 2g Carbohydrate; 1g Dietary Fiber; 20mg Cholesterol; 235mg Sodium.
Exchanges: 1 Grain (Starch); 1/2 Lean Meat; 1/2 Fat.

Spicy Tofu Enchiladas

Recipes:	1	2	3	4	5	6
Servings:	**6**	**12**	**18**	**24**	**30**	**36**
Ingredients:						
Canned kidney beans; drained and divided	15 oz.	30 oz.	45 oz.	60 oz.	75 oz.	90 oz.
Salsa	1 C.	2 C.	3 C.	4 C.	5 C.	6 C.
Salt	1/2 t.	1 t.	1-1/2 t.	2 t.	2-1/2 t.	3 t.
Onion powder	1/4 t.	1/2 t.	3/4 t.	1 t.	1-1/4 t.	1-1/2 t.
Diced onion[1]	1/2 C.	1 C.	1-1/2 C.	2 C.	2-1/2 C.	3 C.
Minced garlic	1/2 t.	1 t.	1-1/2 t.	2 t.	2-1/2 t.	3 t.
Firm tofu, crumbled	1 lb.	2 lbs.	3 lbs.	4 lbs.	5 lbs.	6 lbs.
Cumin	1/2 t.	1 t.	1-1/2 t.	2 t.	2-1/2 t.	3 t.
Chili powder	1 t.	2 t.	1 T.	1 T. + 1 t.	1 T. + 2 t.	2 T.
6 inch corn tortillas	12	24	36	48	60	72
Shredded cheddar cheese[2]	1 C.	2 C.	3 C.	4 C.	5 C.	6 C.
On Hand:						
Enchilada sauce	15 oz.	30 oz.	45 oz.	60 oz.	75 oz.	90 oz.

Assembly Directions:

Place one half of the kidney beans in a bowl and smash them with a fork. Add the salsa and stir until well blended. Add the remaining kidney beans, salt and onion powder.

Spray skillet with cooking spray. Place diced onion, garlic, tofu, cumin and chili powder in skillet and sauté until tofu is lightly browned and onions are translucent.

Add salsa/bean mixture to skillet and cook until mixture is heated through and slightly thickened. This should take 5 to 10 minutes. Allow mixture to cool!

Warm the corn tortillas in microwave to soften them. Place 2 or 3 tablespoons of mixture in the middle of the tortilla and roll up burrito style. Place on a baking sheet. Do this for all of the remaining tortillas.

Freezing Directions:

Flash freeze the enchiladas. When enchiladas are frozen, place in a gallon freezer bag or a rigid freezer container. Place the cheese in a separate freezer bag or snack bag and place inside the container of enchiladas. Seal, label, and freeze.

Serving Directions:

Thaw enchiladas and cheese in the refrigerator. Spray a 9 x 13 pan with cooking spray and place enchiladas in the pan. Pour enchilada sauce over the top. Sprinkle cheese over the enchilada sauce. Bake at 350 degrees for 20 to 30 minutes or until the cheese is melted and sauce begins to bubble.

Notes:

[1] 1 medium onion = 1 C. chopped
[2] 8 oz. cheese = 2 C. shredded

Nutritional Info:

Per Serving: 416 Calories; 19g Fat (40.2% calories from fat); 19g Protein; 45g Carbohydrate; 9g Dietary Fiber; 43mg Cholesterol; 905mg Sodium.
Exchanges: 2-1/2 Grain (Starch); 2-1/2 Lean Meat; 1-1/2 Vegetable; 3 Fat.

Bread & Breakfast Recipes

Breads & Breakfast Recipes

TIPS FOR BREADS & BREAKFAST RECIPES

Yields

- Breads (quick or bread machine) have 12 servings per loaf.
- One muffin is considered a serving. Two crescent rolls are a serving.

Shopping & Cooking Tips

- Single-sized freezer packaging can be a key in getting your family to eat breakfast foods from the freezer. Make it as easy as possible for them to take out a serving, pop it in the microwave or toaster oven and go, go, go! Our Breakfast Burritos (page 118), Breakfast Cookies (page 123), Crunchy Granola Bars (page 127), Little Breakfast Quiches (page 129), and various muffins all qualify as "on the go" foods. For single serving muffins, place each muffin in a sandwich bag and then place the bagged muffins in a larger freezer bag. This makes it extremely easy to just "grab and go" when you are rushed in the morning.
- Waffles and pancakes can be made ahead of time and frozen. Be sure to cool them before freezing. Separate them in small food storage bags (put inside a large freezer bag) so they don't stick together or stack them in a rigid freezer container with layers of plastic wrap or waxed paper between each waffle/pancake. Reheat in the toaster (waffles) or microwave (pancakes and waffles).
- It's also easy to freeze homemade bread. Frozen bread keeps and freshens well. To freeze, allow the loaf to cool before placing it in freezer bags. Remove all of the air from the bag or ice crystals will form during the freezing process. Allow bread to thaw inside plastic bags to re-absorb the moisture lost during the freezing process. To freshen, place on a baking sheet and heat 10 to 15 minutes at 350 degrees.
- To successfully freeze muffins and quick breads, bake them completely, turn them out immediately, and then cool them thoroughly! Place the completely cooled muffins on a tray or baking sheet and open freeze them (no covering) for about a half hour or until they are firm to the touch. Place the frozen muffins into freezer bags or rigid freezer containers, remove any excess air, seal the container and store them in the freezer.
- Nuts keep for a long time in the freezer. When you see them on sale, buy them up, transfer them to quality freezer bags, label them and freeze them for later use.

Healthy Tips

- When you freezer cook, it's easy to "sneak" healthy ingredients in on your family. Because you are working with lots of foods all at one time, they are less likely to notice the whole-wheat flour or the soy milk sitting out on the counter. Experiment with substitutions that will boost the nutritional value of your foods.

30 Day Gourmet Website Recipes & Tips

- For more great 30 Day Gourmet Bread and Breakfast recipes, check out the recipes section of our website at: www.30daygourmet.com
- For more Bread and Breakfast freezing tips and recipes from our cooks, check out our message boards at www.30daygourmet.com
- Check out the eBooks offered on our website for more great Bread & Breakfast recipes and tips.

Use our Master Bread Machine Mix to make a variety of recipes like these calzones.

Super-Easy Freezer Crescent Rolls

Recipes:	1	2	3	4	5	6
Servings:	24	48	72	96	120	144
Makes:	48	96	144	192	240	288
Ingredients:						
Skim milk	2 C.	4 C.	6 C.	8 C.	10 C.	12 C.
Butter or margarine	1/2 C.	1 C.	1-1/2 C.	2 C.	2-1/2 C.	3 C.
Flour, divided	7 C.	14 C.	21 C.	28 C.	35 C.	42 C.
Active dry yeast[1]	2 env.	4 env.	6 env.	8 env.	10 env.	12 env.
Sugar	1/2 C.	1 C.	1-1/2 C.	2 C.	2-1/2 C.	3 C.
Salt	2 t.	1 T. + 1 t.	2 T.	2 T. + 2 t.	3 T. + 1 t.	1/4 C.
Eggs, slightly beaten	2	4	6	8	10	12
Butter or margarine, room temperature	3 T.	1/4 C. + 2 T.	1/2 C. + 1 T.	3/4 C.	3/4 C. + 3 T.	1 C. + 2 T.

Assembly Directions:

Scald the milk by putting it in a saucepan over medium heat. Remove it from the heat when small bubbles start to form around the edges. Add the butter, allowing it to melt in the warm milk. Set aside to cool slightly. In a large bowl, for one recipe mix together 4 C. of flour, yeast, sugar and salt. When the milk has reached a temperature between 120 to 130 degrees (very warm to the touch), add it to the flour mixture. Stir to mix. Mix in the eggs and the remaining 3 C. of flour. Make sure the dough is well mixed, but do not knead. The dough will be sticky.

Cover and let rise for 2 hours in a warm, draft-free place. After 2 hours, punch the dough down, and let it rest for 5 minutes.

Divide the dough into 6 equal pieces. Lightly dust the counter with flour, and roll one piece into a circle as large as you can get it. Spread a thin layer of butter over the circle. Cut the circle into 8 pie-shaped pieces with a pizza cutter. Using your hands, roll up each pie-shaped piece, starting at the wide end and rolling towards the small end. Place it point-side down on a cookie sheet. Repeat this process until all the dough is used up.

Freezing Directions:

Place the cookie sheet(s) of dough rolls into the freezer. When solid, place in a freezer bag or container. Seal, label, and freeze.

Serving Directions:

Spray a cookie sheet with cooking spray and place the needed number of frozen rolls on it. Cover and let rise in a warm, draft-free place for 3-1/2 to 4 hours, or until doubled. (When dough is doubled, you can touch it with your finger and the indentation will stay.) Preheat oven to 350 degrees, and bake the rolls for 10-15 minutes, or until lightly browned. Brush lightly with melted butter and serve.

Notes:

[1] 1 packet of yeast = 2-1/2 t. yeast

Crescent roll tips and variations may be found in the Members' section of our website at www.30DayGourmet.com.

Nutritional Info: 2 rolls per serving

Per Serving: 306 Calories; 3g Fat (7.2% calories from fat); 15g Protein; 61g Carbohydrate; 15g Dietary Fiber; 0mg Cholesterol; 919mg Sodium.
Exchanges: 3 Grain (Starch); 1/2 Lean Meat; 2-1/2 Vegetable.

Pizza Crust

Recipes:	1	2	3	4	5	6
Servings:	16	32	48	64	80	96
Makes:	**2 crusts**	**4 crusts**	**6 crusts**	**8 crusts**	**10 crusts**	**12 crusts**
Ingredients:						
Warm water	1-1/3 C.	2-2/3 C.	4 C.	5-1/3 C.	6-2/3 C.	8 C.
Sugar	1 T.	2 T.	3 T.	1/4 C.	1/4 C. + 1 T.	1/4 C. + 2 T.
Active dry yeast[1]	1 env.	2 env.	3 env.	4 env.	5 env.	6 env.
Oil	1 T.	2 T.	3 T.	1/4 C.	1/4 C. + 1 T.	1/4 C. + 2 T.
Flour	4 C.	8 C.	12 C.	16 C.	20 C.	24 C.
Italian seasoning	1 t.	2 t.	1 T.	1 T. + 1 t.	1 T. + 2 t.	2 T.
Salt	1/2 t.	1 t.	1-1/2 t.	2 t.	2-1/2 t.	1 T.

Assembly Directions:
In a mixer using a dough hook or a large bowl using a wooden spoon, combine warm water and sugar. Stir to mix. Add the yeast and let sit for five minutes while the yeast dissolves.

Add the oil, flour, Italian seasoning, and salt. Mix well until a dough ball forms.

For each recipe, divide the dough into 2 dough balls.

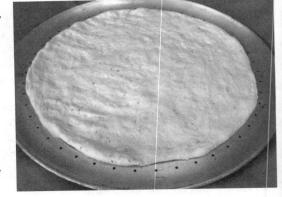

Freezing Directions:
Place each dough ball in a quart freezer bag. Immediately seal, label, and freeze.

Serving Directions:
Remove the dough ball from the freezer 24 hours before using. Leave in freezer bag until 2 hours before use.

Remove dough from the bag, place in a large bowl, cover, and let rise until double in size. This should take one to two hours.

Spray a 16 inch pizza pan, or an 12x17 jelly roll pan with cooking spray. Punch down the dough with a plastic scraper as you remove it to the pizza pan. Spread the dough edge to edge, top with pizza sauce and your favorite pizza toppings. Bake at 425 degrees for 15-20 minutes.

Notes:
[1] 1 packet of yeast = 2-1/2 t. yeast

Nutritional Info: crust only - per slice
Per Serving: 126 Calories; 1g Fat (8.6% calories from fat); 3g Protein; 25g Carbohydrate; 1g Dietary Fiber; 0mg Cholesterol; 68mg Sodium.
Exchanges: 1-1/2 Grain (Starch).

Grandma's Cinnamon Rolls

Recipes:	1	2	3	4	5	6
Servings:	**16**	**32**	**48**	**64**	**80**	**96**
Ingredients:						
Skim milk	1 C.	2 C.	3 C.	4 C.	5 C.	6 C.
Butter or margarine	1/4 C.	1/2 C.	3/4 C.	1 C.	1-1/4 C.	1-1/2 C.
Flour	3-1/2 C.	7 C.	10-1/2 C.	14 C.	17-1/2 C.	21 C.
Yeast, not quick rise	1 env.	2 env.	3 env.	4 env.	5 env.	6 env.
Sugar	1/4 C.	1/2 C.	3/4 C.	1 C.	1-1/4 C.	1-1/2 C.
Salt	1 t.	2 t.	1 T.	1 T. + 1 t.	1 T. + 2 t.	2 T.
Eggs, slightly beaten	1	2	3	4	5	6
Butter or margarine, room temperature	1-1/2 T.	3 T.	1/4 C. + 1-1/2 t.	1/4 C. + 2 T.	1/4 C. + 3-1/2 T.	1/2 C. + 1 T.
Sugar	1/4 C.	1/2 C.	3/4 C.	1 C.	1-1/4 C.	1-1/2 C.
Cinnamon	1 t.	2 t.	1 T.	1 T. + 1 t.	1 T. + 2 t.	2 T.
Lowfat cream cheese	3 oz.	6 oz.	9 oz.	12 oz.	15 oz.	18 oz.
Butter or margarine	1/4 C.	1/2 C.	3/4 C.	1 C.	1-1/4 C.	1-1/2 C.
Powdered sugar	2-1/2 C.	5 C.	7-1/2 C.	10 C.	12-1/2 C.	15 C.
Vanilla	1 t.	2 t.	1 T.	1 T. + 1 t.	1 T. + 2 t.	2 T.

Assembly Directions:

Heat the milk in a saucepan over medium heat. When small bubbles start to form around the edges, remove from heat. Do not allow the milk to boil. Add the butter and allow it to melt. Set aside to cool slightly. In a large bowl, for each recipe, mix together 2 C. of flour along with yeast, sugar and salt. When the milk mixture is between 120 to 130 degrees, add it to the flour mixture. Mix in the eggs and the remaining 1-1/2 C. of flour. Make sure the dough is well mixed, but do not knead. The dough will be sticky.

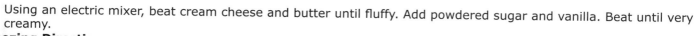

Cover and let rise for 2 hours in a warm, draft-free place. After 2 hours, punch the dough down, and let it rest for 5 minutes.

Lightly dust the counter with flour, and roll dough into a large rectangle about the size of an 12x17 jelly roll pan. Spread a thin layer of butter over the rectangle. Mix sugar and cinnamon in a small bowl. Sprinkle over dough. Leave about 1/2 inch from the edge without sugar. Roll tightly, beginning at the wide side. Seal ends by pinching the edges of the roll together when you are done. Cut into 1-inch slices and place on baking sheets. This should yield 16 or more cinnamon rolls.

Using an electric mixer, beat cream cheese and butter until fluffy. Add powdered sugar and vanilla. Beat until very creamy.

Freezing Directions:

Place the cookie sheet(s) of dough rolls into the freezer. When solid, place in a freezer bag or container. For each recipe, divide the cream cheese frosting in half and place in quart freezer bags. Seal, label, and freeze.

Serving Directions:

Spray an 8-inch cake pan with cooking spray and evenly space 8 rolls around the outer edge and in the middle of the pan. Cover and let rise in a warm, draft-free place for 3-1/2 to 4 hours, or until doubled. (When dough is doubled, you can touch it with your finger and the indentation will stay.) Remove 1 bag of frosting from the freezer and thaw in the refrigerator. Preheat oven to 350 degrees. Bake rolls for 15-20 minutes, or until lightly browned. Spread with frosting and serve.

Nutritional Info:

Per Serving: 306 Calories; 3g Fat (7.2% calories from fat); 15g Protein; 61g Carbohydrate; 15g Dietary Fiber; 0mg Cholesterol; 919mg Sodium.
Exchanges: 3 Grain (Starch); 1/2 Lean Meat; 2-1/2 Vegetable.

Breakfast Burritos

Recipes:	1	2	3	4	5	6
Servings:	**18**	**36**	**54**	**72**	**90**	**108**
Ingredients:						
Eggs	12	24	36	48	60	72
Water	3/4 C.	1-1/2 C.	2-1/4 C.	3 C.	3-3/4 C.	4-1/2 C.
Ground sausage	1/2 lb.	1 lb.	1-1/2 lbs.	2 lbs.	2-1/2 lbs.	3 lbs.
Salsa	1-1/2 C.	3 C.	4-1/2 C.	6 C.	7-1/2 C.	9 C.
Shredded mozzarella cheese[1]	1/2 C.	1 C.	1-1/2 C.	2 C.	2-1/2 C.	3 C.
Shredded cheddar cheese[1]	1/2 C.	1 C.	1-1/2 C.	2 C.	2-1/2 C.	3 C.
Flour tortillas	18	36	54	72	90	108
Optional:						
Frozen hash browns	2 C.	4 C.	6 C.	8 C.	10 C.	12 C.
Diced tomatoes						
Sliced mushrooms						
Chopped green peppers						

Assembly Directions:

In skillet, scramble eggs with water. While eggs are cooling, cook sausage in another pan. Cool and crumble.

Pour eggs and sausage into large bowl. Add salsa, cheeses and your choice of hash browns, diced tomatoes, sautéed mushrooms and/or peppers. Fill each tortilla with about 1/3 C. of mixture and roll up.

Freezing Directions:

Place the rolled up burritos on a baking sheet (seam side down). Flash freeze until firm. Package individually in small freezer bags or together in larger bag. Individual burritos may be wrapped in plastic wrap for a quick microwave warm up.

Serving Directions:

Thaw in the refrigerator overnight. Reheat in the microwave, toaster oven or inside food grill.

Notes:

[1] 8 oz. cheese = 2 C. shredded

Nutritional Info: not including optional ingredients

Per Serving (excluding unknown items): 284 Calories; 13g Fat (42.7% calories from fat); 11g Protein; 29g Carbohydrate; 2g Dietary Fiber; 139mg Cholesterol; 482mg Sodium.
Exchanges: 2 Grain (Starch); 1 Lean Meat; 2 Fat.

Breakfast Quiche

Recipes:	1	2	3	4	5	6
Servings:	**6**	**12**	**18**	**24**	**30**	**36**
Ingredients:						
Evaporated milk	1-1/2 C.	3 C.	4-1/2 C.	6 C.	7-1/2 C.	9 C.
Eggs	3	6	9	12	15	18
Chopped broccoli[1]	1/2 C.	1 C.	1-1/2 C.	2 C.	2-1/2 C.	3 C.
Diced ham[2]	1 C.	2 C.	3 C.	4 C.	5 C.	6 C.
Diced red pepper[3]	1/2 C.	1 C.	1-1/2 C.	2 C.	2-1/2 C.	3 C.
Salt	1/2 t.	1 t.	1-1/2 t.	2 t.	2-1/2 t.	1 T.
Black pepper	1/8 t.	1/4 t.	3/8 t.	1/2 t.	1/2 t. + 1/8 t.	3/4 t.
Shredded Swiss cheese[4]	3/4 C.	1-1/2 C.	2-1/4 C.	3 C.	3-3/4 C.	4-1/2 C.
Pie crust	1	2	3	4	5	6

Assembly Directions:

In a medium bowl, blend the evaporated milk and eggs using a whisk.

Steam broccoli until crisp tender.

Fold broccoli, ham, red pepper, salt, pepper, and Swiss cheese into egg mixture. Mix until combined.

Freezing Directions:

Pour the filling for each recipe into a one gallon freezer bag. Seal, label, and freeze. Keep the pie crust in the freezer or refrigerator, based on when you plan to serve it.

Serving Directions:

Thaw the filling at least overnight in the refrigerator. Thaw the pie shell, if necessary. Pour the filling into the pie crust. Bake at 350 degrees for 35 to 40 minutes or until a knife inserted in the center of the quiche comes out wet but clean.

Notes:

[1] 1lb. fresh or frozen broccoli = 2 C. flowerets
[2] 1 lb. ham = 3 C. diced
[3] 1 large pepper = 1 C. chopped
[4] 8 oz. cheese = 2 C. shredded

You can bake this quiche and then freeze it, if you prefer. Place a piece of waxed paper on top of the baked and cooled quiche. Wrap completely in heavy-duty aluminum foil, or put baked quiche in a two gallon freezer bag. To serve, thaw completely, remove the waxed paper, and then reheat at 350 degrees for 20 minutes.

To reduce the number of calories and the amount of fat, try baking the quiche without the crust. Spray a pie pan with cooking spray. Pour the filling into the pan. Bake at 350 degrees for 35 to 40 minutes.

Nutritional Info: with crust

Per Serving: 310 Calories; 17g Fat (49.4% calories from fat); 17g Protein; 22g Carbohydrate; 1g Dietary Fiber; 128mg Cholesterol; 827mg Sodium.
Exchanges: 1 Grain (Starch); 1-1/2 Lean Meat; 1/2 Non-Fat Milk; 2-1/2 Fat.

Nutritional Info: without crust

Per Serving: 176 Calories; 9g Fat (45.5% calories from fat); 16g Protein; 8g Carbohydrate; trace Dietary Fiber; 128mg Cholesterol; 632mg Sodium.
Exchanges: 1-1/2 Lean Meat; 1/2 Non-Fat Milk; 1 Fat.

Farmer's Breakfast Casserole

Recipes:	1	2	3	4	5	6
Servings:	6	12	18	24	30	36
Ingredients:						
Bread slices, crusts removed if desired	4	8	12	16	20	24
Frozen hash browns	1 C.	2 C.	3 C.	4 C.	5 C.	6 C.
Diced ham[1]	3/4 C.	1-1/2 C.	2-1/4 C.	3 C.	3-3/4 C.	4-1/2 C.
Chopped green peppers[2]	1/3 C.	2/3 C.	1 C.	1-1/3 C.	1-2/3 C.	2 C.
Chopped onion[3]	1/3 C.	2/3 C.	1 C.	1-1/3 C.	1-2/3 C.	2 C.
Diced tomatoes	1/3 C.	2/3 C.	1 C.	1-1/3 C.	1-2/3 C.	2 C.
Shredded Swiss cheese[4]	1/2 C.	1 C.	1-1/2 C.	2 C.	2-1/2 C.	3 C.
Shredded cheddar cheese[4]	1/2 C.	1 C.	1-1/2 C.	2 C.	2-1/2 C.	3 C.
Eggs	3	6	9	12	15	18
Evaporated milk	1 C.	2 C.	3 C.	4 C.	5 C.	6 C.
Onion powder	1/4 t.	1/2 t.	3/4 t.	1 t.	1-1/4 t.	1-1/2 t.
Dry mustard	1/2 t.	1 t.	1-1/2 t.	2 t.	2-1/2 t.	1 T.

Assembly Directions:

Spray a 9" square or round baking pan, or other heatproof baking dish with cooking spray. Cut the bread slices into cubes and place 1/2 of the bread cubes in the dish. Over the bread cubes, layer half of the hash browns, half of the diced ham, half of the green peppers, half of the chopped onions, half of the tomatoes, and half of each shredded cheese. Repeat all the layers ending with a layer of cheese. The pan will be very full. Beat the remaining ingredients together and pour over the pan. If serving the next day, cover the pan loosely with plastic wrap and refrigerate overnight. If not, continue with freezing instructions.

Freezing Directions:

Place the dish inside a labeled one-gallon freezer bag. Seal and freeze.

Serving Directions:

To serve the next day: Bake in a 375 degree preheated oven for 35 – 40 minutes. Cool 5-10 minutes before slicing to serve.

To serve after freezing: Thaw the pan in the refrigerator for about 12 to 14 hours. Remove from bag. Bake in a 375 degree preheated oven for 35 – 40 minutes. Cool 5-10 minutes before slicing to serve.

Notes:

[1] 1 lb. ham = 3 C. diced
[2] 1 large pepper = 1 C. chopped
[3] 1 med. onion = 1 C. chopped
[4] 8 oz. cheese = 2 C. shredded

The doubled recipe will fill a 9x13" baking pan and serve 12 – 14. The casserole may be baked frozen. Bake it at 300 degrees for 25 minutes, then 350 degrees for 35 minutes. A half-pound of bacon or sausage, cooked, drained and crumbled may be substituted for the ham. A cup of sliced summer sausage, or similar sausage may also be substituted. A small can of drained shrimp or crab would also be good in this. A cup of cooked diced broccoli, fresh or canned mushrooms, or sweet bell pepper may be added.

Nutritional Info:

Per Serving: 227 Calories; 9g Fat (34.6% calories from fat); 17g Protein; 20g Carbohydrate; 2g Dietary Fiber; 119mg Cholesterol; 500mg Sodium.
Exchanges: 1 Grain (Starch); 1-1/2 Lean Meat; 1/2 Vegetable; 1/2 Non-Fat Milk; 1 Fat.

French Toast Casserole

Recipes:	1	2	3	4	5	6
Servings:	**6**	**12**	**18**	**24**	**30**	**36**
Ingredients:						
Bread cubes[1]	6 C.	12 C.	18 C.	24 C.	30 C.	36 C.
Blueberries	1 C.	2 C.	3 C.	4 C.	5 C.	6 C.
Eggs	4	8	12	16	20	24
Evaporated milk	1-1/2 C.	3 C.	4-1/2 C.	6 C.	7-1/2 C.	9 C.
Brown sugar	3 T.	1/4 C. + 2 T.	1/2 C. + 1 T.	3/4 C.	3/4 C. + 3 T.	1 C. + 2 T.
Vanilla	1-1/2 t.	1 T.	1 T. + 1-1/2 t.	2 T.	2 T. + 1-1/2 t.	3 T.
Ground cinnamon	1 t.	2 t.	1 T.	1 T. + 1 t.	1 T. + 2 t.	2 T.

Assembly Directions:
Spray an 8x8 pan with cooking spray.

Place bread cubes in bottom of pan. Sprinkle fruit over the bread.

In a bowl, whisk the remaining ingredients. Pour over the bread cubes and fruit. Cover the pan with plastic wrap.

If baking immediately, do not cover pan with plastic wrap. Instead, allow to stand for 15 minutes.

Freezing Directions:
If freezing, place pan in a one gallon freezer bag. Seal, label, and freeze.

Serving Directions:
To bake immediately: Preheat oven to 350 degrees. Bake for 45 minutes or until golden brown. Serve warm with syrup.

To serve after freezing: Thaw in refrigerator for about 12 to 14 hours. Remove from freezer bag and discard plastic wrap. Preheat oven to 350 degrees. Bake for 45 minutes or until golden brown. Serve warm with syrup.

Notes:
[1] 16 oz. loaf bread = 14 C. one inch cubes

A doubled recipe will fill a 9x13 pan and serve 12.

Nutritional Info:
Per Serving: 247 Calories; 5g Fat (17.7% calories from fat); 12g Protein; 38g Carbohydrate; 2g Dietary Fiber; 127mg Cholesterol; 372mg Sodium.
Exchanges: 1-1/2 Grain (Starch); 1/2 Lean Meat; 1/2 Non-Fat Milk; 1/2 Fat; 1/2 Other Carbohydrates.

Chocolate Pecan Pumpkin Bread

Recipes:	1	2	3	4	5	6
Servings:	**12**	**24**	**36**	**48**	**60**	**72**
Ingredients:						
Whole wheat flour	1 C.	2 C.	3 C.	4 C.	5 C.	6 C.
Flour	1 C.	2 C.	3 C.	4 C.	5 C.	6 C.
Cinnamon	1 t.	2 t.	1 T.	1 T. + 1 t.	1 T. + 2 t.	2 T.
Ground nutmeg	1/2 t.	1 t.	1-1/2 t.	2 t.	2-1/2 t.	1 T.
Baking soda	1 t.	2 t.	1 T.	1 T. + 1 t.	1 T. + 2 t.	2 T.
Salt	1/2 t.	1 t.	1-1/2 t.	2 t.	2-1/2 t.	1 T.
Butter or margarine	1/2 C.	1 C.	1-1/2 C.	2 C.	2-1/2 C.	3 C.
Sugar	2 T.	1/4 C.	1/4 C. + 2 T.	1/2 C.	1/2 C. + 2 T.	3/4 C.
Brown sugar	3/4 C.	1-1/2 C.	2-1/4 C.	3 C.	3-3/4 C.	4-1/2 C.
Eggs	2	4	6	8	10	12
Vanilla	1 t.	2 t.	1 T.	1 T. + 1 t.	1 T. + 2 t.	2 T.
Pumpkin puree	1-1/2 C.	3 C.	4-1/2 C.	6 C.	7-1/2 C.	9 C.
Water	1/4 C.	1/2 C.	3/4 C.	1 C.	1-1/4 C.	1-1/2 C.
Miniature chocolate chips	1/2 C.	1 C.	1-1/2 C.	2 C.	2-1/2 C.	3 C.
Chopped pecans (optional)	1/2 C.	1 C.	1-1/2 C.	2 C.	2-1/2 C.	3 C.

Assembly Directions:

Preheat the oven to 350 degrees. Spray a 9x5 inch loaf pan with cooking spray. Combine flours, cinnamon, nutmeg, baking soda and salt in a bowl. Whisk and set aside.

In a mixing bowl, combine butter and sugars and beat for two minutes. Add the eggs and lightly beat until just combined. Mix in vanilla, pumpkin and water -- do not overmix. Gradually beat in the flour mixture.

Stir in the chocolate chips and chopped nuts, if using, by hand.

Pour the batter into the pan and bake for approximately 55 to 65 minutes. Remove from pan and place on a wire rack to cool.

Freezing Directions:

Place cooled bread in a one gallon freezer bag. Seal, label, and freeze.

Serving Directions:

Thaw, slice and enjoy.

Nutritional Info: not including chopped pecans

Per Serving: 257 Calories; 11g Fat (36.6% calories from fat); 4g Protein; 38g Carbohydrate; 3g Dietary Fiber; 31mg Cholesterol; 305mg Sodium.
Exchanges: 1 Grain (Starch); 1/2 Vegetable; 2 Fat; 1-1/2 Other Carbohydrates.

Breakfast Cookies

Recipes:	1	2	3	4	5	6
Servings:	**16**	**32**	**48**	**64**	**80**	**96**
Ingredients:						
Butter or margarine	1/4 C.	1/2 C.	3/4 C.	1 C.	1-1/4 C.	1-1/2 C.
Peanut butter	3/4 C.	1-1/2 C.	2-1/4 C.	3 C.	3-3/4 C.	4-1/2 C.
Brown sugar	1 C.	2 C.	3 C.	4 C.	5 C.	6 C.
Applesauce	1/4 C.	1/2 C.	3/4 C.	1 C.	1-1/4 C.	1-1/2 C.
Vanilla	2 t.	1 T. + 1 t.	2 T.	2 T. + 2 t.	3 T. + 1 t.	1/4 C.
Eggs	2	4	6	8	10	12
Apple juice or water	1/3 C.	2/3 C.	1 C.	1-1/3 C.	1-2/3 C.	2 C.
Salt	1 t.	2 t.	1 T.	1 T. + 1 t.	1 T. + 2 t.	2 T.
Ground cinnamon	1 t.	2 t.	1 T.	1 T. + 1 t.	1 T. + 2 t.	2 T.
Baking soda	2 t.	1 T. + 1 t.	2 T.	2 T. + 2 t.	3 T. + 1 t.	1/4 C.
Milled flax seed	1/3 C.	2/3 C.	1 C.	1-1/3 C.	1-2/3 C.	2 C.
Flour	1 C.	2 C.	3 C.	4 C.	5 C.	6 C.
Whole wheat flour	1 C.	2 C.	3 C.	4 C.	5 C.	6 C.
Old-fashioned rolled oats	2 C.	4 C.	6 C.	8 C.	10 C.	12 C.
Semisweet chocolate chips (optional)	1 C.	2 C.	3 C.	4 C.	5 C.	6 C.
Dried cranberries	1 C.	2 C.	3 C.	4 C.	5 C.	6 C.
Chopped apples[1]	1 C.	2 C.	3 C.	4 C.	5 C.	6 C.

Assembly Directions:

Preheat oven to 350 degrees. In a mixing bowl, cream butter, peanut butter, and sugar until fluffy. Beat in applesauce, vanilla, eggs, and apple juice or water until thoroughly combined. Add salt, cinnamon, and baking soda. Beat until combined. Add flax seed, flours and oats. Beat until combined scraping the bowl at least once with a spatula. Stir in the chocolate chips, cranberries, and apples by hand.

Spray a baking sheet with cooking spray or line with parchment paper. Scoop out dough using a 1/4 cup measuring cup. Bake 8 cookies per sheet. Bake for 20 minutes or until bottoms begin to brown. Remove from baking sheet and cool on a wire rack.

Freezing Directions:

Place cookies in individual snack size bags and then in a larger freezer bag for a quick "grab and go" breakfast. Seal, label, and freeze.

Serving Directions:

Thaw and enjoy!

Notes:

[1] 1 medium apple = 1 C. chopped

Nutritional Info: without chocolate chips

Per Serving: 279 Calories; 11g Fat (35.2% calories from fat); 8g Protein; 39g Carbohydrate; 4g Dietary Fiber; 31mg Cholesterol; 388mg Sodium.
Exchanges: 1-1/2 Grain (Starch); 1/2 Lean Meat; 1/2 Fruit; 2 Fat; 1/2 Other Carbohydrates.

Nutritional Info: with chocolate chips

Per Serving: 329 Calories; 14g Fat (37.6% calories from fat); 8g Protein; 46g Carbohydrate; 5g Dietary Fiber; 31mg Cholesterol; 389mg Sodium.
Exchanges: 1-1/2 Grain (Starch); 1/2 Lean Meat; 1/2 Fruit; 2-1/2 Fat; 1 Other Carbohydrates.

Chocolate Streusel Coffee Cake or Muffins

Recipes:	1	2	3	4	5	6
Servings:	**12**	**24**	**36**	**48**	**60**	**72**
Ingredients:						
Flour	2 C.	4 C.	6 C.	8 C.	10 C.	12 C.
Baking powder	1 t.	2 t.	1 T.	1 T. + 1 t.	1 T. + 2 t.	2 T.
Baking soda	1/2 t.	1 t.	1-1/2 t.	2 t.	2-1/2 t.	1 T.
Salt	1/2 t.	1 t.	1-1/2 t.	2 t.	2-1/2 t.	1 T.
Sugar	1 C.	2 C.	3 C.	4 C.	5 C.	6 C.
Butter or margarine	1/4 C.	1/2 C.	3/4 C.	1 C.	1-1/4 C.	1-1/2 C.
Eggs	2	4	6	8	10	12
Vanilla	1 t.	2 t.	1 T.	1 T. + 1 t.	1 T. + 2 t.	2 T.
Reduced fat sour cream	1 C.	2 C.	3 C.	4 C.	5 C.	6 C.
Streusel Topping:						
Sugar	1/4 C.	1/2 C.	3/4 C.	1 C.	1-1/4 C.	1-1/2 C.
Chopped pecans	1/2 C.	1 C.	1-1/2 C.	2 C.	2-1/2 C.	3 C.
Miniature chocolate chips	1/3 C.	2/3 C.	1 C.	1-1/3 C.	1-2/3 C.	2 C.
Cocoa powder	2 T.	1/4 C.	1/4 C. + 2 T.	1/2 C.	1/2 C. + 2 T.	3/4 C.
Ground cinnamon	3/4 t.	1-1/2 t.	2-1/4 t.	1 T.	1 T. + 3/4 t.	1 T. + 1-1/2 t.

Assembly Directions:

Preheat the oven to 350 degrees. Spray a muffin tin or 9x13 cake pan with cooking spray. Combine flour, baking powder, baking soda, and salt in a bowl. Whisk and set aside.

In a mixing bowl, combine sugar and butter. Beat for two minutes. Add the eggs, vanilla and sour cream and lightly beat until just combined. Gradually beat in the flour mixture.

In a separate bowl, combine the sugar, pecans, chocolate chips, cocoa powder, and cinnamon.

Muffins: Fill each muffin cup until 1/3 full. Sprinkle 1 t. of streusel topping over the batter for each muffin. Add remaining batter. Top with remaining topping mix. Bake for 20 to 23 minutes. Remove muffins from pan and place on a wire rack to cool.

Coffee Cake: Spoon half of the batter into cake pan. Sprinkle half the nut mixture over the batter. Top with remaining batter. Sprinkle with remaining nut mixture. Bake for 25 to 30 minutes or until a toothpick inserted into the center of a muffin comes out clean. Cool completely.

Freezing Directions:

Muffins: Place muffins in a freezer container. Seal, label, and freeze.
Coffee Cake: Place coffee cake in a two gallon freezer bag. Seal, label, and freeze.

Serving Directions:

Thaw muffins or coffee cake overnight. Muffins can also be reheated in a microwave oven 15 seconds on high.

Nutritional Info:

Per Serving: 267 Calories; 10g Fat (32.6% calories from fat); 4g Protein; 42g Carbohydrate; 1g Dietary Fiber; 33mg Cholesterol; 244mg Sodium.
Exchanges: 1 Grain (Starch); 2 Fat; 1-1/2 Other Carbohydrates.

Master Bread Machine Mix

Recipes:	1	2	3	4	5	6
Servings:	72	144	216	288	360	432
Makes:	21 C.	42 C.	63 C.	84 C.	105 C.	126 C.
Ingredients:						
Flour	5 lbs. + 1 C.	10 lbs. + 2 C.	15 lbs. + 3 C.	20 lbs. + 4 C.	25 lbs. + 5 C.	30 lbs. + 6 C.
Sugar or brown sugar	1 C.	2 C.	3 C.	4 C.	5 C.	6 C.
Powdered buttermilk[1]	1 C.	2 C.	3 C.	4 C.	5 C.	6 C.
Salt; heaping measurement	1 t.	2 t.	1 T.	1 T. + 1 t.	1 T. + 2 t.	2 T.

Assembly Directions:

In a large bowl, mix together the flour, sugar, powdered buttermilk and salt. Mix well.

Freezing Directions:

Measure out 3-1/2 C. of the mixture into quart-size zipper bags. Each batch of the mix will yield 6 bags of mix. If you have a few tablespoons of mix left over after measuring out the 6 bags, just divide it between the bags. Put the bags of mix in a 2-gallon freezer bag, or into two 1-gallon freezer bags. Seal, label, and freeze. Or, put the entire mix in an airtight rigid container, and store the whole thing in the freezer.

Serving Directions:

Remove a quart-size bag of the mixture from the freezer. Allow it to come to room temperature. Or, remove the large container of mix from the freezer. Measure out 3-1/2 C. of the mixture, and allow it to come to room temperature. Place the following ingredients in your bread machine in the order recommended by the manufacturer:

1 C. warm water
1 egg
2 T. butter or cooking oil
3-1/2 C. bread mix
1-1/2 t. active dry yeast

Set your bread machine to the appropriate setting and press start. Makes a 1-1/2 pound loaf.

Notes:

This is a very versatile dough that can be used for cinnamon buns, pizza crust, hot pockets, and calzones in addition to bread.

[1] Powdered buttermilk can be found at your local grocery, probably in the baking aisle. They promote it to be used for baking, in place of liquid buttermilk. It has a longer refrigerator-life than liquid buttermilk.

Nutritional Info: Bread Machine Mix

Per Serving: 139 Calories; trace Fat (2.8% calories from fat); 4g Protein; 29g Carbohydrate; 1g Dietary Fiber; 1mg Cholesterol; 40mg Sodium.
Exchanges: 1-1/2 Grain (Starch).

Nutritional Info: Basic Bread Machine Bread

Per Serving: 163 Calories; 3g Fat (15.2% calories from fat); 5g Protein; 29g Carbohydrate; 1g Dietary Fiber; 17mg Cholesterol; 67mg Sodium.
Exchanges: 1-1/2 Grain (Starch); 1/2 Fat.

Herbed Garlic Bread

Recipes:	1	2	3	4	5	6
Servings:	12	24	36	48	60	72
Ingredients:						
French or Italian bread loaf	1	2	3	4	5	6
Butter or margarine	1/2 C.	1 C.	1-1/2 C.	2 C.	2-1/2 C.	3 C.
Minced garlic	1-1/2 t.	1 T.	1 T. + 1-1/2 t.	2 T.	2 T. + 1-1/2 t.	3 T.
Grated Parmesan cheese	3 T.	1/4 C. + 2 T.	1/2 C. + 1 T.	3/4 C.	3/4 C. + 3 T.	1 C. + 2 T.
Dried basil	1/2 t.	1 t.	1-1/2 t.	2 t.	2-1/2 t.	1 T.
Dried parsley	1/2 t.	1 t.	1-1/2 t.	2 t.	2-1/2 t.	1 T.
Dried oregano	1 t.	2 t.	1 T.	1 T. + 1 t.	1 T. + 2 t.	2 T.

Assembly Directions:

Slice loaf of bread in half lengthwise.

In a mixing bowl, beat butter until fluffy. Add garlic, Parmesan cheese, basil, parsley and oregano and beat until combined.

Spread the butter mixture on each half of the bread. Put the two halves of the loaves together to form a complete loaf.

Freezing Directions:

Cover with aluminum foil and place in a freezer bag. Seal, label, and freeze.

Serving Directions:

Do not thaw.

Oven Method: Preheat oven to 450 degrees. Remove bread from freezer bag and remove aluminum foil. Place frozen bread open faced on a baking sheet. Bake for 8 to 10 minutes or until heated through.

Grill Method: Heat grill to medium high heat. Remove bread from freezer bag. Leave aluminum foil on the bread. Place wrapped bread on the grill. Heat 8 to 10 minutes, turning every 4 minutes, or until heated through.

Nutritional Info:

Per Serving: 154 Calories; 7g Fat (39.6% calories from fat); 4g Protein; 19g Carbohydrate; 1g Dietary Fiber; 1mg Cholesterol; 303mg Sodium.
Exchanges: 1-1/2 Grain (Starch); 1-1/2 Fat.

Crunchy Granola Bars

Recipes:	1	2	3	4	5	6
Servings:	**24**	**48**	**72**	**96**	**120**	**144**
Ingredients:						
Canola oil	1/4 C.	1/2 C.	3/4 C.	1 C.	1-1/4 C.	1-1/2 C.
Butter or margarine	1/4 C.	1/2 C.	3/4 C.	1 C.	1-1/4 C.	1-1/2 C.
Sugar	1/2 C.	1 C.	1-1/2 C.	2 C.	2-1/2 C.	3 C.
Honey	1/4 C.	1/2 C.	3/4 C.	1 C.	1-1/4 C.	1-1/2 C.
Salt	1/2 t.	1 t.	1-1/2 t.	2 t.	2-1/2 t.	1 T.
Cinnamon	1 t.	2 t.	1 T.	1 T. + 1 t.	1 T. + 2 t.	2 T.
Old-fashioned rolled oats	5 C.	10 C.	15 C.	20 C.	25 C.	30 C.
Whole wheat flour	1/2 C.	1 C.	1-1/2 C.	2 C.	2-1/2 C.	3 C.
Milled flax seed	1/2 C.	1 C.	1-1/2 C.	2 C.	2-1/2 C.	3 C.
Eggs	2	4	6	8	10	12
Baking soda	1 t.	2 t.	1 T.	1 T. + 1 t.	1 T. + 2 t.	2 T.

Assembly Directions:

Preheat oven to 300 degrees. In a saucepan, gently heat the oil, butter, sugar, and honey. Stir in the salt and cinnamon. When the butter melts and the sugar dissolves, stir in the oats, flour, and flax seed. Mix well and allow to cool slightly. Mix in the eggs and baking soda.

Spray a 15x10 jelly roll pan with cooking spray. Press the granola mixture firmly into the pan. Use a rolling pin to make sure the mixture is pressed tightly into the pan. Pay special attention to the corners and the edges.

Bake for 1 hour. Remove from the oven and cut into 24 bars. Allow to cool in the pan. When the bars are completely cold, remove from the pan.

Freezing Directions:

Place the granola bars into freezer bags or containers. Seal, label, and freeze.

Serving Directions:

Thaw and enjoy!

Nutritional Info:

Per Serving: 159 Calories; 6g Fat (35.5% calories from fat); 4g Protein; 22g Carbohydrate; 3g Dietary Fiber; 16mg Cholesterol; 131mg Sodium.
Exchanges: 1 Grain (Starch); 1 Fat; 1/2 Other Carbohydrates.

Cranberry Orange Muffins

Recipes:	1	2	3	4	5	6
Servings:	12	24	36	48	60	72
Ingredients:						
Butter or margarine	1/2 C.	1 C.	1-1/2 C.	2 C.	2-1/2 C.	3 C.
Sugar	1 C.	2 C.	3 C.	4 C.	5 C.	6 C.
Egg	1	2	3	4	5	6
Orange juice	1/4 C.	1/2 C.	3/4 C.	1 C.	1-1/4 C.	1-1/2 C.
Nonfat vanilla yogurt	3/4 C.	1-1/2 C.	2-1/4 C.	3 C.	3-3/4 C.	4-1/2 C.
Grated orange peel	1 T.	2 T.	3 T.	1/4 C.	1/4 C. + 1 T.	1/4 C. + 2 T.
Flour	1 C.	2 C.	3 C.	4 C.	5 C.	6 C.
Whole wheat flour	1 C.	2 C.	3 C.	4 C.	5 C.	6 C.
Baking soda	1 t.	2 t.	1 T.	1 T. + 1 t.	1 T. + 2 t.	2 T.
Baking powder	1 t.	2 t.	1 T.	1 T. + 1 t.	1 T. + 2 t.	2 T.
Dried cranberries	1/2 C.	1 C.	1-1/2 C.	2 C.	2-1/2 C.	3 C.
Chopped pecans, optional	1/4 C.	1/2 C.	3/4 C.	1 C.	1-1/4 C.	1-1/2 C.

Assembly Directions:
Preheat oven to 350 degrees.

In a mixing bowl, cream butter and sugar. Beat in egg, orange juice, yogurt, and orange peel. Add flours and baking soda. Mix until just combined. Add cranberries and pecans. Mix by hand.

Spray muffin tins with cooking spray or line with paper liners. Fill muffin tins two-thirds full. Bake for 20 to 25 minutes or until a toothpick inserted into the center of a muffin comes out clean.

Cool for 5 minutes before removing to a wire rack.

Freezing Directions:
Place the muffins in a freezer bag or container. For single servings, place each muffin in a sandwich bag and then place the bagged muffins in a larger freezer bag. Seal, label, and freeze.

Serving Directions:
Thaw muffins overnight or reheat in a microwave oven 15 seconds on high.

Nutritional Info:
Per Serving: 230 Calories; 8g Fat (31.8% calories from fat); 4g Protein; 36g Carbohydrate; 2g Dietary Fiber; 16mg Cholesterol; 212mg Sodium.
Exchanges: 1 Grain (Starch); 1-1/2 Fat; 1-1/2 Other Carbohydrates.

Little Breakfast Quiches

Recipes:	1	2	3	4	5	6
Servings:	**12**	**24**	**36**	**48**	**60**	**72**
Ingredients:						
Lowfat cottage cheese	16 oz.	32 oz.	48 oz.	64 oz.	80 oz.	96 oz.
Eggs	4	8	12	16	20	24
Skim milk	1/4 C.	1/2 C.	3/4 C.	1 C.	1-1/4 C.	1-1/2 C.
Flour	1/4 C.	1/2 C.	3/4 C.	1 C.	1-1/4 C.	1-1/2 C.
Baking powder	1 t.	2 t.	1 T.	1 T. + 1 t.	1 T. + 2 t.	2 T.
Salt	1/4 t.	1/2 t.	3/4 t.	1 t.	1-1/4 t.	1-1/2 t.
Shredded cheddar cheese[1]	1 C.	2 C.	3 C.	4 C.	5 C.	6 C.
Bacon; cooked and crumbled	6 slices	12 slices	18 slices	24 slices	30 slices	36 slices
Chopped onion[2]	1/4 C.	1/2 C.	3/4 C.	1 C.	1-1/4 C.	1-1/2 C.

Assembly Directions:

Process cottage cheese in a food processor until smooth. Transfer to large bowl.

In medium bowl, beat eggs. Add milk, flour, baking powder and salt to eggs and mix until smooth.

Add egg mixture to cottage cheese and mix. Stir in shredded cheese, bacon and onions.

Freezing Directions:

Pour mixture into a gallon freezer bag. Seal, label, and freeze.

Serving Directions:

Thaw overnight in the refrigerator. Preheat oven to 375 degrees. Line muffin tins with foil liners. Bake for 12-15 minutes or until edges are lightly browned.

Notes:

[1] 8 oz. cheese = 2 C. shredded
[2] 1 med. onion = 1 C. chopped

Nutritional Info:

Per Serving: 118 Calories; 7g Fat (50.9% calories from fat); 10g Protein; 4g Carbohydrate; trace Dietary Fiber; 77mg Cholesterol; 366mg Sodium.
Exchanges: 1-1/2 Lean Meat; 1 Fat.

Miniature Chocolate Chip Muffins

Recipes:	1	2	3	4	5	6
Servings:	15	30	45	60	75	90
Makes: muffins	30	60	90	120	150	180
Ingredients:						
Flour	2 C.	4 C.	6 C.	8 C.	10 C.	12 C.
Sugar	3/4 C.	1-1/2 C.	2-1/4 C.	3 C.	3-3/4 C.	4-1/2 C.
Baking powder	2 t.	1 T. + 1 t.	2 T.	2 T. + 2 t.	3 T. + 1 t.	1/4 C.
Salt	1/2 t.	1 t.	1-1/2 t.	2 t.	2-1/2 t.	1 T.
Skim milk	1 C.	2 C.	3 C.	4 C.	5 C.	6 C.
Canola oil	1/3 C.	2/3 C.	1 C.	1-1/3 C.	1-2/3 C.	2 C.
Egg	1	2	3	4	5	6
Miniature chocolate chips	3/4 C.	1-1/2 C.	2-1/4 C.	3 C.	3-3/4 C.	4-1/2 C.

Assembly Directions:

Preheat oven to 350 degrees.

In a large bowl, combine the flour, sugar, baking powder and salt. Combine the ingredients using a whisk or fork.

In a separate bowl, beat together the milk, oil, and egg. Pour egg mixture into the flour mixture. Stir to combine.

Fold in chocolate chips.

Spray miniature muffin tins with cooking spray. Spoon batter into miniature muffin tins filling to the top. Bake for 12 to 16 minutes or until a toothpick inserted into the center of a muffin comes out clean.

Remove from tins and allow to cool on a wire rack.

Freezing Directions:

For individual servings, place muffins in snack bags two at a time. Place snack bags in a gallon freezer bag. Seal, label, and freeze.

Serving Directions:

Thaw in the refrigerator overnight. Or if packing for lunches, place in lunchbox directly from freezer. The muffins will thaw in time for lunch. Or if eating immediately, microwave on high for 15 seconds.

Nutritional Info: 2 muffins per serving

Per Serving: 194 Calories; 8g Fat (35.6% calories from fat); 3g Protein; 29g Carbohydrate; trace Dietary Fiber; 13mg Cholesterol; 154mg Sodium.
Exchanges: 1 Grain (Starch); 1-1/2 Fat; 1 Other Carbohydrates.

Pizza Bread

Recipes:	1	2	3	4	5	6
Servings:	**12**	**24**	**36**	**48**	**60**	**72**
Ingredients:						
Warm water	1 C.	2 C.	3 C.	4 C.	5 C.	6 C.
Active dry yeast	1-1/2 t.	1 T.	1 T. + 1-1/2 t.	2 T.	2 T. + 1-1/2 t.	3 T.
Egg	1	2	3	4	5	6
Canola oil	2 T.	1/4 C.	1/4 C. + 2 T.	1/2 C.	1/2 C. + 2 T.	3/4 C.
Master Bread Machine Mix[1]	3-1/2 C.	7 C.	10-1/2 C.	14 C.	17-1/2 C.	21 C.
Pepperoni slices	32	64	96	128	160	192
Italian seasoning	1 t.	2 t.	1 T.	1 T. + 1 t.	1 T. + 2 t.	2 T.
Shredded mozzarella cheese[2]	1/2 C.	1 C.	1-1/2 C.	2 C.	2-1/2 C.	3 C.
Dried parsley	1 t.	2 t.	1 T.	1 T. + 1 t.	1 T. + 2 t.	2 T.
Flour	2 T.	1/4 C.	1/4 C. + 2 T.	1/2 C.	1/2 C. + 2 T.	3/4 C.
Minced garlic	1/2 t.	1 t.	1-1/2 t.	2 t.	2-1/2 t.	1 T.
Pizza sauce	1/4 C.	1/2 C.	3/4 C.	1 C.	1-1/4 C.	1-1/2 C.

Assembly Directions:

This first step can be done by hand with a wooden spoon, with a bread machine set on the dough setting or a heavy duty mixer with a dough hook. In a large bowl, combine the water and yeast. Let sit for 5 minutes or until yeast is dissolved. Add egg and oil. Combine thoroughly. Add bread mix and stir to combine. Once a dough ball starts to form, knead by hand for 5 minutes. Cover with a wet cloth and allow to rise in a warm place until doubled in size.

Preheat oven to 350 degrees. Quarter the pepperoni slices. Add to a medium sized bowl with Italian seasoning, mozzarella, parsley, flour, garlic and pizza sauce. Stir to combine.

Divide the dough in half. On a floured surface, roll each half out into 2 rectangles about 4 inches wide and 18 inches long. Divide the filling evenly between the two rectangles. Roll up lengthwise and seal to form two "ropes". Spray a baking sheet with cooking spray. Place the two ropes side by side on the sheet. Cross the ropes at 1/3 and 2/3 of the length. Make several slits in the top of the braid.

Bake for 30 to 35 minutes or until golden brown. Remove from oven and allow to cool.

Freezing Directions:

Place pizza bread in a gallon freezer bags. Seal, label, and freeze.

Serving Directions:

Thaw overnight in the refrigerator. Preheat oven to 350 degrees. Remove bread from the freezer bag. Wrap in aluminum foil and bake for 15 to 20 minutes or until hot. Cut into slices and serve.

Notes:

[1] The recipe for Master Bread Machine mix can be found on page 125. Two 11 oz. packages of refrigerated French or Italian bread dough can be used instead.
[2] 8 oz. cheese = 2 C. shredded

Nutritional Info:

Per Serving: 256 Calories; 11g Fat (37.4% calories from fat); 9g Protein; 30g Carbohydrate; 1g Dietary Fiber; 31mg Cholesterol; 402mg Sodium.
Exchanges: 1-1/2 Grain (Starch); 1 Lean Meat; 1-1/2 Fat.

Whole Wheat Apple Crunch Muffins

Recipes:	1	2	3	4	5	6
Servings:	**16**	**32**	**48**	**64**	**80**	**96**
Ingredients:						
Flour	1 C.	2 C.	3 C.	4 C.	5 C.	6 C.
Whole wheat flour	1 C.	2 C.	3 C.	4 C.	5 C.	6 C.
Sugar	1 C.	2 C.	3 C.	4 C.	5 C.	6 C.
Baking powder	2 t.	1 T. + 1 t.	2 T.	2 T. + 2 t.	3 T. + 1 t.	1/4 C.
Baking soda	1/2 t.	1 t.	1-1/2 t.	2 t.	2-1/2 t.	1 T.
Salt	1/2 t.	1 t.	1-1/2 t.	2 t.	2-1/2 t.	1 T.
Cinnamon	1 t.	2 t.	1 T.	1 T. + 1 t.	1 T. + 2 t.	2 T.
Eggs	2	4	6	8	10	12
Canola oil	1/4 C.	1/2 C.	3/4 C.	1 C.	1-1/4 C.	1-1/2 C.
Applesauce	1/2 C.	1 C.	1-1/2 C.	2 C.	2-1/2 C.	3 C.
Chopped apples[1]	2 C.	4 C.	6 C.	8 C.	10 C.	12 C.
Crunch Topping:						
Old-fashioned rolled oats	1/2 C.	1 C.	1-1/2 C.	2 C.	2-1/2 C.	3 C.
Flour	1/2 C.	1 C.	1-1/2 C.	2 C.	2-1/2 C.	3 C.
Brown sugar	1/2 C.	1 C.	1-1/2 C.	2 C.	2-1/2 C.	3 C.
Cinnamon	1/2 t.	1 t.	1-1/2 t.	2 t.	2-1/2 t.	1 T.
Butter or margarine	1/4 C.	1/2 C.	3/4 C.	1 C.	1-1/4 C.	1-1/2 C.

Assembly Directions:

Preheat the oven to 350 degrees. Spray a muffin pan with cooking spray. Combine first measure of flour, whole wheat flour, sugar, baking powder, baking soda, salt, and first measure of cinnamon in a bowl. Whisk and set aside.

In a second bowl, beat eggs, oil and applesauce. Pour egg mixture into flour mixture and mix until just combined. Fold in apples.

In a separate bowl, combine the oats, second measure of flour, brown sugar, and second measure of cinnamon. Cut the butter into the oat mixture using a fork or pastry knife until coarse crumbs form.

Fill each muffin cup 2/3 full. Top each muffin with oatmeal mixture. Bake for 20 to 23 minutes. Remove muffins from pan and place on a wire rack to cool.

Freezing Directions:

For individual servings, place muffins in sandwich bags. Place sandwich bags in a gallon freezer bag. Seal, label, and freeze.

Serving Directions:

Thaw in the refrigerator overnight. Or if packing for lunches, place in lunchbox directly from freezer. The muffins will thaw in time for lunch. Or if eating immediately, microwave on high for 15 seconds.

Notes:

[1] 1 medium apple = 1 C. chopped

Nutritional Info:

Per Serving: 223 Calories; 7g Fat (28.7% calories from fat); 3g Protein; 37g Carbohydrate; 2g Dietary Fiber; 23mg Cholesterol; 210mg Sodium.
Exchanges: 1 Grain (Starch); 1/2 Fruit; 1-1/2 Fat; 1 Other Carbohydrates.

Strawberry Stuffed French Toast

Recipes:	1	2	3	4	5	6
Servings:	**10**	**20**	**30**	**40**	**50**	**60**
Ingredients:						
Reduced fat cream cheese, softened	8 oz.	16 oz.	24 oz.	32 oz.	40 oz.	48 oz.
Powdered sugar	1/2 C.	1 C.	1-1/2 C.	2 C.	2-1/2 C.	3 C.
Vanilla	1 t.	2 t.	1 T.	1 T. + 1 t.	1 T. + 2 t.	2 T.
Sliced strawberries	2 C.	4 C.	6 C.	8 C.	10 C.	12 C.
French or Italian bread loaf	1	2	3	4	5	6
Eggs	5	10	15	20	25	30
Skim milk	1 C.	2 C.	3 C.	4 C.	5 C.	6 C.
Vanilla	1 T.	2 T.	3 T.	1/4 C.	1/4 C. + 1 T.	1/4 C. + 2 T.
On Hand:						
Sliced strawberries for garnish						
Powdered sugar for garnish						

Assembly Directions:
In a mixing bowl, beat cream cheese until smooth. Add the powdered sugar and first measure of vanilla. Beat until creamy. Fold in sliced strawberries.

Cut a small diagonal slice off of each end of the loaf of bread. Discard. Cut the bread diagonally into 10 thick slices. Cut each slice in half starting at the top side of the loaf but leave 1/4 inch uncut at the bottom of the slice. This will form a pocket for the filling. Divide the filling evenly between the slices spreading to cover each pocket with the filling. Place the slices in a 9x13 baking dish.

In a medium bowl, mix together the eggs, milk and second measure of vanilla using a whisk. Pour the egg mixture over the bread. Using tongs, turn the slices over to coat both sides. Cover with plastic wrap and refrigerate for 4 hours.

Freezing Directions:
Place French toast slices on a baking sheet. Flash freeze. When solid, remove from sheet and place in freezer bags or containers. Seal, label, and freeze.

Serving Directions:
Preheat oven to 375 degrees. Spray a baking sheet with cooking spray. Place frozen stuffed French toast slices on baking sheet. Bake for 15 to 20 minutes on each side until golden brown. Garnish with fresh sliced strawberries and powdered sugar.

Nutritional Info:
Per Serving: 242 Calories; 8g Fat (30.0% calories from fat); 10g Protein; 31g Carbohydrate; 2g Dietary Fiber; 107mg Cholesterol; 433mg Sodium.
Exchanges: 1-1/2 Grain (Starch); 1/2 Lean Meat; 1 Fat; 1/2 Other Carbohydrates.

Banana Bread or Muffins

Recipes:	1	2	3	4	5	6
Servings:	**12**	**24**	**36**	**48**	**60**	**72**
Ingredients:						
Butter or margarine	1/4 C.	1/2 C.	3/4 C.	1 C.	1-1/4 C.	1-1/2 C.
Sugar	1 C.	2 C.	3 C.	4 C.	5 C.	6 C.
Eggs	2	4	6	8	10	12
Bananas, mashed	2	4	6	8	10	12
Unsweetened applesauce	1/4 C.	1/2 C.	3/4 C.	1 C.	1-1/4 C.	1-1/2 C.
Skim milk	1/4 C.	1/2 C.	3/4 C.	1 C.	1-1/4 C.	1-1/2 C.
Baking soda	1 t.	2 t.	1 T.	1 T. + 1 t.	1 T. + 2 t.	2 T.
Flour	2 C.	4 C.	6 C.	8 C.	10 C.	12 C.

Assembly Directions:

Preheat oven to 350 degrees.

Cream butter and sugar until fluffy. Add eggs one at a time and beat until well blended.

Add bananas, applesauce, milk and baking soda. Beat until combined.

Add the flour and beat until well blended.

Muffins: Fill greased or paper-lined muffin tins two-thirds full. Bake for 20 to 25 minutes or until a toothpick inserted into the center of a muffin comes out clean.

Bread: Spray a 9x5 loaf pan with cooking spray. Fill pan with batter. Bake for one hour or until a toothpick inserted into the center of the loaf comes out clean.

Cool for 5 minutes before removing to a wire rack.

Freezing Directions:

For individual servings, place muffins or bread slices in sandwich bags. Place sandwich bags in a gallon freezer bag. Seal, label, and freeze.

Loaves can also be frozen whole in a gallon freezer bag.

Serving Directions:

Thaw in the refrigerator overnight. Or if packing for lunches, place in lunchbox directly from freezer. The muffins will thaw in time for lunch. Or if eating immediately, microwave on high for 15 seconds.

Nutritional Info:

Per Serving: 207 Calories; 5g Fat (20.7% calories from fat); 3g Protein; 38g Carbohydrate; 1g Dietary Fiber; 31mg Cholesterol; 162mg Sodium.
Exchanges: 1 Grain (Starch); 1/2 Fruit; 1 Fat; 1 Other Carbohydrates.

Soup & Sandwich Recipes

Soup & Sandwich Recipes

TIPS FOR SOUP & SANDWICH RECIPES

Yields

- 1 cup of soup or chili is considered a standard serving.
- 1/4 to 1/2 cup of barbecue or pulled beef is considered a standard serving.

Shopping & Cooking Tips

- Soups and sandwiches seem to be making a comeback. Gone are the days of canned tomato soup and a boring grilled cheese sandwich. Today, it's Panini and bread bowls and little crocks of thick, rich soups. Save lots of money and make them at home!
- Package your soups to minimize thawing, reheating and then refrigerating leftovers. It's easy to package soup in individual freezer containers for work or school. Larger freezer containers work great for family sized meals.
- You can also freeze soup in freezer bags. Double-bagging it will prevent any small punctures from creating a mess in your freezer. Thaw your frozen soup by running the bag under hot water for a few minutes.
- It's fine to freeze soups containing milk. When they are thawed, they may look curdled or separated, but once you heat them thru, they re-combine and are fine.
- You can freeze sandwiches of all kinds. Avoid soggy bread by using "day-old" and by not spreading mayonnaise on the bread before freezing. Butter and peanut butter work fine but mayo separates and soaks into the bread. Just wrap them individually in plastic wrap or sandwich bags and then put them into a rigid freezer container so that they don't get squished in the freezer.
- For PB&J's, put peanut butter on both pieces of bread, with the jelly in the middle of the two and do not cut the sandwich until it is time to eat it. This will prevent the bread from getting soggy.

Healthy Tips

- Homemade soup is so much healthier than the store brands. Make your own healthy substitutions. Low fat, low salt, low anything-you-like. Soups are also a great way to sneak some extra nutrition and fiber in on your family.

Website Recipes & Tips

- For more great 30 Day Gourmet Soup and Sandwich recipes, check out the recipes section of our website at: www.30daygourmet.com
- For more Soup and Sandwich freezing tips and recipes from our cooks, check out our message boards at www.30daygourmet.com
- The *Souper Freezer Soups*, *Freezer Lunches to Go*, and *Slow Cooker Freezer Favorites* eBooks offered on our website have lots more great Soup and Sandwich recipes and tips.

Nothing beats a bowl of homemade soup!

Shrimp Jambalaya

Recipes:	1	2	3	4	5	6
Servings:	**12**	**24**	**36**	**48**	**60**	**72**
Ingredients:						
Polish kielbasa, cut in 1-inch slices	1 lb.	2 lbs.	3 lbs.	4 lbs.	5 lbs.	6 lbs.
Canola oil	2 T.	1/4 C.	1/4 C. + 2 T.	1/2 C.	1/2 C. + 2 T.	3/4 C.
Chopped green peppers[1]	1 C.	2 C.	3 C.	4 C.	5 C.	6 C.
Chopped celery[2]	1 C.	2 C.	3 C.	4 C.	5 C.	6 C.
Chopped onion[3]	1 C.	2 C.	3 C.	4 C.	5 C.	6 C.
Minced garlic	1-1/2 t.	1 T.	1 T. + 1-1/2 t.	2 T.	2 T. + 1-1/2 t.	3 T.
Canned diced tomatoes, low sodium	14.5 oz.	29 oz.	43.5 oz.	58 oz.	72.5 oz.	87 oz.
Chicken bouillon granules	2 T.	1/4 C.	1/4 C. + 2 T.	1/2 C.	1/2 C. + 2 T.	3/4 C.
Dried thyme	1/2 t.	1 t.	1-1/2 t.	2 t.	2-1/2 t.	1 T.
Dried oregano	1/2 t.	1 t.	1-1/2 t.	2 t.	2-1/2 t.	1 T.
Cayenne pepper	1/4 t.	1/2 t.	3/4 t.	1 t.	1-1/4 t.	1-1/2 t.
Dried basil	1/2 t.	1 t.	1-1/2 t.	2 t.	2-1/2 t.	1 T.
Black pepper	1/2 t.	1 t.	1-1/2 t.	2 t.	2-1/2 t.	1 T.
Frozen cooked shrimp	1 lb.	2 lbs.	3 lbs.	4 lbs.	5 lbs.	6 lbs.
On Hand:						
Water	7 C.	14 C.	21 C.	28 C.	35 C.	42 C.
Long grain white rice	1-1/2 C.	3 C.	4-1/2 C.	6 C.	7-1/2 C.	9 C.

Assembly Directions:

In a large frying pan, cook sausage in oil over medium-high heat until sausage is lightly browned.

Add the green peppers, celery, onion, and garlic. Cook 5 minutes or until the onions are translucent. Remove from heat and allow to cool.

Add the tomatoes, chicken bouillon granules, thyme, oregano, cayenne pepper, basil, and black pepper. Stir to combine.

Freezing Directions:

Pour sausage mixture into a gallon freezer bag or freezer container. Attach frozen shrimp to bag/container. Seal, label, and freeze.

Serving Directions:

Thaw sausage mixture and shrimp in the refrigerator overnight. Place the sausage mixture in a large stockpot. Add the water and bring to a boil. Add the rice. Bring back to a boil. Reduce heat to medium-low and cook for 45 minutes. Remove the tails from the shrimp. Add to soup and cook an additional 5 to 7 minutes or until shrimp are hot.

Notes:

[1] 1 large pepper = 1 C. diced
[2] 1 rib celery = 1/2 C. diced
[3] 1 medium onion = 1 C. chopped

Nutritional Info:

Per Serving: 264 Calories; 11g Fat (39.3% calories from fat); 15g Protein; 24g Carbohydrate; 1g Dietary Fiber; 83mg Cholesterol; 746mg Sodium.
Exchanges: 1 Grain (Starch); 2 Lean Meat; 1/2 Vegetable; 1-1/2 Fat.

Mediterranean Gourmet Burgers

Recipes:	1	2	3	4	5	6
Servings:	**6**	**12**	**18**	**24**	**30**	**36**
Ingredients:						
Lean ground beef	1 lb.	2 lbs.	3 lbs.	4 lbs.	5 lbs.	6 lbs.
Minced onion[1]	1/2 C.	1 C.	1-1/2 C.	2 C.	2-1/2 C.	3 C.
Worcestershire sauce	1 T.	2 T.	3 T.	1/4 C.	1/4 C. + 1 T.	1/4 C. + 2 T.
Ground cumin or chili powder	1/4 t.	1/2 t.	3/4 t.	1 t.	1-1/4 t.	1-1/2 t.
Crumbled Feta cheese[2]	1/4 C.	1/2 C.	3/4 C.	1 C.	1-1/4 C.	1-1/2 C.
Seasoned salt	1/2 t.	1 t.	1-1/2 t.	2 t.	2-1/2 t.	1 T.
Black pepper	1/4 t.	1/2 t.	3/4 t.	1 t.	1-1/4 t.	1-1/2 t.
Minced garlic	1 t.	2 t.	1 T.	1 T. + 1 t.	1 T. + 2 t.	2 T.
Chopped black olives[3] (optional)	1/4 C.	1/2 C.	3/4 C.	1 C.	1-1/4 C.	1-1/2 C.
On Hand:						
Spinach leaves	1 C.	2 C.	3 C.	4 C.	5 C.	6 C.
Provolone or mozzarella cheese slices	6	12	18	24	30	36
Portobello mushrooms, sautéed	4 oz.	8 oz.	12 oz.	16 oz.	20 oz.	24 oz.
Hamburger buns	6	12	18	24	30	36

Assembly Directions:
In a large bowl, combine ground beef, onion, Worcestershire sauce, cumin, Feta cheese, seasoned salt, pepper, garlic and olives. Mix together with your hands or a wooden spoon. Divide mixture evenly to form 6 balls. Press flat with a hamburger press or by hand between 2 sheets of waxed paper.

Freezing Directions:
Stack patties and separate with squares of waxed paper or freezer paper. Place the hamburger stacks in a freezer bag or container. Seal, label, and freeze.

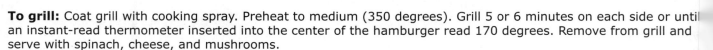

Serving Directions:
Thaw overnight in the refrigerator. Separate patties and discard wax or freezer paper between patties.

To grill: Coat grill with cooking spray. Preheat to medium (350 degrees). Grill 5 or 6 minutes on each side or until an instant-read thermometer inserted into the center of the hamburger read 170 degrees. Remove from grill and serve with spinach, cheese, and mushrooms.

To cook on stovetop: Cook in a skillet over medium heat 5 to 6 minutes on each side or until an instant-read thermometer inserted into the center of the hamburger read 170 degrees. Remove from pan and serve with spinach, cheese, and mushrooms.

Notes:
[1] 1 medium onion = 1 C. chopped
[2] 8 oz. Feta = 2 C. crumbled
[3] 15 large or 36 small olives = 1 C. chopped

Nutritional Info: including all on hand ingredients
Per Serving: 418 Calories; 22g Fat (48.2% calories from fat); 27g Protein; 26g Carbohydrate; 2g Dietary Fiber; 73mg Cholesterol; 713mg Sodium.
Exchanges: 1-1/2 Grain(Starch); 3 Lean Meat; 1/2 Vegetable; 2-1/2 Fat.

Tuscan White Bean Soup

Recipes:	1	2	3	4	5	6
Servings:	**6**	**12**	**18**	**24**	**30**	**36**
Ingredients:						
Dry Great Northern beans	1-1/4 C.	2-1/2 C.	3-3/4 C.	5 C.	6-1/4 C.	7-1/2 C.
Cold water	4 C.	8 C.	12 C.	16 C.	20 C.	24 C.
Sweet Italian sausage links, cut into 1-inch slices	3	6	9	12	15	18
Beef bouillon granules	1 T.	2 T.	3 T.	1/4 C.	1/4 C. + 1 T.	1/4 C. + 2 T.
Chopped onion[1]	1 C.	2 C.	3 C.	4 C.	5 C.	6 C.
Minced garlic	1 t.	2 t.	1 T.	1 T. + 1 t.	1 T. + 2 t.	2 T.
Italian seasoning	1 t.	2 t.	1 T.	1 T. + 1 t.	1 T. + 2 t.	2 T.
On Hand:						
Water	5-1/2 C.	11 C.	16-1/2 C.	22 C.	27-1/2 C.	33 C.
Zucchini, sliced	1	2	3	4	5	6
Packed fresh spinach	2 C.	4 C.	6 C.	8 C.	10 C.	12 C.
Canned diced tomatoes	14 oz.	28 oz.	42 oz.	56 oz.	70 oz.	84 oz.
Fresh shredded Parmesan cheese, optional						

Assembly Directions:

Rinse dry beans and remove any foreign debris such as rocks. Place beans and cold water in a large stockpot. Bring to a boil. Reduce heat and simmer 10 minutes. Remove from heat. Cover and let stand 1 hour. Drain and rinse beans.

In a medium skillet, cook the sausage until lightly browned. Drain well and allow to cool. Add sausage, beef bouillon granules, chopped onion, garlic and Italian seasoning to beans. Stir to combine.

Freezing Directions:

Place the bean and sausage mixture in a freezer bag or container. Seal, label, and freeze.

Serving Directions:

Thaw the bean and sausage mixture overnight in the refrigerator.

To cook in a 5-quart slow cooker: In the slow cooker, combine sausage and bean mixture, water, and zucchini. Cover and cook on low for 9 to 10 hours or on high for 5 to 6 hours or until the beans are tender. If using the low setting, turn to high. Add spinach and undrained tomatoes. Stir to combine. Cover and cook 15 to 30 minutes until heated through. Serve with Parmesan cheese.

To cook on stovetop: In a large stockpot, combine sausage and bean mixture, water, and zucchini. Bring to a boil. Reduce heat to medium-low. Cover and cook for 1 hour or until the beans are tender. Add spinach and undrained tomatoes. Stir to combine. Cover and cook 15 to 30 minutes until heated through. Serve with Parmesan cheese.

Notes:

[1] 1 medium onion = 1 C. chopped

Nutritional Info: not including shredded Parmesan cheese

Per Serving: 290 Calories; 13g Fat (38.2% calories from fat); 15g Protein; 30g Carbohydrate; 9g Dietary Fiber; 29mg Cholesterol; 570mg Sodium.
Exchanges: 1-1/2 Grain (Starch); 1 Lean Meat; 1 Vegetable; 2 Fat.

Sweet BBQ Joes

Recipes:	1	2	3	4	5	6
Servings:	6	12	18	24	30	36
Ingredients:						
Lean ground beef	1-1/2 lbs.	3 lbs.	4-1/2 lbs.	6 lbs.	7-1/2 lbs.	9 lbs.
Chopped onion[1]	3/4 C.	1-1/2 C.	2-1/4 C.	3 C.	3-3/4 C.	4-1/2 C.
Ketchup	1 C.	2 C.	3 C.	4 C.	5 C.	6 C.
Celery seeds	1 t.	2 t.	1 T.	1 T. + 1 t.	1 T. + 2 t.	2 T.
White vinegar	1 T.	2 T.	3 T.	1/4 C.	1/4 C. + 1 T.	1/4 C. + 2 T.
Sugar	2 T.	1/4 C.	1/4 C. + 2 T.	1/2 C.	1/2 C. + 2 T.	3/4 C.
Worcestershire sauce	2 T.	1/4 C.	1/4 C. + 2 T.	1/2 C.	1/2 C. + 2 T.	3/4 C.
Yellow mustard	1-1/2 T.	3 T.	1/4 C. + 1-1/2 t.	1/4 C. + 2 T.	1/4 C. + 3-1/2 T.	1/2 C. + 1 T.
On Hand:						
Hamburger buns	6	12	18	24	30	36

Assembly Directions:

In a large skillet, brown ground beef and onions. Remove from heat and drain fat from pan.

Return to heat and add ketchup, celery seeds, vinegar, sugar, Worcestershire sauce, and mustard. Bring to a boil over medium-high heat. Reduced to medium-low and cook for 15 minutes, stirring occasionally. Remove from heat and allow to cool.

Freezing Directions:

Meal-sized portion: Pour sandwich filling into meal-sized freezer bags or containers. Seal, label, and freeze.

Individual servings: Scoop out filling and place in muffin tins. Flash freeze. When solid, fill sink with about 1 inch of hot water. Gently set muffin tin in hot water in sink for 30 seconds. Do not get any water on the filling itself. Remove from water and remove the individual servings from the pan with a fork. Place in freezer bags or containers. Seal, label, and freeze.

Serving Directions:

Thaw in the microwave or overnight in the refrigerator. Reheat over very low heat on the stove or microwave on medium high in a non-plastic dish until heated through. Stir the mixture several times during thawing and reheating. Heap the sandwich filling onto opened sandwich buns and enjoy.

Notes:

[1] 1 medium onion = 1 C. chopped

This is a great recipe to pack for lunch. Heat up an individual serving and place in a preheated thermos.

Packaging the filling in individual servings is very convenient for those busy nights when everyone is eating at different times.

Nutritional Info: including hamburger buns

Per Serving: 439 Calories; 18g Fat (37.1% calories from fat); 29g Protein; 40g Carbohydrate; 2g Dietary Fiber; 79mg Cholesterol; 879mg Sodium.
Exchanges: 1-1/2 Grain(Starch); 3-1/2 Lean Meat; 1/2 Vegetable; 1-1/2 Fat; 1 Other Carbohydrates.

Taco Chili

Recipes:	1	2	3	4	5	6
Servings:	**12**	**24**	**36**	**48**	**60**	**72**
Ingredients:						
Lean ground beef	2 lbs.	4 lbs.	6 lbs.	8 lbs.	10 lbs.	12 lbs.
Taco seasoning envelope	1	2	3	4	5	6
Canned crushed tomatoes, undrained	28 oz.	56 oz.	84 oz.	112 oz.	140 oz.	168 oz.
Salsa	15 oz.	30 oz.	45 oz.	60 oz.	75 oz.	90 oz.
Canned corn, undrained	15 oz.	30 oz.	45 oz.	60 oz.	75 oz.	90 oz.
Canned kidney beans, undrained	16 oz.	32 oz.	48 oz.	64 oz.	80 oz.	96 oz.
Canned black beans, drained and rinsed	15 oz.	30 oz.	45 oz.	60 oz.	75 oz.	90 oz.
On Hand:						
Reduced fat sour cream	8 oz.	16 oz.	24 oz.	32 oz.	40 oz.	48 oz.
Shredded cheddar cheese	1 C.	2 C.	3 C.	4 C.	5 C.	6 C.
Tortilla chips for scooping	15 oz.	30 oz.	45 oz.	60 oz.	75 oz.	90 oz.

Assembly Directions:
Brown ground beef. Meanwhile, in a large bowl, combine the taco seasoning, tomatoes, salsa, corn, kidney beans and black beans. Stir to mix. When the ground beef is cooked, drain off any fat, then add it to the bowl of other ingredients and stir to combine.

Freezing Directions:
Freeze in freezer bags or containers based on your family size. Seal, label, and freeze.

Serving Directions:
Thaw overnight in the refrigerator.

Stovetop: Heat mixture in a saucepan on the stovetop until it's hot and bubbly.

Microwave: Heat on high for 5 to 6 minutes in a non-plastic microwave safe bowl. Stir frequently.

Slow Cooker: Pour into slow cooker. Heat on high for 1 to 2 hours or on low for 3 to 4 hours or until chili is hot.

Spoon into bowls. Top each bowl with a spoonful of sour cream and a sprinkle of shredded cheddar cheese. Serve with tortilla chips on the side for scooping to eat it… don't use a spoon!

Notes:
This recipe is very versatile, and quick and easy to put together. You can control the spiciness by choosing mild or hot salsa. If you really like salsa, add a bigger jar. If you really like hot and spicy, add a 4 ounce can of drained, diced green chilies. You can also add a can of sliced black olives (drained), if your family likes them.

Nutritional Info:
Per Serving: 499 Calories; 24g Fat (42.3% calories from fat); 27g Protein; 46g Carbohydrate; 9g Dietary Fiber; 64mg Cholesterol; 1054mg Sodium.
Exchanges: 2-1/2 Grain (Starch); 3 Lean Meat; 1 Vegetable; 3 Fat.

Teriyaki Sliders

Recipes:	1	2	3	4	5	6
Servings:	**6**	**12**	**18**	**24**	**30**	**36**
Makes	**12**	**24**	**36**	**48**	**60**	**72**
Ingredients:						
Ground turkey or beef	2 lbs.	4 lbs.	6 lbs.	8 lbs.	10 lbs.	12 lbs.
Teriyaki sauce	1/4 C.	1/2 C.	3/4 C.	1 C.	1-1/4 C.	1-1/2 C.
Minced garlic	1-1/2 t.	1 T.	1 T. + 1-1/2 t.	2 T.	2 T. + 1-1/2 t.	3 T.
Ground ginger	1/4 t.	1/2 t.	3/4 t.	1 t.	1-1/4 t.	1-1/2 t.
Poultry seasoning	1/4 t.	1/2 t.	3/4 t.	1 t.	1-1/4 t.	1-1/2 t.
Dried parsley	1 t.	2 t.	1 T.	1 T. + 1 t.	1 T. + 2 t.	2 T.
Split dinner rolls	12	24	36	48	60	72

Assembly Directions:
Combine ground turkey or beef, teriyaki sauce, garlic, ginger, poultry seasoning, and parsley in a large bowl. Divide mixture evenly to form 12 small 1/2 inch thick patties per recipe.

Freezing Directions:
Freeze raw burgers to cook later OR cook burgers on grill, stovetop, or broiler. Cool.

To grill: Coat grill with cooking spray. Preheat to medium (350 degrees). Grill five or six minutes on each side or until thermometer reads 170 degrees. Remove from grill and cool.

To cook on stovetop: Cook in a skillet over medium heat 5 to 6 minutes on each side or until an instant-read thermometer inserted into the center of the hamburger read 170 degrees.

Place burgers in a gallon freezer bag. Leave the rolls in their original package and place inside the bag with the burgers. Seal, label, and freeze.

Serving Directions:
Thaw bag overnight in the refrigerator. Cook or warm burgers. Split rolls with a serrated knife if necessary. Serve on bun with desired toppings.

Notes:
These are a fun change of pace for lunch. Place the hot burgers in a warmed thermos and close lid. Split rolls with a serrated knife if necessary. Place rolls in a sandwich bag and pack separately with burgers. You can also add any toppings to the rolls before placing in the sandwich bag.

King's Hawaiian® and Sara Lee® rolls work well for this recipe.

Nutritional Info: turkey
Per Serving: 407 Calories; 17g Fat (37.3% calories from fat); 32g Protein; 31g Carbohydrate; 2g Dietary Fiber; 120mg Cholesterol; 898mg Sodium.
Exchanges: 2 Grain (Starch); 3-1/2 Lean Meat; 1/2 Vegetable; 1 Fat.

Nutritional Info: beef
Per Serving: 504 Calories; 25g Fat (44.8% calories from fat); 38g Protein; 31g Carbohydrate; 2g Dietary Fiber; 106mg Cholesterol; 844mg Sodium.
Exchanges: 2 Grain (Starch); 4-1/2 Lean Meat; 1/2 Vegetable; 2 Fat.

Homestyle Chicken Noodle Soup

Recipes:	1	2	3	4	5	6
Servings:	6	12	18	24	30	36
Ingredients:						
Boneless, skinless chicken breasts	3	6	9	12	15	18
Water	2 C.	4 C.	6 C.	8 C.	10 C.	12 C.
Chopped onion[1]	1 C.	2 C.	3 C.	4 C.	5 C.	6 C.
Minced garlic	1/2 t.	1 t.	1-1/2 t.	2 t.	2-1/2 t.	1 T.
Sliced carrots[2]	1 C.	2 C.	3 C.	4 C.	5 C.	6 C.
Sliced celery[3]	1/2 C.	1 C.	1-1/2 C.	2 C.	2-1/2 C.	3 C.
Dried parsley	2 t.	1 T. + 1 t.	2 T.	2 T. + 2 t.	3 T. + 1 t.	1/4 C.
Dried thyme	1 t.	2 t.	1 T.	1 T. + 1 t.	1 T. + 2 t.	2 T.
Water	2 C.	4 C.	6 C.	8 C.	10 C.	12 C.
Chicken broth	48 oz.	96 oz.	144 oz.	192 oz.	240 oz.	288 oz.
Thick, wide egg noodles	3 C.	6 C.	9 C.	12 C.	15 C.	18 C.

Assembly Directions:

Cut chicken into bite-sized pieces. Place in a stockpot. Cook chicken in first measure of water with onion and garlic. When chicken is no longer pink in the middle, add carrots, celery, parsley, thyme, second measure of water and chicken broth. Bring to a boil. Stir in uncooked noodles. Return to boiling. Reduce heat to medium and simmer uncovered for 15 minutes or until pasta and vegetables are tender. Remove from heat and allow to cool.

Freezing Directions:

Pour soup into freezer bags or containers. Seal, label, and freeze.

Serving Directions:

Thaw soup overnight in the refrigerator. Soup can be reheated in a saucepan on the stovetop or in a microwave oven. Heat until steaming but not boiling.

Notes:

[1] 1 medium onion = 1 C. chopped
[2] 1 carrots = 1/2 C. sliced
[3] 1 rib celery = 1/2 C. sliced

You can speed up preparation by using a food processor to slice the vegetables.

If you have a picky eater who does not like carrots, they can be shredded instead of sliced. The onions can be processed in a food processor so that they are very fine.
Package the soup in individual servings for lunches, for seniors, or for college students.

Nutritional Info:

Per Serving: 168 Calories; 2g Fat (10.4% calories from fat); 17g Protein; 20g Carbohydrate; 2g Dietary Fiber; 53mg Cholesterol; 446mg Sodium.
Exchanges: 1 Grain (Starch); 2 Lean Meat; 1 Vegetable.

Polynesian Turkey Burgers

Recipes:	1	2	3	4	5	6
Servings:	6	12	18	24	30	36
Ingredients:						
Ground turkey	1-1/2 lbs.	3 lbs.	4-1/2 lbs.	6 lbs.	7-1/2 lbs.	9 lbs.
Dry bread crumbs	1 C.	2 C.	3 C.	4 C.	5 C.	6 C.
Reduced sodium soy sauce	1 T.	2 T.	3 T.	1/4 C.	1/4 C. + 1 T.	1/4 C. + 2 T.
Ground ginger	1/2 t.	1 t.	1-1/2 t.	2 t.	2-1/2 t.	1 T.
Sweet and sour sauce; divided	1 C.	2 C.	3 C.	4 C.	5 C.	6 C.
Crushed pineapple; drained	1 C.	2 C.	3 C.	4 C.	5 C.	6 C.

Assembly Directions:

Burgers: For each recipe, combine ground turkey, dry bread crumbs, soy sauce, ground ginger and 1/4 C. of sweet and sour sauce. Shape into 6 burgers.

Sauce: For each recipe, combine 3/4 C. sweet and sour sauce with 1 C. drained, crushed pineapple.

Freezing Directions:

Burgers: 1. Freeze raw burgers to cook later OR
2. Cook burgers on grill, stovetop, or broiler. Cool.

Place burgers in freezer bag or rigid containers. Add bagged sauce. Label and freeze.

Sauce: Pour into quart-sized freezer bag. Label and freeze with burgers.

Serving Directions:

Thaw burgers and sauce. Cook or warm burgers. Warm sauce in microwave or on stovetop.

Notes:

These taste great and are a family favorite. The kids eat them on buns with ketchup and mustard. The adults smother them with the sauce. Yummy! Ground turkey is usually much cheaper than ground beef and better for you!

Nutritional Info:

Per Serving: 316 Calories; 10g Fat (30.0% calories from fat); 23g Protein; 32g Carbohydrate; 1g Dietary Fiber; 90mg Cholesterol; 492mg Sodium.
Exchanges: 1 Grain (Starch); 2-1/2 Lean Meat; 1/2 Fruit; 1/2 Fat; 1 Other Carbohydrates.

Cheddar Broccoli Soup

Recipes:	1	2	3	4	5	6
Servings:	**6**	**12**	**18**	**24**	**30**	**36**
Ingredients:						
Frozen broccoli or Fresh broccoli	20 oz. or 1 bunch	40 oz. or 2 bunches	60 oz. or 3 bunches	80 oz. or 4 bunches	100 oz. or 5 bunches	120 oz. or 6 bunches
Water	1 C.	2 C.	3 C.	4 C.	5 C.	6 C.
Chopped onion[1]	1/4 C.	1/2 C.	3/4 C.	1 C.	1-1/4 C.	1-1/2 C.
Butter or margarine	1/4 C.	1/2 C.	3/4 C.	1 C.	1-1/4 C.	1-1/2 C.
Chicken bouillon granules	2 T.	1/4 C.	1/4 C. + 2 T.	1/2 C.	1/2 C. + 2 T.	3/4 C.
Hot water	1 C.	2 C.	3 C.	4 C.	5 C.	6 C.
Flour	1/2 C.	1 C.	1-1/2 C.	2 C.	2-1/2 C.	3 C.
Skim milk	2 C.	4 C.	6 C.	8 C.	10 C.	12 C.
Shredded cheddar cheese[2]	2 C.	4 C.	6 C.	8 C.	10 C.	12 C.
Ground nutmeg	1/8 t.	1/4 t.	3/8 t.	1/2 t.	1/2 t. + 1/8 t.	3/4 t.

Assembly Directions:

If using fresh broccoli, cut it into chunks, including the stalk. Cook broccoli in water until tender. Don't drain. Puree the broccoli and water in a food processor; set aside. (You should have about 2 C. pureed broccoli per batch.) Sauté onion in butter until tender. Dissolve bouillon in hot water; set aside. Stir flour into butter/onion mixture. Gradually add the milk and water/bouillon, stirring constantly. Continue stirring until well blended and thick. Add the cheese, nutmeg and pureed broccoli. Cook until cheese melts and soup is hot. Don't boil the soup.

Freezing Directions:

Allow soup to cool completely. Package it for freezing based on how you want to serve it. If you will serve it all at once, freeze it in a 1 or 2-gallon freezer bag, or large rigid container. If you want single servings, freeze it in quart freezer bags or 2 C. rigid containers. Seal, label, and freeze.

Serving Directions:

Thaw large containers or gallon freezer bags at least overnight in the refrigerator. Single servings can be thawed in the refrigerator or the microwave. Heat the soup in the microwave or on the stovetop until heated through. Do not boil. To keep warm for a gathering, keep the soup in a slow cooker on low.

Notes:

[1] 1 medium onion = 1 C. chopped
[2] 8 oz. cheese = 2 C. shredded

If you like pieces of broccoli in your soup, reserve 1/4 to 1/3 C. of small broccoli florets and don't puree them. Add them to the soup when you add the pureed broccoli.

The individual servings are ideal for lunches, seniors, or college students.

Nutritional Info:

Per Serving: 319 Calories; 21g Fat (57.8% calories from fat); 16g Protein; 18g Carbohydrate; 3g Dietary Fiber; 41mg Cholesterol; 762mg Sodium.
Exchanges: 1/2 Grain (Starch); 1-1/2 Lean Meat; 1 Vegetable; 1/2 Non-Fat Milk; 3 Fat.

Kickin' White Chicken Chili

Recipes:	1	2	3	4	5	6
Servings:	6	12	18	24	30	36
Makes:	9 C.	18 C.	27 C.	36 C.	45 C.	54 C.
Ingredients:						
Canola oil	1 T.	2 T.	3 T.	1/4 C.	1/4 C. + 1 T.	1/4 C. + 2 T.
Chopped onion[1]	1 C.	2 C.	3 C.	4 C.	5 C.	6 C.
Chopped celery[2]	1/2 C.	1 C.	1-1/2 C.	2 C.	2-1/2 C.	3 C.
Minced garlic	1 t.	2 t.	1 T.	1 T. + 1 t.	1 T. + 2 t.	2 T.
Boneless, skinless chicken breasts; cubed	1-1/2 lbs.	3 lbs.	4-1/2 lbs.	6 lbs.	7-1/2 lbs.	9 lbs.
Canned, chopped green chilies; drained	4 oz.	8 oz.	12 oz.	16 oz.	20 oz.	24 oz.
Chili powder	1 T.	2 T.	3 T.	1/4 C.	1/4 C. + 1 T.	1/4 C. + 2 T.
Dried oregano	1 t.	2 t.	1 T.	1 T. + 1 t.	1 T. + 2 t.	2 T.
Ground cumin	1 t.	2 t.	1 T.	1 T. + 1 t.	1 T. + 2 t.	2 T.
Salt	1/2 t.	1 t.	1-1/2 t.	2 t.	2-1/2 t.	1 T.
Cayenne pepper	1/4 t.	1/2 t.	3/4 t.	1 t.	1-1/4 t.	1-1/2 t.
Chicken broth	4 C.	8 C.	12 C.	16 C.	20 C.	24 C.
Canned Great Northern beans, drained	30 oz.	60 oz.	90 oz.	120 oz.	150 oz.	180 oz.
Dried cilantro	1 T.	2 T.	3 T.	1/4 C.	1/4 C. + 1 T.	1/4 C. + 2 T.

Assembly Directions:
In a large stockpot over medium high heat, combine oil, onion, celery, garlic, and chicken. Cook, stirring constantly for 5 minutes.
Add the green chilies, chili powder, oregano, cumin, salt, and cayenne pepper. Cook, stirring for 2 minutes. Add the chicken broth, Great Northern beans, and cilantro. Bring to a boil. Reduce heat to medium and simmer for 15 minutes. Remove from heat and allow to cool.

Freezing Directions:
Package it for freezing based on how you want to serve it. If you will serve it all at once, freeze it in a 1 or 2-gallon freezer bag, or large rigid container. If you want single servings, freeze it in quart freezer bags or 2 C. rigid containers. Seal, label, and freeze.

Serving Directions:
Thaw large containers or gallon freezer bags at least overnight in the refrigerator. Single servings can be thawed in the refrigerator or the microwave. Heat the soup in the microwave or on the stovetop until heated through.

Notes:
[1] 1 medium onion = 1 C. chopped
[2] 1 rib celery = 1/2 C. sliced

Nutritional Info:
Per Serving: 368 Calories; 6g Fat (15.0% calories from fat); 44g Protein; 35g Carbohydrate; 8g Dietary Fiber; 69mg Cholesterol; 610mg Sodium.
Exchanges: 2 Grain (Starch); 5 Lean Meat; 1/2 Vegetable; 1/2 Fat.

30 Day Gourmet © 201

Sides & Salad Recipes

Sides & Salad Recipes

TIPS FOR SIDES & SALAD RECIPES

Yields

- One 16 ounce can, or 10 ounces of frozen vegetables, serves three to four adults.
- 1 pound of fresh vegetables with little waste (green beans or carrots for example), or 2 pounds with shells or heavy peels (peas, beets, and winter squash for example) serves three to four adults.
- 1/2 C. is a standard serving size for mashed potatoes, baked beans and veggie casseroles.
- 1/2 cup is a standard serving size for fruit salads.
- Can and bag sizes seem to be constantly changing now. Don't fret over using a 10-3/4 oz. can of soup when the recipe calls for a 10 oz. can. Close is good enough!

Shopping & Cooking Tips

- Meats may be added to many of the side dishes in this section if you want to add protein.
- If your family members can't agree on side dishes at meal time, freeze your sides in 1-2 portion containers and serve a variety.
- All fresh vegetables except chopped onion, green pepper, and celery must be blanched before being added to foods going into the freezer. See page 223 in the Appendix for a vegetable blanching chart.
- Chopped ham or chicken can be added to the Homestyle Mac and Cheese for a great main dish.

Rice freezes well and is a great side dish to have on hand.

- Rice freezes great! Fully cook it and when cooled, package it in various sized freezer bags. Remove all of the air and freeze the bags flat. Rice can be reheated on the stovetop or in the microwave and served with steamed vegetables, bean burritos, tacos, vegetarian chili, or used to fill cabbage rolls, make fried rice or rice pudding.
- Freezing uncooked rice is fine too. Buy it in bulk and store it in the freezer safely for up to 2 years.

Healthy Tips

- Making these dishes ahead really helps to plan your "5 a day" servings of fruits and veggies!
- Save time and money by freezing homegrown fruit and vegetables. Tomatoes, beans, zucchini, apples, blueberries, strawberries and many others can all be frozen for later use and are much healthier for you all the way around.

Buying fruits and vegetables in season to freeze can save a lot of money!

Website Recipes & Tips

- For more great 30 Day Gourmet Side and Salad recipes, check out the recipes section of our website at: www.30daygourmet.com
- For more Side and Salad freezing tips and recipes from our cooks, check out the message boards at www.30daygourmet.com
- Check out the *Vegetarian Freezer Cooking*, *Slow Cooker Freezer Favorites*, and *Freezer Desserts to Die For!* offered on our website for more great Side and Salad recipes and tips.

Lime Rice

Recipes:	1	2	3	4	5	6
Servings:	4	8	12	16	20	24
Ingredients:						
Water	2 C.	4 C.	6 C.	8 C.	10 C.	12 C.
Basmati or Jasmine rice	1 C.	2 C.	3 C.	4 C.	5 C.	6 C.
Lime peel	1 t.	2 t.	1 T.	1 T. + 1 t.	1 T. + 2 t.	2 T.
Lime juice	2 T.	1/4 C.	1/4 C. + 2 T.	1/2 C.	1/2 C. + 2 T.	3/4 C.
Chopped cilantro	2 T.	1/4 C.	1/4 C. + 2 T.	1/2 C.	1/2 C. + 2 T.	3/4 C.

Assembly Directions:

Rinse the rice with cold water thoroughly before cooking to remove the excess starch. Wash two to three times or until the rinse water is no longer milky.

Stovetop: In a large saucepan, bring water to boil. Stir in rice. Cover. Reduce heat and simmer for 15-20 minutes or until all the water is absorbed.

Microwave: In a 2-quart microwave safe dish, combine 2 cups of water with 1 cup of rice. (It is recommended that only 1 cup of rice be prepared in the microwave at one time.) Cover and cook on high for 5 minutes. Cook at 50 percent power for 15 minutes. Remove from microwave and let stand for 5 minutes.

Once rice is cooked, stir in lime peel, lime peel, and cilantro. Allow to cool.

Freezing Directions:

Package rice in freezer bags or containers. Seal, label, and freeze.

Serving Directions:

Thaw overnight in the refrigerator. Put rice in a 2-quart microwave safe dish. Microwave on high for 4 to 6 minutes or until rice is hot.

Notes:

This rice is a great change of pace. It goes great with fish and Mexican main dishes. It tastes very similar to rice that you may find at some Mexican burrito restaurants.

If your rice is too sticky, try reducing the amount of water to 1-1/2 C. to 1-3/4 C. per recipe.

Nutritional Info:

Per Serving: 157 Calories; 1g Fat (5.8% calories from fat); 4g Protein; 33g Carbohydrate; trace Dietary Fiber; 0mg Cholesterol; 34mg Sodium.
Exchanges: 2 Grain (Starch).

Twice Baked Potatoes

Recipes:	1	2	3	4	5	6
Servings:	**24**	**48**	**18**	**24**	**30**	**36**
Ingredients:						
Russet potatoes	12	24	36	48	60	72
Butter or margarine	6 T.	3/4 C.	1 C. + 2 T.	1-1/2 C.	1-3/4 C. + 2 T.	2-1/4 C.
Skim milk	1/4 C.	1/2 C.	3/4 C.	1 C.	1-1/4 C.	1-1/2 C.
Reduced fat sour cream	1 C.	2 C.	3 C.	4 C.	5 C.	6 C.
Green onions, sliced	3	6	9	12	15	18
Shredded cheddar cheese[1]	1-1/2 C.	3 C.	4-1/2 C.	6 C.	7-1/2 C.	9 C.
Salt and pepper, to taste						

Assembly Directions:

Scrub potatoes, removing any bad portions with a knife and prick 5 or 6 times with the tip of a sharp knife.

Oven: Bake the potatoes in a preheated 425 degree oven for about 75 minutes.

Microwave: Cook 6 potatoes at a time on high for 12 to 15 minutes or until potatoes are tender.

Cool the potatoes at least until they are easily handled. Cut the cooled potatoes in half and carefully scoop the insides into a bowl, leaving an empty shell. Add the butter to the bowl of potatoes and mash by hand or with an electric mixer. Add milk and sour cream. Continue mashing. Add more milk if needed, but not any more than necessary. The more milk you add, the softer the thawed potato filling will be. Stir in green onions and cheese by hand. Add salt and pepper. Fill the shells with the potato mixture.

Freezing Directions:

Place filled potato shells on a baking sheet and place in the freezer. Flash freeze. When solid, place the potatoes in a freezer bag or freezer container. Seal, label, and freeze.

Serving Directions:

Take out as many as needed and thaw in the refrigerator overnight. Preheat oven to 350 degrees. Bake for 25 minutes or until potatoes are heated through and begin to brown.

Notes:

[1] 8 oz. cheese = 2 C. shredded

The potatoes can be reheated for 2 to 3 minutes in the microwave.

Nutritional Info:

Per Serving: 107 Calories; 5g Fat (45.0% calories from fat); 3g Protein; 12g Carbohydrate; 1g Dietary Fiber; 16mg Cholesterol; 81mg Sodium.
Exchanges: 1 Grain (Starch); 1/2 Lean Meat; 1 Fat.

Homestyle Mac and Cheese

Recipes:	1	2	3	4	5	6
Servings:	**10**	**20**	**30**	**40**	**50**	**60**
Ingredients:						
Macaroni, dry	16 oz.	32 oz.	48 oz.	64 oz.	80 oz.	96 oz.
Chicken flavored Fat Free White Sauce[1]	1-1/2 C.	3 C.	4-1/2 C.	6 C.	7-1/2 C.	9 C.
Shredded extra sharp cheddar cheese[2]	2 C.	4 C.	6 C.	8 C.	10 C.	12 C.
Shredded lowfat sharp cheddar cheese[2]	2 C.	4 C.	6 C.	8 C.	10 C.	12 C.
Evaporated milk	12 oz.	24 oz.	36 oz.	48 oz.	60 oz.	72 oz.
Skim milk	1 C.	2 C.	3 C.	4 C.	5 C.	6 C.

Assembly Directions:
Cook macaroni according to package directions. While macaroni is cooking, add White Sauce, grated cheeses, evaporated milk, and milk to slow cooker, on low. Stir to combine. When macaroni is cooked, drain and add to slow cooker. Stir to mix. Cook on low 3 hours. Cool.

Freezing Directions:
Put into freezer bags or rigid containers, dividing it into appropriate serving sizes for your family. Seal, label, and freeze.

Serving Directions:
Thaw overnight in the refrigerator. Spray a baking dish with cooking spray, and put thawed macaroni in it. Bake at 350 degrees for 25-30 minutes, or until heated through.

Notes:
[1] A recipe for Fat Free White Sauce can be found on page 161.
[2] 8 oz. cheese = 2 C. shredded

This is a very easy and versatile recipe. Have it going in the slow cooker on Assembly Day and you can make several batches in a day.

Variations:
1. Mexican Mac 'n Cheese: Substitute Pepper Jack cheese for the Extra-Sharp Cheddar cheese. You can also add a can of drained, chopped green chilies, if desired.
2. Broccoli Mac 'n Cheese: Add 2 C. of cooked, chopped broccoli to the mac and cheese before freezing.
3. Main Dish: Add a cup of cooked, chopped chicken or ham to make this a main dish.

Nutritional Info:
Per Serving: 383 Calories; 13g Fat (30.5% calories from fat); 22g Protein; 44g Carbohydrate; 1g Dietary Fiber; 41mg Cholesterol; 409mg Sodium.
Exchanges: 2-1/2 Grain (Starch); 1-1/2 Lean Meat; 1/2 Non-Fat Milk; 1-1/2 Fat.

Very Berry Fruit Salad

Recipes:	1	2	3	4	5	6
Servings:	16	32	48	64	80	96
Ingredients:						
Reduced fat cream cheese, softened	8 oz.	16 oz.	24 oz.	32 oz.	40 oz.	48 oz.
Sugar	3/4 C.	1-1/2 C.	2-1/4 C.	3 C.	3-3/4 C.	4-1/2 C.
Crushed pineapple	20 oz.	40 oz.	60 oz.	80 oz.	100 oz.	120 oz.
Frozen strawberries without syrup, thawed	10 oz.	20 oz.	30 oz.	40 oz.	50 oz.	60 oz.
Frozen raspberries, thawed	10 oz.	20 oz.	30 oz.	40 oz.	50 oz.	60 oz.
Frozen blueberries, thawed	10 oz.	20 oz.	30 oz.	40 oz.	50 oz.	60 oz.
Reduced fat sour cream	1-1/2 C.	3 C.	4-1/2 C.	6 C.	7-1/2 C.	9 C.

Assembly Directions:
Beat cream cheese and sugar until fluffy. Drain pineapple, and then add pineapple, strawberries, raspberries, and blueberries to the cream cheese mixture. Mix well by hand. Fold in sour cream. Spread in 9x13 pan.

Freezing Directions:
Cover with aluminum foil or place pan in a 2-gallon freezer bag. Seal, label, and freeze.

Serving Directions:
To serve, thaw 15-30 minutes before cutting.

Notes:
This salad is a great way to incorporate fruit into your family's diet. It's cool enough to be offered as a frozen treat instead of ice cream.

One recipe can be made in two 8x8 pans.

Nutritional Info:
Per Serving: 139 Calories; 3g Fat (19.1% calories from fat); 2g Protein; 27g Carbohydrate; 2g Dietary Fiber; 10mg Cholesterol; 86mg Sodium.
Exchanges: 1/2 Lean Meat; 1 Fruit; 1/2 Fat; 1/2 Other Carbohydrates.

Garlic Green Beans with Red Peppers

Recipes:	1	2	3	4	5	6
Servings:	6	12	18	24	30	36
Ingredients:						
Fresh green beans	1 lb.	2 lbs.	3 lbs.	4 lbs.	5 lbs.	6 lbs.
Chopped red bell pepper[1]	1 C.	2 C.	3 C.	4 C.	5 C.	6 C.
Chopped sweet onion[2]	1/4 C.	1/2 C.	3/4 C.	1 C.	1-1/4 C.	1-1/2 C.
On Hand:						
Butter or margarine	2 T.	1/4 C.	1/4 C. + 2 T.	1/2 C.	1/2 C. + 2 T.	3/4 C.
Minced garlic	1-1/2 t.	1 T.	1 T. + 1-1/2 t.	2 T.	2 T. + 1-1/2 t.	3 T.
Salt and pepper to taste						

Assembly Directions:

Wash green beans in cold water. Snip both ends and break in half.

Bring a saucepan of lightly salted water to a boil. Add beans, red bell pepper, and sweet onion. Boil for 1 minute. Strain. Allow to cool.

Freezing Directions:

Place vegetable mix in freezer bags or containers. Seal, label, and freeze.

Serving Directions:

Thaw overnight in the refrigerator. In a large skillet, melt butter over medium heat. Add garlic and cook for 1 to 2 minutes. Add vegetable mixture. Toss to coat with garlic mixture. Continue to cook the vegetables until heated through. Season with salt and pepper.

Notes:

[1] 1 large pepper = 1 C. chopped
[2] 1 medium onion = 1 C. chopped

Nutritional Info:

Per Serving: 95 Calories; 6g Fat (51.5% calories from fat); 2g Protein; 10g Carbohydrate; 4g Dietary Fiber; 16mg Cholesterol; 66mg Sodium.
Exchanges: 2 Vegetable; 1 Fat.

Fried Rice

Recipes:	1	2	3	4	5	6
Servings:	4	8	12	16	20	24
Ingredients:						
Frozen peas and carrots[1]	1 C.	2 C.	3 C.	4 C.	5 C.	6 C.
Cold cooked rice	3 C.	6 C.	9 C.	12 C.	15 C.	18 C.
On Hand:						
Canola oil, divided	2 T.	1/4 C.	1/4 C. + 2 T.	1/2 C.	1/2 C. + 2 T.	3/4 C.
Eggs	2	4	6	8	10	12
Reduced sodium soy sauce	3 T.	1/4 C. + 2 T.	1/2 C. + 1 T.	3/4 C.	3/4 C. + 3 T.	1 C. + 2 T.
Black pepper	1 dash	1/8 t.	1/4 t.	1/4 t. + 1/8 t.	1/2 t.	1/2 t. + 1/8 t.

Assembly Directions:
In a large bowl, combine the peas and carrots, and rice. Mix well.

Freezing Directions:
Place rice mixture in a freezer bag or container. Seal, label, and freeze.

Serving Directions:
Thaw bag of rice mixture in refrigerator overnight.

Heat 1 T. oil in a large skillet. Dump rice mixture into the skillet. Cook and stir over medium heat, breaking up any chunks of rice, until hot, about 5 minutes. Push rice mixture to the side of the skillet.

Add 1 T. oil to the empty side of the skillet and add the eggs. Cook and stir until eggs are thickened but still moist. Combine eggs with the rice mixture. Turn off heat. Stir in soy sauce and pepper. Serve.

Notes:
[1] You can find bags of mixed frozen peas and carrots in your grocer's frozen vegetable section. You could also use 1/2 C. of frozen peas, and 1/2 C. of cooked chopped carrots per recipe instead.

You can use white rice or a mixture of white and brown rice for this recipe. You can also pre-make the entire recipe and freeze it, so you just have to reheat it but it tastes fresher if you make it per the directions above. This recipe only takes about 10 minutes to make, so it's very quick and easy!

Nutritional Info:
Per Serving: 273 Calories; 10g Fat (31.6% calories from fat); 8g Protein; 38g Carbohydrate; 2g Dietary Fiber; 94mg Cholesterol; 510mg Sodium.
Exchanges: 2-1/2 Grain (Starch); 1/2 Lean Meat; 1-1/2 Fat.

Garlic Smashed Red Potatoes

Recipes:	1	2	3	4	5	6
Servings:	6	12	18	24	30	36
Ingredients:						
Red potatoes	2-1/2 lbs.	5 lbs.	7-1/2 lbs.	10 lbs.	12-1/2 lbs.	15 lbs.
Butter or margarine	1/2 C.	1 C.	1-1/2 C.	2 C.	2-1/2 C.	3 C.
Reduced fat sour cream	1/4 C.	1/2 C.	3/4 C.	1 C.	1-1/4 C.	1-1/2 C.
Evaporated milk	1/4 C.	1/2 C.	3/4 C.	1 C.	1-1/4 C.	1-1/2 C.
Minced garlic	1-1/2 t.	1 T.	1 T. + 1-1/2 t.	2 T.	2 T. + 1-1/2 t.	3 T.
Salt and pepper to taste						

Assembly Directions:

Wash potatoes and quarter if large. Do not peel the potatoes. Place in a large stockpot. Cover with water and bring to a boil. Cook for 10 to 20 minutes or until tender when poked with a fork. Drain potatoes. Place in a large bowl.

Mash the potatoes with a potato masher or the back of a wooden spoon. Add the butter cut in pats, sour cream, evaporated milk, garlic, salt, and pepper. Stir by hand to combine. Make sure the butter melts completely. Allow to cool.

Freezing Directions:

Place in freezer bags or rigid containers. Seal, label, and freeze.

Serving Directions:

Thaw overnight in the refrigerator. Reheat in the microwave oven or bake at 375 degrees for 30 to 40 minutes until the top is golden brown.

Notes:

You can also make these with a mixer. Make sure to beat them on the lowest speed and don't over beat the potatoes.

Nutritional Info:

Per Serving: 298 Calories; 16g Fat (46.0% calories from fat); 5g Protein; 36g Carbohydrate; 3g Dietary Fiber; 1mg Cholesterol; 204mg Sodium.
Exchanges: 2 Grain (Starch); 3 Fat.

Broccoli Pesto Pasta

Recipes:	1	2	3	4	5	6
Servings:	**6**	**12**	**18**	**24**	**30**	**36**
Ingredients:						
Penne pasta, uncooked	8 oz.	16 oz.	24 oz.	32 oz.	40 oz.	48 oz.
Olive oil	1 T.	2 T.	3 T.	1/4 C.	1/4 C. + 1 T.	1/4 C. + 2 T.
Minced garlic	1/2 t.	1 t.	1-1/2 t.	2 t.	2-1/2 t.	1 T.
Chopped red bell pepper[1]	1/2 C.	1 C.	1-1/2 C.	2 C.	2-1/2 C.	3 C.
Chopped broccoli[2]	3 C.	6 C.	9 C.	12 C.	15 C.	18 C.
Pesto sauce[3]	1/2 C.	1 C.	1-1/2 C.	2 C.	2-1/2 C.	3 C.
Grated Parmesan cheese	1/3 C.	2/3 C.	1 C.	1-1/3 C.	1-2/3 C.	2 C.

Assembly Directions:

In large pot, boil pasta for 8-10 minutes. Drain pasta, return to pot.

In a large skillet, heat oil over medium heat. Sauté garlic, red bell pepper, and broccoli about 4 minutes.

Add the pesto, Parmesan, and the broccoli mixture to the pasta. Stir to mix. Sprinkle top with extra Parmesan.

Freezing Directions:

Place the pasta in a freezer bag or container. Seal, label, and freeze.

Serving Directions:

Thaw the pasta mixture overnight in the refrigerator.

Bake in oven 350 degrees for 30 minutes.

Notes:

[1] 1 large pepper = 1 C. chopped
[2] 1 lb. fresh or frozen broccoli = 2 C. flowerets
[3] A recipe for Pesto Sauce can be found on page 162.

Nutritional Info:

Per Serving: 297 Calories; 14g Fat (41.1% calories from fat); 11g Protein; 33g Carbohydrate; 3g Dietary Fiber; 9mg Cholesterol; 235mg Sodium.
Exchanges: 2 Grain (Starch); 1/2 Lean Meat; 1/2 Vegetable; 2 Fat.

Freezer Cole Slaw

Recipes:	1	2	3	4	5	6
Servings:	10	20	30	40	50	60
Ingredients:						
Bagged cole slaw mix	3 lbs.	6 lbs.	9 lbs.	12 lbs.	15 lbs.	18 lbs.
Salt	1/2 t.	1 t.	1-1/2 t.	2 t.	2-1/2 t.	1 T.
Sugar	2 C.	4 C.	6 C.	8 C.	10 C.	12 C.
Cider vinegar	1 C.	2 C.	3 C.	4 C.	5 C.	6 C.
Celery seed	1 t.	2 t.	1 T.	1 T. + 1 t.	1 T. +2 t.	2 T.
Water	1/2 C.	1 C.	1-1/2 C.	2 C.	2-1/2 C.	3 C.

Assembly Directions:

Dump the cole slaw mix in a large bowl. Sprinkle with salt and stir to mix. Let sit 1 hour.

Meanwhile, in a small saucepan, mix the sugar, vinegar, celery seed and water. Stir to mix. Heat to boiling. Boil 1 minute. Set aside to cool.

When the hour is up, drain any excess water that has accumulated from the cole slaw mix. Pour cooled dressing over cole slaw mix and stir to combine.

Freezing Directions:

Divide into freezer bags or rigid containers based on your family size. Seal, label and freeze.

Serving Directions:

Thaw 24 hours in the refrigerator. Dump slaw into a bowl. Stir to mix, and serve.

Notes:

This recipe is so easy and goes together very quickly. It's amazing how crisp the cabbage stays after being frozen! You can also use a fresh head of cabbage that you shred yourself... you might need two heads per batch.

Nutritional Info:

Per Serving: 193 Calories; trace Fat (1.8% calories from fat); 2g Protein; 49g Carbohydrate; 3g Dietary Fiber; 0mg Cholesterol; 132mg Sodium.
Exchanges: 1-1/2 Vegetable; 3 Other Carbohydrates.

Honey Ginger Carrots

Recipes:	1	2	3	4	5	6
Servings:	**4**	**8**	**12**	**16**	**20**	**24**
Ingredients:						
Baby carrots	1 lb.	2 lbs.	3 lbs.	4 lbs.	5 lbs.	6 lbs.
Butter or margarine	1 T.	2 T.	3 T.	1/4 C.	1/4 C. + 1 T.	1/4 C. + 2 T.
Honey	1/4 C.	1/2 C.	3/4 C.	1 C.	1-1/4 C.	1-1/2 C.
Lemon juice	1 T.	2 T.	3 T.	1/4 C.	1/4 C. + 1 T.	1/4 C. + 2 T.
Salt	1/2 t.	1 t.	1-1/2 t.	2 t.	2-1/2 t.	1 T.
Ground ginger	1/2 t.	1 t.	1-1/2 t.	2 t.	2-1/2 t.	1 T.

Assembly Directions:

Bring a large pot of water to a boil. Add carrots and cook until tender but still firm, about 5 minutes. Drain.

In a large skillet over low heat, melt butter with honey. Stir in lemon juice, salt, and ground ginger. Stir in carrots and simmer until heated through.

Allow to cool.

Freezing Directions:

Place carrot mixture in a freezer bag or container. Seal, label, and freeze.

Serving Directions:

Thaw the carrot mixture overnight in the refrigerator. Reheat in a saucepan on the stovetop or in a microwave safe bowl in the microwave oven.

Nutritional Info:

Per Serving: 135 Calories; 3g Fat (18.9% calories from fat); 1g Protein; 28g Carbohydrate; 3g Dietary Fiber; 0mg Cholesterol; 336mg Sodium.
Exchanges: 2 Vegetable; 1/2 Fat; 1 Other Carbohydrates.

Sauce & Marinade Recipes

Sauce & Marinade Recipes

TIPS FOR SAUCES & MARINADE RECIPES

Shopping & Cooking Tips

- Freezing meats in homemade marinade is one of the easiest and most economical ways to begin stocking your freezer. To save time, prepare the marinade for several meals in one large glass measuring cup with a good handle and a large pouring spout. Use some simple math and the "close is good" method to distribute the marinade into each bag or rigid container.

- If you are going to be marinating lots of meat, a trip to a buying club like Sam's or Costco or to a store such as GFS Marketplace is a good idea. You can save quite a bit of money by purchasing items such as red wine vinegar, soy sauce, Worcestershire sauce, broths, and spices in bulk.

- Freeze sauces and marinades in thin, flat layers using quality freezer bags. They will thaw much quicker and retain quality much longer this way rather than using your whipped topping tubs.

- Having sauces ready to go in the freezer makes all the difference when you need to get dinner on the table quickly. Spaghetti and Fettuccine and easy meals when the sauce is already done.

Healthy Tips

- Our White Sauce is a great substitute for "cream of" soups. Make up a big batch and then divide it into 1-1/2 C. portions to use them as a substitute for a can of soup.

- Making your own sauces and marinades gives you the flexibility to change your ingredients according to your health goals. You can easily cut down on the salt or increase the vegetables without spending extra time or money.

- Save time and money by freezing homegrown fruits and vegetables. Spaghetti sauce, pizza sauce, applesauce, jams, jellies, and butters can all be frozen for later use and are much healthier for you all the way around.

Website Recipes & Tips

- For more great 30 Day Gourmet Sauce & Marinade recipes, check out the recipes section of our website at: www.30daygourmet.com

- For more Sauce & Marinade freezing tips and recipe from our cooks, check out our message boards at www.30daygourmet.com

Save time and money by making jams, jellies, and butters when fruit is in season.

White Sauce and Fat Free White Sauce

Recipes:	1	2	3	4	5	6
Servings:	10	20	30	40	50	60
Makes:	6 C.	12 C.	18 C.	24 C.	30 C.	36 C.
Ingredients:						
Butter, margarine, or cooking oil	3/4 C.	1-1/2 C.	2-1/4 C.	3 C.	3-3/4 C.	4-1/2 C.
Flour	3/4 C.	1-1/2 C.	2-1/4 C.	3 C.	3-3/4 C.	4-1/2 C.
Chicken or Beef flavoring: Bouillon granules Or	2 T.	1/4 C.	1/4 C. + 2 T.	1/2 C.	1/2 C. + 2 T.	3/4 C.
Bouillon cubes Or	6	12	18	24	30	36
Broth powder	1/4 C.	1/2 C.	3/4 C.	1 C.	1-1/4 C.	1-1/2 C.
Milk, warmed	6 C.	12 C.	18 C.	24 C.	30 C.	36 C.

Assembly Directions for White Sauce:
Melt the butter/margarine. Add flour and broth flavoring, then microwave for about 60-90 seconds until the mixture is bubbly. Add 2 C. of the milk and microwave for 2 minutes. Repeat until there are 6 C. of milk in the bowl. Microwave and stir in 2-minute increments until thick. A 6-cup batch will take about 15 minutes.

Assembly Directions for Fat Free White Sauce:
Since the fat free sauce has no butter, just warm up 2 C. of the milk for 60-90 seconds. Then stir the flour and broth flavoring into the warm milk. Follow the directions above.

Freezing Directions:
When combined with other foods in recipes like Wet Tacos (page 52) and Crab and Portobello Stuffed Chicken (page 85), this sauce freezes well. We would not recommend freezing it separately.

Notes:
We used to make this White Sauce on the stove. All of that stirring without scorching almost drove us nuts even though the finished product was always worth it. Then we learned to do this in the microwave. It's best to make it in 6-cup batches in a glass measuring cup.

This is a great substitute for canned, creamed soups (1-1/2 C. of white sauce = 1 small can of soup) and saves money. If you use skim milk and canola oil, it is lower in fat and much better for your health, too. It can be seasoned with salt and pepper or other seasonings.

Optional: For more flavor and vitamins, add any of these finely minced vegetables: Sautéed or steamed onion, celery, mushrooms, or broccoli.
Optional: For a cheese sauce, just add shredded cheddar, Swiss or grated parmesan cheese in desired amounts while sauce is still hot. Stir until melted.

Nutritional Info: White Sauce
Per Serving: 249 Calories; 19g Fat (67.4% calories from fat); 6g Protein; 14g Carbohydrate; trace Dietary Fiber; 20mg Cholesterol; 455mg Sodium.
Exchanges: 1/2 Grain (Starch); 1/2 Non-Fat Milk; 3-1/2 Fat.

Nutritional Info: Fat Free White Sauce
Per Serving: 100 Calories; 1g Fat (5.0% calories from fat); 6g Protein; 17g Carbohydrate; trace Dietary Fiber; 3mg Cholesterol; 299mg Sodium.
Exchanges: 1/2 Grain (Starch); 1/2 Non-Fat Milk.

Pesto Sauce

Recipes:	1	2	3	4	5	6
Servings:	20	40	60	80	100	120
Ingredients:						
Packed fresh basil leaves	4 C.	8 C.	12 C.	16 C.	20 C.	24 C.
Minced garlic	2 t.	1 T. + 1 t.	2 T.	2 T. + 2 t.	3 T. + 1 t.	1/4 C.
Pine nuts	1/3 C.	2/3 C.	1 C.	1-1/3 C.	1-2/3 C.	2 C.
Olive oil	1/2 C.	1 C.	1-1/2 C.	2 C.	2-1/2 C.	3 C.
Salt	1/2 t.	1 t.	1-1/2 t.	2 t.	2-1/2 t.	1 T.
Black pepper	Dash	1/8 t.	1/4 t.	1/4 t. + 1/8 t.	1/2 t.	1/2 t. + 1/8 t.
Grated Parmesan cheese	3/4 C.	1-1/2 C.	2-1/4 C.	3 C.	3-3/4 C.	4-1/2 C.

Assembly Directions:

Put the basil, garlic, pine nuts, oil, salt, and pepper in a food processor. Blend for about 20 seconds to make a smooth, even puree.

Transfer to a bowl and using a wooden spoon, beat in the grated Parmesan cheese. You could use the food processor, processing about 10 seconds, but the texture will not be the same. One recipe will make about 1-1/4 C.

Freezing Directions:

Pour pesto into a freezer container. Top with a little olive oil and cover with plastic wrap. Press the wrap directly onto the surface of the pesto to prevent discoloration. Place lid on container. Label and freeze.

Freezer life for pesto is 3 months.

Serving Directions:

Thaw overnight in the refrigerator. Stir to mix pesto.

If using pesto as a pasta sauce, place it in the serving bowl. Add 2 T. of the cooking water from the pasta to the pesto and blend. Toss the drained pasta with the pesto sauce.

One recipe of pesto is enough for one pound of pasta.

Notes:

Pesto has many uses. Try it as a sandwich spread. Mix it with olive oil or mayonnaise to make salad dressing or as a topping for pasta salad. Mix with olive oil and drizzle over fresh grilled meat.

Late summer is the best time of the year to prepare pesto. The herb crops are mature and available from your garden or local markets. Spinach, tarragon, cilantro, and parsley can be substituted for all or part of the basil in the recipe.

Try the Broccoli Pesto Pasta recipe on page 156.

Nutritional Info: one tablespoon

Per Serving: 76 Calories; 7g Fat (86.3% calories from fat); 2g Protein; 1g Carbohydrate; trace Dietary Fiber; 2mg Cholesterol; 109mg Sodium.
Exchanges: 1-1/2 Fat.

Zippy Spaghetti Sauce

Recipes:	1	2	3	4	5	6
Servings:	6	12	18	24	30	36
Ingredients:						
Cooked lean ground beef[1]	2-1/2 C.	5 C.	7-1/2 C.	10 C.	12-1/2 C.	15 C.
Diced onion[2]	1/2 C.	1 C.	1-1/2 C.	2 C.	2-1/2 C.	3 C.
Minced garlic	2 t.	1 T. + 1 t.	2 T.	2 T. + 2 t.	3 T. + 1 t.	1/4 C.
Minced green pepper (optional)[3]	1/2 C.	1 C.	1-1/2 C.	2 C.	2-1/2 C.	3 C.
Tomato sauce	8 oz.	16 oz.	24 oz.	32 oz.	40 oz.	48 oz.
Tomato paste	6 oz.	12 oz.	18 oz.	24 oz.	30 oz.	36 oz.
Water	1 C.	2 C.	3 C.	4 C.	5 C.	6 C.
Dried oregano	1 t.	2 t.	1 T.	1 T. + 1 t.	1 T. + 2 t.	2 T.
Dried basil	1/4 t.	1/2 t.	3/4 t.	1 t.	1-1/4 t.	1-1/2 t.
Sugar (optional)	1 t.	2 t.	1 T.	1 T. + 1 t.	1 T. + 2 t.	2 T.
Black pepper	1/4 t.	1/2 t.	3/4 t.	1 t.	1-1/4 t.	1-1/2 t.

Assembly Directions:
Combine cooked ground beef, onion, garlic, green pepper (optional), tomato sauce, tomato paste, water, oregano, basil, sugar (optional) and pepper in a saucepan or slow cooker. Simmer one hour in saucepan or 6 hours to overnight on low in the slow cooker. The longer this sauce simmers, the thicker it gets. Cool completely.

Freezing Directions:
Pour cooled sauce into a 1-gallon freezer bag or a rigid container. Seal, label and freeze.

Serving Directions:
Thaw. Heat in a saucepan over medium heat, or in the microwave.

Notes:
[1] 1 lb. ground beef = 2-1/2 C. browned
[2] 1 medium onion = 1 C. chopped
[3] 1 large green pepper = 1 C. chopped

Try this recipe when making Baked Ziti (page 108), Cheese-Filled Shells (page (103), Cheesy Chicken and Penne (page 81), Lasagna Rollups (page 65), Lazy Day Lasagna (page 47), Spaghetti Pie (page 62), and Spinach Lasagna (page 105).

Nutritional Info: with meat
Per Serving: 210 Calories; 11g Fat (44.8% calories from fat); 18g Protein; 11g Carbohydrate; 2g Dietary Fiber; 53mg Cholesterol; 499mg Sodium.
Exchanges: 2-1/2 Lean Meat; 2 Vegetable; 1/2 Fat.

Nutritional Info: without meat
Per Serving: 48 Calories; trace Fat (4.8% calories from fat); 2g Protein; 11g Carbohydrate; 2g Dietary Fiber; 0mg Cholesterol; 455mg Sodium.
Exchanges: 2 Vegetable.

Easy Pineapple Marinade

Recipes:	1	2	3	4	5	6
Servings:	6	12	18	24	30	36
Ingredients:						
Pineapple juice	16 oz.	32 oz.	48 oz.	64 oz.	80 oz.	96 oz.
Reduced sodium soy sauce	1/2 C.	1 C.	1-1/2 C.	2 C.	2-1/2 C.	3 C.
Ground ginger	1 t.	2 t.	1 T.	1 T. + 1 t.	1 T. + 2 t.	2 T.
Minced garlic	1/2 t.	1 t.	1-1/2 t.	2 t.	2-1/2 t.	1 T.
Reduced fat Italian salad dressing	1/3 C.	2/3 C.	1 C.	1-1/3 C.	1-2/3 C.	2 C.
Chicken breasts, pork chops, or steaks	6	12	18	24	30	36

Assembly Directions:

Combine all marinade ingredients. Place the meat of your choice in a gallon freezer bag or container. Pour marinade (about 3 cups per recipe) over the meat.

Freezing Directions:

Seal, label, and freeze.

Serving Directions:

Thaw overnight in the refrigerator. Grill, broil, or pan fry meat until browned. Discard marinade.

Nutritional Info: chicken breasts

Per Serving: 200 Calories; 3g Fat (13.2% calories from fat); 29g Protein; 13g Carbohydrate; trace Dietary Fiber; 69mg Cholesterol; 982mg Sodium.
Exchanges: 4 Lean Meat; 1/2 Vegetable; 1/2 Fruit; 1/2 Fat.

Nutritional Info: pork loin chops (1-1/2 lbs. per recipe)

Per Serving: 186 Calories; 7g Fat (36.9% calories from fat); 15g Protein; 13g Carbohydrate; trace Dietary Fiber; 32mg Cholesterol; 937mg Sodium.
Exchanges: 2 Lean Meat; 1/2 Vegetable; 1/2 Fruit; 1/2 Fat.

Nutritional Info: trimmed flank steaks (2 lbs. per recipe)

Per Serving: 304 Calories; 13g Fat (38.4% calories from fat); 32g Protein; 13g Carbohydrate; trace Dietary Fiber; 76mg Cholesterol; 1016mg Sodium.
Exchanges: 4-1/2 Lean Meat; 1/2 Vegetable; 1/2 Fruit; 1/2 Fat.

Cherry or Raspberry Ham Glaze

Recipes:	1	2	3	4	5	6
Servings:	**15**	**30**	**45**	**60**	**75**	**90**
Ingredients:						
Water	1/4 C.	1/2 C.	3/4 C.	1 C.	1-1/4 C.	1-1/2 C.
White vinegar	6 T.	3/4 C.	1 C. + 2 T.	1-1/2 C.	1-3/4 C. + 2 T.	2-1/4 C.
Honey	3 T.	1/4 C. + 2 T.	1/2 C. + 1 T.	3/4 C.	3/4 C. + 3 T.	1 C. + 2 T.
Cherry or raspberry preserves	18 oz.	36 oz.	54 oz.	72 oz.	90 oz.	108 oz.
Cinnamon	1 t.	2 t.	1 T.	1 T. + 1 t.	1 T. + 2 t.	2 T.
Ground cloves	1 t.	2 t.	1 T.	1 T. + 1 t.	1 T. + 2 t.	2 T.
Ground nutmeg	1 t.	2 t.	1 T.	1 T. + 1 t.	1 T. + 2 t.	2 T.
On Hand:						
Spiral sliced ham or semi-boneless ham	5 lbs.	10 lbs.	15 lbs.	20 lbs.	25 lbs.	30 lbs.

Assembly Directions:
In a saucepan, use a whisk to combine water, vinegar, honey, preserves, cinnamon, cloves, and nutmeg.

Bring to a boil. Reduce heat and simmer for 2 minutes. Remove from heat and allow to cool.

Freezing Directions:
Pour sauce into a freezer bag or container. Seal, label and freeze.

Serving Directions:
Thaw glaze in refrigerator overnight. Cook ham according to instructions on packaging. During last 30 minutes of cooking, pour 1/4 C. of the glaze over the ham. Remove ham from oven. Stir ham drippings into remaining glaze and serve with ham.

Nutritional Info:
Per Serving: 373 Calories; 16g Fat (38.7% calories from fat); 27g Protein; 31g Carbohydrate; 1g Dietary Fiber; 86mg Cholesterol; 2007mg Sodium.
Exchanges: 4 Lean Meat; 1 Fat; 1-1/2 Other Carbohydrates.

Flavored Butters

Recipes:	1	2	3	4	5	6
Servings:	**6**	**12**	**18**	**24**	**30**	**36**
Orange Cinnamon Butter Ingredients:						
Butter or margarine	1/4 C.	1/2 C.	3/4 C.	1 C.	1-1/4 C.	1-1/2 C.
Cinnamon	1 t.	2 t.	1 T.	1 T. + 1 t.	1 T. + 2 t.	2 T.
Brown sugar	2 T.	1/4 C.	1/4 C. + 2 T.	1/2 C.	1/2 C. + 2 T.	3/4 C.
Frozen orange juice concentrate	1 t.	2 t.	1 T.	1 T. + 1 t.	1 T. + 2 t.	2 T.
Lime juice	1 t.	2 t.	1 T.	1 T. + 1 t.	1 T. + 2 t.	2 T.
Grated orange peel	1 T.	2 T.	3 T.	1/4 C.	1/4 C. + 1 T.	1/4 C. + 2 T
Cashew Butter Ingredients:						
Dry-roasted cashews	4 oz.	8 oz.	12 oz.	16 oz.	20 oz.	24 oz.
Butter or margarine	1/4 C.	1/2 C.	3/4 C.	1 C.	1-1/4 C.	1-1/2 C.
Honey	2 t.	1 T. + 1 t.	2 T.	2 T. + 2 t.	3 T. + 1 t.	1/4 C.
Pistachio Butter Ingredients:						
Pistachio nuts	2 T.	1/4 C.	1/4 C. + 2 T.	1/2 C.	1/2 C. + 2 T.	3/4 C.
Butter or margarine	1/4 C.	1/2 C.	3/4 C.	1 C.	1-1/4 C.	1-1/2 C.
Chopped fresh parsley	1 T.	2 T.	3 T.	1/4 C.	1/4 C. + 1 T.	1/4 C. + 2 T

Assembly Directions:

Orange Cinnamon Butter: Using a mixer, beat butter, cinnamon and brown sugar until butter is fluffy. Beat in orange juice concentrate, lime juice, and orange peel until combined.

Cashew Butter: Using a food processor, chop cashews into pea sized pieces. Add the butter and honey. Pulse to combine.

Pistachio Butter: Using a food processor, chop pistachios into pea sized pieces. Add the butter and parsley. Pulse to combine.

Freezing Directions:
Place butter on a sheet of plastic wrap. Roll into a log. Put butter logs into freezer bags or rigid containers. Seal, label, and freeze.

Serving Directions:
Thaw overnight in the refrigerator.
Try the Orange Cinnamon Butter on chicken, pork, or carrots. Try the Cashew Butter on chicken, fish, green beans, or carrots. Try the Pistachio Butter on chicken, pork, or pasta.

Nutritional Info: Orange Cinnamon Butter
Per Serving: 83 Calories; 8g Fat (80.9% calories from fat); trace Protein; 4g Carbohydrate; trace Dietary Fiber; 21mg Cholesterol; 79mg Sodium.
Exchanges: 1-1/2 Fat.

Nutritional Info: Cashew Butter
Per Serving: 183 Calories; 16g Fat (76.7% calories from fat); 3g Protein; 8g Carbohydrate; 1g Dietary Fiber; 0mg Cholesterol; 92mg Sodium.
Exchanges: 1/2 Grain (Starch); 3 Fat.

Nutritional Info: Pistachio Butter
Per Serving: 84 Calories; 9g Fat (93.6% calories from fat); 1g Protein; 1g Carbohydrate; trace Dietary Fiber; 21mg Cholesterol; 79mg Sodium.
Exchanges: 2 Fat.

Gringo Enchilada Sauce

Recipes:	1	2	3	4	5	6
Servings:	6	12	18	24	30	36
Makes:	1-3/4 C.	3-1/2 C.	5-1/4 C.	7 C.	8-3/4 C.	10-1/2 C.
Ingredients:						
Canola oil	1 T.	2 T.	3 T.	1/4 C.	1/4 C. + 1 T.	1/4 C. + 2 T.
Minced garlic	1 t.	2 t.	1 T.	1 T. + 1 t.	1 T. + 2 t.	2 T.
Minced onion[1]	1 t.	2 t.	1 T.	1 T. + 1 t.	1 T. + 2 t.	2 T.
Dried oregano	1/2 t.	1 t.	1-1/2 t.	2 t.	2-1/2 t.	1 T.
Chili powder	2-1/2 t.	1 T. + 2 t.	2 T. + 1-1/2 t.	3 T. + 1 t.	4 T. + 1/2 t.	5 T.
Dried basil	1/2 t.	1 t.	1-1/2 t.	2 t.	2-1/2 t.	1 T.
Black pepper	1/8 t.	1/4 t.	3/8 t.	1/2 t.	1/2 t. + 1/8 t.	3/4 t.
Salt	1/8 t.	1/4 t.	3/8 t.	1/2 t.	1/2 t. + 1/8 t.	3/4 t.
Cumin	1/4 t.	1/2 t.	3/4 t.	1 t.	1-1/4 t.	1-1/2 t.
Dried parsley	1 t.	2 t.	1 T.	1 T. + 1 t.	1 T. + 2 t.	2 T.
Salsa	1/4 C.	1/2 C.	3/4 C.	1 C.	1-1/4 C.	1-1/2 C.
Tomato sauce	6 oz.	12 oz.	18 oz.	24 oz.	30 oz.	36 oz.
Water	1-1/2 C.	3 C.	4-1/2 C.	6 C.	7-1/2 C.	9 C.

Assembly Directions:
Heat the oil in a large saucepan over medium heat. Add the garlic and sauté for 1 to 2 minutes. Add the onion, oregano, chili powder, basil, ground black pepper, salt, cumin, parsley, salsa and tomato sauce. Mix together and then stir in the water. Bring to a boil, reduce heat to low and simmer for 15 to 20 minutes.

Freezing Directions:
Cool sauce. Place in a quart freezer bag or freezer container. Seal, label and freeze.

Serving Directions:
Thaw sauce in refrigerator.

Notes:
[1] 1 medium onion = 1 C. chopped

Use this sauce in any recipe that calls for enchilada sauce. Try the Wet Tacos recipe on page 52.

Nutritional Info:
Per Serving: 38 Calories; 3g Fat (54.9% calories from fat); 1g Protein; 4g Carbohydrate; 1g Dietary Fiber; 0mg Cholesterol; 276mg Sodium.
Exchanges: 1/2 Vegetable; 1/2 Fat.

Wild Mushroom Sauce

Recipes:	1	2	3	4	5	6
Servings:	4	8	12	16	20	24
Ingredients:						
Canola oil	2 t.	1 T. + 1 t.	2 T.	2 T. + 2 t.	3 T. + 1 t.	1/4 C.
Minced green onion[1]	1/4 C.	1/2 C.	3/4 C.	1 C.	1-1/4 C.	1-1/2 C.
Minced garlic	1/2 t.	1 t.	1-1/2 t.	2 t.	2-1/2 t.	1 T.
Mixed fresh mushrooms	8 oz.	16 oz.	24 oz.	32 oz.	40 oz.	48 oz.
White pepper	1/8 t.	1/4 t.	3/8 t.	1/2 t.	1/2 t. + 1/8 t.	3/4 t.
Dried parsley	1 t.	2 t.	1 T.	1 T. + 1 t.	1 T. + 2 t.	2 T.
Dried thyme	1/4 t.	1/2 t.	3/4 t.	1 t.	1-1/4 t.	1-1/2 t.
Worcestershire sauce	2 t.	1 T. + 1 t.	2 T.	2 T. + 2 t.	3 T. + 1 t.	1/4 C.
Beef broth	2/3 C.	1-1/3 C.	2 C.	2-2/3 C.	3-1/3 C.	4 C.
On Hand:						
Cornstarch	1 t.	2 t.	1 T.	1 T. + 1 t.	1 T. + 2 t.	2 T.
Water	1 T.	2 T.	3 T.	1/4 C.	1/4 C. + 1 T.	1/4 C. + 2 T.

Assembly Directions:
Heat the oil in a skillet over medium heat. Add onion and garlic. Cook for 2 minutes. Slice mushrooms. Add the mushrooms, pepper, parsley and thyme. Cook for 3 minutes. Add Worcestershire sauce and beef broth. Cook for 5 minutes. Cool.

Freezing Directions:
Place into freezer bags or rigid containers. Seal, label, and freeze.

Serving Directions:
Thaw overnight in the refrigerator. Pour mushroom mixture into a saucepan. Bring to a boil. Dissolve cornstarch in water. Add to skillet, stirring until thickened. Serve sauce over meat or noodles.

Notes:
[1] 7 medium green onions = 1/2 C. sliced

Serve this sauce over any grilled or broiled beef or pork.

Nutritional Info:
Per Serving: 52 Calories; 3g Fat (40.5% calories from fat); 3g Protein; 5g Carbohydrate; 1g Dietary Fiber; 0mg Cholesterol; 242mg Sodium.
Exchanges: 1/2 Vegetable; 1/2 Fat.

30 Day Gourmet © 2012

Sweet and Sour Sauce

Recipes:	1	2	3	4	5	6
Servings:	4	8	12	16	20	24
Ingredients:						
Canned pineapple tidbits	20 oz.	40 oz.	60 oz.	80 oz.	100 oz.	120 oz.
White vinegar	2 T.	1/4 C.	1/4 C. + 2 T.	1/2 C.	1/2 C. + 2 T.	3/4 C.
Reduced sodium soy sauce	1 T.	2 T.	3 T.	1/4 C.	1/4 C. + 1 T.	1/4 C. + 2 T.
Brown sugar	1 T.	2 T.	3 T.	1/4 C.	1/4 C. + 1 T.	1/4 C. + 2 T.
On Hand:						
Cornstarch	2 T.	1/4 C.	1/4 C. + 2 T.	1/2 C.	1/2 C. + 2 T.	3/4 C.
Cold water	2 T.	1/4 C.	1/4 C. + 2 T.	1/2 C.	1/2 C. + 2 T.	3/4 C.

Assembly Directions:
Drain the juice from the pineapple tidbits into a one cup or larger measuring cup. Add enough water to the juice to make one cup of liquid per recipe. Combine the pineapple tidbits, pineapple juice, vinegar, soy sauce, and brown sugar.

Freezing Directions:
Pour pineapple mixture into a freezer bag or container. Seal, label, and freeze.

Serving Directions:
Thaw in the refrigerator overnight. Pour the pineapple mixture into a saucepan. Bring to a boil. Mix the cornstarch with the cold water until the lumps dissolve. Add the cornstarch mixture to the pineapple mixture. Cook, stirring constantly, until the sauce thickens slightly, about 1 to 2 minutes. Remove skillet from heat and serve at once.

Notes:
This sauce is great over chicken or pork.

Nutritional Info:
Per Serving: 62 Calories; trace Fat (0.8% calories from fat); trace Protein; 15g Carbohydrate; trace Dietary Fiber; 0mg Cholesterol; 152mg Sodium.
Exchanges: 1/2 Fruit.

Alfredo Sauce

Recipes:	1	2	3	4	5	6
Servings:	6	12	18	24	30	36
Makes:	1-1/2 C.	3 C.	4-1/2 C.	6 C.	7-1/2 C.	9 C.
Alfredo Sauce:						
Half-n-half or light cream	1 C.	2 C.	3 C.	4 C.	5 C.	6 C.
Grated Parmesan cheese	1 C.	2 C.	3 C.	4 C.	5 C.	6 C.
Butter or margarine	3 T.	6 T.	9 T.	12 T.	15 T.	18 T.
Light Alfredo Sauce:						
Butter or margarine	2 T.	1/4 C.	1/4 C. + 2 T.	1/2 C.	1/2 C. + 2 T.	3/4 C.
Minced garlic	1-1/2 t.	1 T.	1 T. + 1-1/2 t.	2 T.	2 T. + 1-1/2 t.	3 T.
Dried basil	1-1/2 t.	1 T.	1 T. + 1-1/2 t.	2 T.	2 T. + 1-1/2 t.	3 T.
Dried parsley	1-1/2 t.	1 T.	1 T. + 1-1/2 t.	2 T.	2 T. + 1-1/2 t.	3 T.
Evaporated milk	12 oz.	24 oz.	36 oz.	48 oz.	60 oz.	72 oz.
Grated Parmesan cheese	1/4 C.	1/2 C.	3/4 C.	1 C.	1-1/4 C.	1-1/2 C.
Salt	1/2 t.	1 t.	1-1/2 t.	2 t.	2-1/2 t.	1 T.
Black pepper	Dash	1/8 t.	1/4 t.	1/4 t. + 1/8 t.	1/2 t.	1/2 t. + 1/8 t.

Assembly Directions:

Alfredo Sauce: Put Half-n-Half, Parmesan and butter in a saucepan. Heat on medium-low, and stir to combine. Heat until heated through; do not allow it to come to a boil. Set aside to cool.

Light Alfredo Sauce: Heat butter in a saucepan over medium heat. Add garlic and cook for 2 minutes. Add basil and parsley. Stir to combine. Stir in milk, Parmesan cheese, and salt. Cover over medium heat until slightly thickened; stirring constantly. Do not let the sauce boil. Sprinkle with pepper. Allow sauce to cool. One recipe makes approximately 1-1/2 cups of sauce.

Freezing Directions:

Pour sauce into quart freezer bags or freezer containers. Seal, label, and freeze.

Serving Directions:

Thaw overnight in the refrigerator. Heat sauce in a saucepan over low heat. Do not let the sauce boil.

Notes:

Try this recipe when making Chicken Broccoli Fettuccine (page 87) or Shrimp Carbonara (page 92).

Nutritional Info: Alfredo Sauce

Per Serving: 164 Calories; 14g Fat (78.1% calories from fat); 7g Protein; 2g Carbohydrate; 0g Dietary Fiber; 25mg Cholesterol; 331mg Sodium.
Exchanges: 1 Lean Meat; 2-1/2 Fat.

Nutritional Info: Light Alfredo Sauce

Per Serving: 102 Calories; 5g Fat (39.8% calories from fat); 7g Protein; 8g Carbohydrate; trace Dietary Fiber; 14mg Cholesterol; 374mg Sodium.
Exchanges: 1/2 Lean Meat; 1/2 Non-Fat Milk; 1/2 Fat.

Appetizer Recipes

Appetizer Recipes

TIPS FOR APPETIZERS

Serving Tips

When planning an "appetizers only" event, how much should you prepare?

- Appetizers: 6-7 per person/hour
- Sweets: 3-5 per person
- Beverages: 1 cup beverage per person/hour

Party Appetizer Tips:

- Serve a balance of foods made ahead of time and foods prepared that day. Offer cold dishes that are prepared in advance as well as some hot from the oven.
- Be sure that you have something for vegetarians. Fruit slices and a simple veggie tray are an easy way to add color, variety and good nutrition for all your guests.
- Make appetizers small enough to be eaten in one bite for less mess.
- Garnish serving trays with kale, olives, parsley or lemon peel and line bowls with cabbage leaves.
- Rather than having one table, place appetizers in multiple locations. This encourages your guests to move around more.
- Serve cold foods such as vegetables, shrimp and cubed cheese in a ring of ice.
- Stash fresh trays of appetizers in the kitchen so you can quickly refill.
- Provide easy-to-find receptacles for used napkins, skewers, or other consumable items.

Shopping & Cooking Tips

- Almost any type of appetizer freezes well. Think about the appetizers that you see now in the buying clubs and places like GFS Marketplace. They are all frozen and just require thawing and/or baking.
- For freshest flavor, do not pre-bake appetizers. Just pre-assemble them and bake them on the day that you will serve them.

Short list of appetizers that freeze well:

- Sausage Balls
- Meatballs
- Fruit or Meat Puffs
- Mini Quiches
- Spinach Balls
- Party Sandwiches
- Cheeseballs
- Hot & Cold Dips
- Stuffed Mushrooms
- Quesadillas
- Buffalo Wings
- Pot Stickers & Eggrolls

Website Recipes & Tips

- For more great 30 Day Gourmet Appetizer recipes, check out the recipes section of our website at: www.30daygourmet.com
- For more Appetizer freezing tips and recipes from our cooks, check out the Cooking-Appetizers section of our message boards at www.30daygourmet.com

Serve appetizers and dips in interesting "containers" such as bread, pumpkins or watermelons.

ot Spinach Artichoke Dip

Recipes:	1	2	3	4	5	6
Servings:	32	64	96	128	160	192
Makes:	4 C.	8 C.	12 C.	16 C.	20 C.	24 C.
Ingredients:						
Butter or margarine	2 T.	1/4 C.	1/4 C. + 2 T.	1/2 C.	1/2 C. + 2 T.	3/4 C.
Minced garlic	2 t.	1 T. + 1 t.	2 T.	2 T. + 2 t.	3 T. + 1 t.	1/4 C.
Frozen chopped spinach, partially thawed	10 oz.	20 oz.	30 oz.	40 oz.	50 oz.	60 oz.
Canned artichoke hearts, drained and chopped	14 oz.	28 oz.	42 oz.	56 oz.	70 oz.	84 oz.
Lowfat cream cheese	8 oz.	16 oz.	24 oz.	32 oz.	40 oz.	48 oz.
Reduced fat sour cream	16 oz.	32 oz.	48 oz.	64 oz.	80 oz.	96 oz.
Grated Parmesan cheese	3/4 C.	1-1/2 C.	2-1/4 C.	3 C.	3-3/4 C.	4-1/2 C.
Salt	1/2 t.	1 t.	1-1/2 t.	2 t.	2-1/2 t.	1 T.

Assembly Directions:
Melt the butter in a saucepan over low heat. Add the garlic and heat for a few minutes. Add the spinach and artichoke hearts, stirring to mix. Cook until the spinach is completely thawed and isn't in chunks anymore. Add the cream cheese, sour cream, and Parmesan cheese. Stir until the cheeses are melted. Add the salt and stir to mix.

Freezing Directions:
Allow the dip to cool. Pour into a rigid container. Seal, label and freeze. The dip can be frozen in a freezer bag but it is easier to scrape the dip out of a rigid container after it has thawed.

Serving Directions:
Thaw overnight in the refrigerator.

Heat it on the stovetop or in the microwave. Serve the dip hot, with tortilla chips for scooping. You can also serve it with corn chips, breadsticks or crackers. Serve it with sour cream and/or salsa on the side. To keep it warm for a gathering, put the dip in a slow cooker on low.

Notes:
Most people think they won't like this dip, just because they don't usually eat spinach and artichokes. But once they try it, they're hooked! Make sure you buy chopped or cut spinach, not whole leaf. Canned artichokes are better for this recipe than marinated artichokes in a jar but if all your store has are marinated ones, you can use them. Just rinse the marinade off before you chop the artichokes. If you use artichokes in a jar instead of a can, the jar will probably be 2 oz. or so smaller than the can. You should be fine to use the smaller amount in the jar, in place of the 14 oz. can. To quickly chop the artichoke hearts, use your food processor.

Nutritional Info: per 2 tablespoons
Per Serving: 43 Calories; 3g Fat (57.4% calories from fat); 2g Protein; 2g Carbohydrate; trace Dietary Fiber; 7mg Cholesterol; 158mg Sodium.
Exchanges: 1/2 Lean Meat; 1/2 Fat.

Basic Fruit Dip

Recipes:	1	2	3	4	5	6
Servings:	**16**	**32**	**48**	**64**	**80**	**96**
Makes:	**2 C.**	**4 C.**	**6 C.**	**8 C.**	**10 C.**	**12 C.**
Ingredients:						
Reduced fat cream cheese, softened	8 oz.	16 oz.	24 oz.	32 oz.	40 oz.	48 oz.
Sugar	3 T.	1/4 C. + 2 T.	1/2 C. + 1 T.	3/4 C.	3/4 C. + 3 T.	1 C. + 2 T.
Reduced fat sour cream	1 C.	2 C.	3 C.	4 C.	5 C.	6 C.
Vanilla	1 t.	2 t.	1 T.	1 T. + 1 t.	1 T. + 2 t.	2 T.
Optional Add Ins:						
Peanut butter Or	2 T.	1/4 C.	1/4 C. + 2 T.	1/2 C.	1/2 C. + 2 T.	3/4 C.
Fruit preserves	2 T.	1/4 C.	1/4 C. + 2 T.	1/2 C.	1/2 C. + 2 T.	3/4 C.

Assembly Directions:
Beat cream cheese and sugar with an electric mixer until smooth. Add sour cream and vanilla. Continue to beat until light and fluffy.

Optional Add Ins:
Peanut Butter: Beat peanut butter with cream cheese and sugar. Continue with the recipe.

Fruit Preserves: Fold in fruit preserves after beating sour cream and vanilla. Mix until combined.

Freezing Directions:
Place in a quart freezer bag or freezer container. Seal, label and freeze.

Serving Directions:
Thaw overnight in refrigerator.

Nutritional Info: plain
Per Serving: 48 Calories; 3g Fat (52.0% calories from fat); 2g Protein; 4g Carbohydrate; 0g Dietary Fiber; 9mg Cholesterol; 83mg Sodium.
Exchanges: 1/2 Lean Meat; 1/2 Fat.

Nutritional Info: peanut butter
Per Serving: 60 Calories; 4g Fat (56.2% calories from fat); 2g Protein; 4g Carbohydrate; trace Dietary Fiber; 9mg Cholesterol; 93mg Sodium.
Exchanges: 1/2 Lean Meat; 1/2 Fat.

Nutritional Info: fruit
Per Serving: 54 Calories; 3g Fat (45.8% calories from fat); 2g Protein; 6g Carbohydrate; trace Dietary Fiber; 9mg Cholesterol; 84mg Sodium.
Exchanges: 1/2 Lean Meat; 1/2 Fat; 1/2 Other Carbohydrates.

Traditional Egg Rolls

Recipes:	1	2	3	4	5	6
Servings:	21	42	63	84	105	126
Ingredients:						
Ground pork	1 lb.	2 lbs.	3 lbs.	4 lbs.	5 lbs.	6 lbs.
Grated cabbage[1]	3 C.	6 C.	9 C.	12 C.	15 C.	18 C.
Grated carrots[2]	1-1/2 C.	3 C.	4-1/2 C.	6 C.	7-1/2 C.	9 C.
Grated onion[3]	1/4 C.	1/2 C.	3/4 C.	1 C.	1-1/4 C.	1-1/2 C.
Minced garlic	1 t.	2 t.	1 T.	1 T. + 1 t.	1 T. + 2 t.	2 T.
Reduced sodium soy sauce	1 T.	2 T.	3 T.	1/4 C.	1/4 C. + 1 T.	1/4 C. + 2 T.
Ground ginger	1-1/2 t.	1 T.	1 T. + 1-1/2 t.	2 T.	2 T. + 1-1/2 t.	3 T.
Onion powder	1/2 t.	1 t.	1-1/2 t.	2 t.	2-1/2 t.	1 T.
Garlic powder	1/2 t.	1 t.	1-1/2 t.	2 t.	2-1/2 t.	1 T.
Egg roll wrappers	21	42	63	84	105	126

Assembly Directions:

Brown ground pork in a large pot. Drain off excess fat. Add cabbage, carrots, onions, garlic, soy sauce, ginger, onion powder, and garlic powder and cook for about 15 minutes. Cool.

Place one wrapper flat on a flat surface. Spread about 1/4 c. filling across one end of the square, leaving about an inch on each of the three sides. Fold over the 2 sides, then the end of the square. Roll up towards the other end. Press gently to seal and flatten slightly. Repeat this with the remaining filling and wrappers.

To deep fry, heat oil in a large pot or wok. Fry egg rolls until they start to turn brown, about 15 minutes. You may have to turn them over to brown evenly.

To pan fry, heat oil in a frying pan. Fry egg rolls on one side until starting to brown. Flip them over and fry on the second side.

For an alternative that is lower in fat and faster to make, these can be oven-fried. Lightly grease a baking dish; place egg rolls on the greased surface and brush each lightly with oil. Preheat oven to 350 degrees and bake for about 15 minutes, turning once after about the first 10 minutes.

Freezing Directions:

Egg rolls can be frozen before or after frying. In either case, lay them out flat on a baking sheet. Flash freeze. Place in a freezer bag or container. Seal, label, and freeze.

Serving Directions:

Thaw in the refrigerator overnight. To reheat fried egg rolls, bake in a 350 degree oven for about 10 minutes or about 15-20 minutes if heating still-frozen egg rolls. Raw frozen egg rolls can be cooked as above, but it may take a few more minutes. Cook until light brown.

Notes:

[1] 1 lb. cabbage = 4 C. shredded
[2] 1 medium carrot = 1/2 C. grated
[3] 1 onion = 1 C. chopped

Nutritional Info: baked

Per Serving: 211 Calories; 9g Fat (40.6% calories from fat); 10g Protein; 20g Carbohydrate; 1g Dietary Fiber; 28mg Cholesterol; 237mg Sodium.
Exchanges: 1 Grain (Starch); 1 Lean Meat; 1/2 Vegetable; 1-1/2 Fat.

Hot Pizza Dip

Recipes:	1	2	3	4	5	6
Servings:	**12**	**24**	**36**	**48**	**60**	**72**
Makes:	**3 C.**	**6 C.**	**9 C.**	**12 C.**	**15 C.**	**18 C.**
Ingredients:						
Reduced fat cream cheese, softened	8 oz.	16 oz.	24 oz.	32 oz.	40 oz.	48 oz.
Reduced fat sour cream	4 oz.	8 oz.	12 oz.	16 oz.	20 oz.	24 oz.
Garlic powder	1/8 t.	1/4 t.	3/8 t.	1/2 t.	1/2 t. + 1/8 t.	3/4 t.
Dried oregano	1/4 t.	1/2 t.	3/4 t.	1 t.	1-1/4 t.	1-1/2 t.
Pizza sauce	3/4 C.	1-1/2 C.	2-1/4 C.	3 C.	3-3/4 C.	4-1/2 C.
Diced pepperoni	1/2 C.	1 C.	1-1/2 C.	2 C.	2-1/2 C.	3 C.
Chopped onion[1]	1/4 C.	1/2 C.	3/4 C.	1 C.	1-1/4 C.	1-1/2 C.
Chopped green peppers[2]	1/4 C.	1/2 C.	3/4 C.	1 C.	1-1/4 C.	1-1/2 C.
Shredded mozzarella cheese[3]	1 C.	2 C.	3 C.	4 C.	5 C.	6 C.

Assembly Directions:

In a small mixing bowl, combine the cream cheese, sour cream, garlic powder and oregano. Spread the mixture in a 9" glass pie plate. Spread the pizza sauce over the cream cheese mixture. Evenly sprinkle the pepperoni, onion and pepper on top of the pizza sauce. Bake at 350 degrees for 18 minutes. Remove from the oven and set aside to cool.

Freezing Directions:

Cover the top of the cooled pie plate with waxed paper or plastic wrap. Then cover the whole dish in foil. Or, put the covered plate in a one- or two-gallon freezer bag. Put the mozzarella cheese in a one-quart freezer bag. Seal, label and freeze.

Serving Directions:

Thaw dish and bag of mozzarella cheese at least overnight in the refrigerator. If the dish is wrapped in waxed paper or plastic wrap, remove it before baking. Bake in the oven at 350 degrees for 15 minutes. Remove from the oven, sprinkle the mozzarella cheese on top, and return to the oven for 8-10 minutes. Serve hot with tortilla chips for dipping.

Notes:

[1] 1 medium onion = 1 C. chopped
[2] 1 large pepper = 1 C. chopped
[3] 8 oz. cheese = 2 C. shredded

This dish is a great appetizer! Tortilla chips are a great choice for "dippers", but you could also use breadsticks, crackers, or even pizza veggies such as broccoli florets, mushroom halves, green pepper strips, etc.

Nutritional Info:

Per Serving: 123 Calories; 9g Fat (64.6% calories from fat); 7g Protein; 4g Carbohydrate; trace Dietary Fiber; 22mg Cholesterol; 407mg Sodium.
Exchanges: 1 Lean Meat; 1/2 Vegetable; 1 Fat.

Sausage Stuffed Mushrooms

Recipes:	1	2	3	4	5	6
Servings:	4	8	12	16	20	24
Ingredients:						
Fresh mushrooms	12 oz.	24 oz.	36 oz.	48 oz.	60 oz.	72 oz.
Turkey sausage	8 oz.	16 oz.	24 oz.	32 oz.	40 oz.	48 oz.
Minced onion	1 T.	2 T.	3 T.	1/4 C.	1/4 C. + 1 T.	1/4 C. + 2 T.
Minced garlic	1/2 t.	1 t.	1-1/2 t.	2 t.	2-1/2 t.	1 T.
Dried parsley	1 t.	2 t.	1 T.	1 T. + 1 t.	1 T. + 2 t.	2 T.
Grated Parmesan cheese	1/4 C.	1/2 C.	3/4 C.	1 C.	1-1/4 C.	1-1/2 C.

Assembly Directions:

Wash mushrooms and gently pat dry. Remove stems and set caps aside.

Coarsely chop the mushroom stems. Brown sausage, chopped mushroom stems, onion, and garlic in a frying pan until the sausage is no longer pink. Drain off any excess fat. Place sausage mixture in a food processor and chop on pulse for 1 to 2 seconds. Stir in parsley and Parmesan cheese. Pulse again for 1 second.

Fill mushroom caps with filling.

Freezing Directions:

Place mushroom caps on a baking sheet. Make sure that the mushrooms do not touch. Flash freeze. When solid, remove mushrooms from baking sheet and place in a freezer bag or container. Seal, label, and freeze.

Serving Directions:

Thaw overnight in the refrigerator. Preheat oven to 350 degrees. Place mushrooms on a baking sheet. Bake for 15 to 20 minutes.

Notes:

This is a great recipe to make ahead for holiday family gatherings.

Nutritional Info:

Per Serving: 181 Calories; 13g Fat (62.0% calories from fat); 12g Protein; 5g Carbohydrate; 1g Dietary Fiber; 49mg Cholesterol; 478mg Sodium.
Exchanges: 1-1/2 Lean Meat; 1 Vegetable; 1-1/2 Fat.

Shrimp and Pork Pot Stickers

Recipes:	1	2	3	4	5	6
Servings:	**12**	**24**	**36**	**48**	**60**	**72**
Makes:	**48**	**96**	**144**	**192**	**240**	**288**
Ingredients:						
Frozen cooked shrimp	6 oz.	12 oz.	18 oz.	24 oz.	30 oz.	36 oz.
Canned, sliced water chestnuts	1/2 C.	1 C.	1-1/2 C.	2 C.	2-1/2 C.	3 C.
Cooked ground pork[1]	1 C.	2 C.	3 C.	4 C.	5 C.	6 C.
Chopped green onions[2]	3/4 C.	1-1/2 C.	2-1/4 C.	3 C.	3-3/4 C.	4-1/2 C.
Reduced sodium soy sauce	2 T.	1/4 C.	1/4 C. + 2 T.	1/2 C.	1/2 C. + 2 T.	3/4 C.
Ground ginger	1 t.	2 t.	1 T.	1 T. + 1 t.	1 T. + 2 t.	2 T.
Sesame oil	1 t.	2 t.	1 T.	1 T. + 1 t.	1 T. + 2 t.	2 T.
Wonton wrappers	48	96	144	192	240	288
On Hand:						
Canola oil	1 T.	2 T.	3 T.	1/4 C.	1/4 C. + 1 T.	1/4 C. + 2 T.

Assembly Directions:

Place shrimp in a colander and run cold water over them. Remove the tails from the shrimp. Combine shrimp, water chestnuts, ground pork, green onions, soy sauce, ginger, and sesame seed oil in a food processor. Process a few seconds or until mixture is fine but not smooth.

Place one wrapper flat on a flat surface. Put about 1/2 tablespoon of filling in the middle of the wrapper. Moisten the edges of the wrapper. Fold wrapper in half and form small pleats around the edge of the wrapper. Repeat this with the remaining filling and wrappers.

Freezing Directions:

Place pot stickers on a baking sheet. Flash freeze. When solid, place in a freezer bag or freezer container. Seal, label and freeze.

Serving Directions:

Thaw in refrigerator overnight.

Heat vegetable oil in a nonstick skillet over medium high heat. Arrange pot stickers in pan and fry 2 or 3 minutes or until the undersides are pale brown.

Add 1/2 C. of water to the skillet, tipping it to distribute the water evenly. Cover and cook until the liquid has evaporated and the pot stickers are crisp and golden, about 7 to 10 minutes.

Remove pot stickers from skillet and serve immediately. Repeat procedure with remaining pot stickers.

Notes:

[1] 7 medium green onions = 1/2 C. sliced
[2] 1 lb. ground pork = 2-1/2 C. browned

Nutritional Info: per 4 pot stickers

Per Serving: 184 Calories; 6g Fat (30.8% calories from fat); 11g Protein; 20g Carbohydrate; 1g Dietary Fiber; 42mg Cholesterol; 295mg Sodium.
Exchanges: 1 Grain (Starch); 1 Lean Meat; 1/2 Fat.

Mango Salsa

Recipes:	1	2	3	4	5	6
Servings:	**8**	**16**	**24**	**32**	**40**	**48**
Ingredients:						
Frozen diced mango[1]	2 C.	4 C.	6 C.	8 C.	10 C.	12 C.
Red bell pepper, diced[2]	1	2	3	4	5	6
Minced red onion[3]	1/4 C.	1/2 C.	3/4 C.	1 C.	1-1/4 C.	1-1/2 C.
Frozen corn	1 C.	2 C.	3 C.	4 C.	5 C.	6 C.
Canned kidney beans, drained and rinsed	15 oz.	30 oz.	45 oz.	60 oz.	75 oz.	90 oz.
On Hand:						
Chopped fresh cilantro	2 T.	1/4 C.	1/4 C. + 2 T.	1/2 C.	1/2 C. + 2 T.	3/4 C.
Canned green chilies	4 oz.	8 oz.	12 oz.	16 oz.	20 oz.	24 oz.
Lime juice	1/4 C.	1/2 C.	3/4 C.	1 C.	1-1/4 C.	1-1/2 C.
Lemon juice	2 T.	1/4 C.	1/4 C. + 2 T.	1/2 C.	1/2 C. + 2 T.	3/4 C.
Salt and pepper to taste						

Assembly Directions:
In a large bowl, combine mango, red pepper, red onion, frozen corn, and kidney beans. Stir to mix.

Freezing Directions:
Place mango mixture into freezer bags or rigid containers. Seal, label, and freeze.

Serving Directions:
Thaw overnight in the refrigerator. Place mango mixture in a serving bowl. Add cilantro, green chilies, lime juice, and lemon juice. Stir to mix. Add salt and pepper to taste. Serve with tortilla chips.

Notes:
[1] 16 oz. frozen mango chunks = 2-1/4 C.
[2] 1 large red pepper = 1 C. diced
[3] 1 medium onion = 1 C. diced

The salsa can also be made without the corn and kidney beans. Try it either way!

Nutritional Info: with corn and kidney beans
Per Serving: 102 Calories; 1g Fat (4.1% calories from fat); 4g Protein; 23g Carbohydrate; 5g Dietary Fiber; 0mg Cholesterol; 184mg Sodium.
Exchanges: 1 Grain (Starch); 1/2 Vegetable; 1/2 Fruit.

Nutritional Info: without corn and kidney beans (8 servings per recipe)
Per Serving: 39 Calories; trace Fat (3.5% calories from fat); 1g Protein; 10g Carbohydrate; 2g Dietary Fiber; 0mg Cholesterol; 2mg Sodium.
Exchanges: 1/2 Vegetable; 1/2 Fruit.

Chicken Quesadillas

Recipes:	1	2	3	4	5	6
Servings:	8	16	24	32	40	48
Ingredients:						
Chicken, cooked and finely minced[1]	1-1/2 C.	3 C.	4-1/2 C.	6 C.	7-1/2 C.	9 C.
Reduced fat sour cream	1/4 C.	1/2 C.	3/4 C.	1 C.	1-1/4 C.	1-1/2 C.
Thick and chunky salsa	1 C.	2 C.	3 C.	4 C.	5 C.	6 C.
Shredded cheddar cheese[2]	1/2 C.	1 C.	1-1/2 C.	2 C.	2-1/2 C.	3 C.
Shredded Pepper Jack cheese[2]	1/2 C.	1 C.	1-1/2 C.	2 C.	2-1/2 C.	3 C.
Chili powder	1 t.	2 t.	1 T.	1 T. + 1 t.	1 T. + 2 t.	2 T.
Flour tortillas	8	16	24	32	40	48

Assembly Directions:
In a mixing bowl, mix chicken, sour cream, salsa, cheeses and chili powder.

Freezing Directions:
Place chicken mixture in a quart-sized freezer or storage bag. Seal. Place quart-sized freezer bag inside of a gallon sized freezer bag. Add tortillas. Seal, label, and freeze.

Serving Directions:
Thaw contents of the quesadilla kit. Remove tortillas and separate. Lay them out on a flat surface, such as a clean counter, and divide the filling evenly between the tortillas. Fold each tortilla in half.

Spray a fry pan with cooking spray. Cook the quesadillas one at a time in the pan, lightly browning them on each side. The cheese in the filling should melt. After each one is done, remove it from the pan. Using a pizza cutter, cut each quesadilla into 3 pieces.

Notes:
[1] 1 large chicken breast = 3/4 C. cooked and chopped
[2] 8 oz. cheese = 2 C. shredded

You can easily mince chicken in a food processor or mini-chopper.

Kids love these! It's nice to have the filling totally ready and in a kit form. It makes it a convenient recipe to serve when you have unexpected company or for those football Saturdays.

Nutritional Info:
Per Serving: 217 Calories; 8g Fat (34.3% calories from fat); 15g Protein; 20g Carbohydrate; 2g Dietary Fiber; 37mg Cholesterol; 400mg Sodium.
Exchanges: 1 Grain (Starch); 1-1/2 Lean Meat; 1/2 Vegetable; 1 Fat.

Spicy Buffalo Wings

Recipes:	1	2	3	4	5	6
Servings:	9	18	27	36	45	54
Ingredients:						
Chicken wings	6 lbs.	12 lbs.	18 lbs.	24 lbs.	30 lbs.	36 lbs.
Butter or margarine	3 C.	6 C.	9 C.	12 C.	15 C.	18 C.
Worcestershire sauce	1 C.	2 C.	3 C.	4 C.	5 C.	6 C.
Cayenne pepper	2 T.	1/4 C.	1/4 C. + 2 T.	1/2 C.	1/2 C. + 2 T.	3/4 C.
Garlic salt	1 T.	2 T.	3 T.	1/4 C.	1/4 C. + 1 T.	1/4 C. + 2 T.
Louisiana-style hot sauce	12 oz.	24 oz.	36 oz.	48 oz.	60 oz.	72 oz.

Assembly Directions:

Warm the butter, Worcestershire sauce, cayenne pepper, garlic salt, and hot sauce together in a large saucepan on the stove. Place the wings (thawed if needed) in a large bowl or container. Add the warmed ingredients to the chicken wings and turn with a spatula to ensure even coating. Marinate in this mixture for 30 minutes.

Preheat the oven to 425 degrees. Place the wings on cookie sheets or baking pans and bake them for 20 minutes. Turn the chicken wings over and bake for an additional 40 minutes. Remove from the oven and cool.

Freezing Directions:

Place chicken wings into freezer bags or rigid containers. Seal, label, and freeze.

Serving Directions:

Thaw overnight in the refrigerator.

Preheat oven to 400 degrees. Reheat wings about 15 minutes or until heated through.

Notes:

Even though this recipe is multiplied for serving up to 54 adults, we recommend that unless you have a commercial kitchen with huge ovens and pans, you only use the equivalents for shopping purposes!

Assemble this recipe in containers that will easily accommodate the ingredients. For example, a single recipe of these wings will take up an entire rack of your oven.

Nutritional Info:

Nutritional analysis does not include the butter in the marinade.
Per Serving: 210 Calories; 12g Fat (53.8% calories from fat); 17g Protein; 6g Carbohydrate; 1g Dietary Fiber; 52mg Cholesterol; 1995mg Sodium.
Exchanges: 2-1/2 Lean Meat; 1 Fat; 1/2 Other Carbohydrates.

Spicy Cheese Bites

Recipes:	1	2	3	4	5	6
Servings:	**32**	**64**	**96**	**128**	**160**	**192**
Ingredients:						
Mozzarella or Pepper Jack cheese	8 oz.	16 oz.	24 oz.	32 oz.	40 oz.	48 oz.
Wonton wrappers	32	64	96	128	160	192
Canola oil for frying						

Assembly Directions:

Cut an 8 oz. block of cheese into 32 cubes. Place cheese cube in center of wrapper. Moisten edges of wrapper with water. Fold wonton wrapper in half leaving the moistened edges exposed. Fold the left and right sides of the triangle towards the center of the triangle forming an "envelope". Fold the top of the triangle down to close the bundle. Repeat with the remaining cheese cubes and wontons.

Freezing Directions:

Place cheese bites in a freezer bag or freezer container. Seal, label and freeze.

Serving Directions:

Thaw cheese bites in refrigerator. Pour oil to depth of 1-1/2 inches into a wok or large skillet. Heat to 375 degrees. Fry wontons six at a time, 30 seconds on each side or until golden. Drain on paper towels. Serve immediately.

Notes:

This is a great appetizer to have on hand around the holidays or for football Saturdays.

Nutritional Info:

Nutritional analysis includes oil at 20 percent absorption rate.
Per Serving: 73 Calories; 5g Fat (58.5% calories from fat); 3g Protein; 5g Carbohydrate; trace Dietary Fiber; 5mg Cholesterol; 83mg Sodium.
Exchanges: 1/2 Grain (Starch); 1/2 Lean Meat; 1 Fat.

Snack Recipes

Snack Recipes

TIPS FOR SNACK RECIPES

Yields

- For young kids, the key to successful freezer snacks is packaging. Make it look cute and fun! Use the printed snack sized freezer bags. It's fine to use food storage bags, too, as long as all of the little bags are stored inside a freezer bag.
- Individual packaging is helpful for portion control. 2 chocolate chip cookies in a little bag, one brownie in a ziptop bag, you get the idea. We're slipping into a "super sizing" mentality here in the USA!

Shopping & Cooking Tips

- The snacks you make at home will always be cheaper and healthier than the ones you buy pre-packaged at the store or the restaurant.
- It's easy to replicate many of the pre-packaged snacks that your family loves to eat. You'll eat healthier, save money, and save time because the snacks are already in the freezer. For example, substitute:
  Yogurt Fruit Snack Cups (page 185) for Gogurt ®
  Snackin' Mix (page 187) for Chex Mix®
  Italian Chicken Bites (page 189) for fast food Chicken Nuggets
- If there are pre-packaged snacks that you just LOVE, buy them when they are on sale and then package them in individual servings for the freezer. You will still save time and money!
- Adults eat snacks too! Don't just plan for the kids.
- Cutting down on the fat and calories in snacks is easy when you make them at home. Bake instead of fry. Substitute healthier ingredients.

Healthy Tips

- Honey may be used in place of corn syrup in many recipes. Honey, however, has a stronger flavor so you might buy the lightest color or clover honey which will be the mildest.
- Unsweetened applesauce can be substituted for up to 1/2 the oil in most recipes. Just be sure the recipe is not really high in fat in the first place, or the texture of the revised recipe may be disappointing.
- Whole-wheat flour is a good substitute for white flour

whenever possible. The fiber and nutrients in the whole-wheat flour are great for our bodies! In baked goods, you can use a mixture of 1/2 whole-wheat flour and 1/2 white flour. The kids rarely know the difference. If you choose to use whole-wheat flour, you need to refrigerate it if it wi not be used within 30 days. The natural oil in the wheat germ is very perishable.

- Wheat germ is good for all of us. It can be sprinkled into lots of recipes (cookies, breads, snack bars, etc.) without even tasting it. Try adding one tablespoon of raw or toasted wheat germ to each cup of flour or other dry ingredients.
- Try to make sure that the snacks your children eat have a redeeming nutritional value. If they are eating a snack loaded with butter or chocolate, what does it have in it that is good for the body? Oats, nuts, whole-wheat flour, raisins or other fruits can make a bad-for-you food into a acceptable food with a few added ingredients!

30 Day Gourmet Website Recipes & Tips

- For more great 30 Day Gourmet Snack recipes, check out the recipes section of our website at: www.30daygourmet.com
- For more Snack freezing tips and recipes from our cooks, check out the Cooking-Snacks section of our message boards at www.30daygourmet.com
- Check out the *Freezer Lunches to Go, Freezer Cooking for Daycare Providers & Busy Parents* eBooks offered on our website for more great Snack recipes and tips.

Make healthier versions of the snacks your family loves. Individual packaging makes it easy to "grab and go".

Yogurt Fruit Snack Cups

Recipes:	1	2	3	4	5	6
Servings:	24	48	72	96	120	144
Ingredients:						
Bananas[1]	3	6	9	12	15	18
Nonfat strawberry yogurt	24 oz.	48 oz.	72 oz.	96 oz.	120 oz.	144 oz.
Frozen sliced strawberries, slightly thawed and undrained	16 oz.	32 oz.	48 oz.	64 oz.	80 oz.	96 oz.
Canned crushed pineapple, in juice and undrained	8 oz.	16 oz.	24 oz.	32 oz.	40 oz.	48 oz.

Assembly Directions:
Dice or mash bananas and place in a large mixing bowl. Stir in yogurt, strawberries and pineapple.

Freezing Directions:
Spoon into paper lined muffin-tin cups and freeze at least 3 hours or until firm. Remove frozen cups and store in a plastic freezer bag in the freezer or use individual containers. Seal, label, and freeze.

Serving Directions:
Remove paper cups and let stand 10 minutes. You want to eat these slushy and not completely thawed.

Notes:
[1] 1 medium banana = 1/3 C. mashed

Microwave them for 15 seconds to soften them up when taken out of the freezer. It makes a great afternoon snack for the kids. Try it!

Nutritional Info: including all on hand ingredients
Per Serving: 61 Calories; trace Fat (2.2% calories from fat); 2g Protein; 14g Carbohydrate; 1g Dietary Fiber; 1mg Cholesterol; 17mg Sodium.
Exchanges: 1 Fruit.

Fruit 'n' Nut Chocolaty Oat Bars

Recipes:	1	2	3	4	5	6
Servings:	**24**	**48**	**72**	**96**	**120**	**144**
Ingredients:						
Whole wheat flour	1-1/4 C.	2-1/2 C.	3-3/4 C.	5 C.	6-1/4 C.	7-1/2 C.
Ground cinnamon	1 t.	2 t.	1 T.	1 T. + 1 t.	1 T. + 2 t.	2 T.
Ground cloves	1/4 t.	1/2 t.	3/4 t.	1 t.	1-1/4 t.	1-1/2 t.
Ground ginger	1/4 t.	1/2 t.	3/4 t.	1 t.	1-1/4 t.	1-1/2 t.
Baking soda	1/2 t.	1 t.	1-1/2 t.	2 t.	2-1/2 t.	1 T.
Salt	1/4 t.	1/2 t.	3/4 t.	1 t.	1-1/4 t.	1-1/2 t.
Light butter (stick)	1/2 C.	1 C.	1-1/2 C.	2 C.	2-1/2 C.	3 C.
Packed brown sugar	2/3 C.	1-1/3 C.	2 C.	2-2/3 C.	3-1/3 C.	4 C.
Egg	1	2	3	4	5	6
Mashed ripe bananas[1]	1-2/3 C.	3-1/3 C.	5 C.	6-2/3 C.	8 C.	9-2/3 C.
Uncooked oats (quick or old fashioned)	1-1/2 C.	3 C.	4-1/2 C.	6 C.	7-1/2 C.	9 C.
Dried cranberries	1/2 C.	1 C.	1-1/2 C.	2 C.	2-1/2 C.	3 C.
Chopped, toasted walnuts	1/2 C.	1 C.	1-1/2 C.	2 C.	2-1/2 C.	3 C.
Semi-sweet chocolate chips	1/2 C.	1 C.	1-1/2 C.	2 C.	2-1/2 C.	3 C.

Assembly Directions:
Preheat oven to 350 degrees. Lightly spray a 13x9x2 baking pan with nonstick cooking spray. Stir dry ingredients together in medium bowl and set aside.

Beat butter and brown sugar in large bowl until well blended. Add egg and bananas. Mix well. Add flour mixture beating on low just until well blended. Stir in oats, cranberries, walnuts and chocolate chips. Spread evenly in sprayed pan.

Bake 20-25 minutes until edges are golden brown and toothpick comes out clean. Cool completely. Cut into 24 bars.

Freezing Directions:
Put each bar in a snack size bag. Put all bars into a gallon size, labeled freezer bag.

Serving Directions:
Thaw overnight in refrigerator.

Notes:
[1] 1 medium banana = 1/3 C. mashed

Nutritional Info:
Per Serving: 130 Calories; 5g Fat (33.4% calories from fat); 3g Protein; 20g Carbohydrate; 2g Dietary Fiber; 14mg Cholesterol; 78mg Sodium.
Exchanges: 1/2 Grain (Starch); 1 Fat; 1/2 Other Carbohydrates.

Snackin' Mix

Recipes:	1	2	3	4	5	6
Servings:	18	36	54	72	90	108
Makes:	9 C.	18 C.	27 C.	36 C.	45 C.	54 C.
Ingredients:						
Waffle-type cereal	7 C.	14 C.	21 C.	28 C.	35 C.	42 C.
Nuts, mixed nuts or peanuts	1 C.	2 C.	3 C.	4 C.	5 C.	6 C.
Pretzels, thin sticks or twists	1 C.	2 C.	3 C.	4 C.	5 C.	6 C.
Butter or margarine, melted	3 T.	1/4 C. + 2 T.	1/2 C. + 1 T.	3/4 C.	3/4 C. + 3 T.	1 C. + 2 T.
Garlic salt	1/4 t.	1/2 t.	3/4 t.	1 t.	1-1/4 t.	1-1/2 t.
Onion salt	1/4 t.	1/2 t.	3/4 t.	1 t.	1-1/4 t.	1-1/2 t.
Lemon juice	2 t.	1 T. + 1 t.	2 T.	2 T. + 2 t.	3 T. + 1 t.	1/4 C.
Worcestershire sauce	1 T.	2 T.	3 T.	1/4 C.	1/4 C. + 1 T.	1/4 C. + 2 T.

Assembly Directions:
Combine cereal, nuts and pretzels in large bowl. Set aside. In glass measuring cup, melt butter and add remaining ingredients. Pour over cereal mixture until evenly coated. Microwave on high for 2 minutes. Stir and microwave for an additional 2-3 minutes. Spread in a single layer on paper towels or waxed paper to cool.

Freezing Directions:
Freeze in rigid containers to prevent crushing or in small quantity freezer bags for easy snacking. Mix may also be stored at room temperature in an airtight container or in food storage bags.

Serving Directions:
Thaw and enjoy!

Notes:
The little snack-sized bags are easy to grab for lunch boxes, car trips or a quick outside snack!
Use some of the wheat or multi-bran waffle type cereals for more fiber.
After cooling, add small candy coated chocolates for color (and appeal).
Our recipe has less oil so it's safer in the mini-van!
If mix becomes stale, it can be re-crisped for a few minutes in a 350 degree oven.
Add small crackers (cheese or other varieties) in place of some of the pretzels if you like.
Using the microwave for this recipe is SO much faster than the old oven method. The mixture will still be "mushy" after the first 2 minutes but it will crisp up by the end of the cooking and cooling time.

Nutritional Info: 1/2 C. per serving
Per Serving: 138 Calories; 6g Fat (39.4% calories from fat); 3g Protein; 18g Carbohydrate; 1g Dietary Fiber; 0mg Cholesterol; 298mg Sodium.
Exchanges: 1 Grain (Starch); 1/2 Lean Meat; 1 Fat.

Fruity Empanadas

Recipes:	1	2	3	4	5	6
Servings:	30	60	90	120	150	180
Makes:	2-1/2 dozen	5 dozen	7-1/2 dozen	10 dozen	12-1/2 dozen	15 dozen
Ingredients:						
Butter, softened	1/2 C.	1 C.	1-1/2 C.	2 C.	2-1/2 C.	3 C.
Reduced fat cream cheese, softened	3 oz.	6 oz.	9 oz.	12 oz.	15 oz.	18 oz.
Flour	1 C.	2 C.	3 C.	4 C.	5 C.	6 C.
Fruit preserves	1 C.	2 C.	3 C.	4 C.	5 C.	6 C.
Granulated sugar	1/3 C.	2/3 C.	1 C.	1-1/3 C.	1-2/3 C.	2 C.
Cinnamon	1 t.	2 t.	1 T.	1 T. + 1 t.	1 T. + 2 t.	2 T.

Assembly Directions:

Cream the butter and cream cheese together until well blended and no lumps appear. Beat in the flour until just blended. Form the dough into a ball and wrap it in foil or plastic wrap. Refrigerate the dough 8 hours or overnight, or the dough can be frozen at this point. *See note below.

After the dough has chilled for at least 8 hours, preheat oven to 375 degrees. Remove the dough from the refrigerator and allow it to sit at room temperature for 30 minutes. Roll the chilled dough to about 1/8 inch thick or a little thinner. Cut the dough with a 3 or 4 inch round cookie or biscuit cutter. Place about 1/2 teaspoon of preserves in the center of each circle of dough. With a small pastry brush or your finger, moisten the dough all the way around the outer edge. Fold the dough in half (covering the preserves). Press the edges of the dough together to seal the preserves inside.

Bake on an ungreased baking sheet for 15-20 minutes until lightly browned. If you notice that the preserves are leaking out, you have not sealed the edges completely. Combine the granulated sugar and the cinnamon. When the cookies are baked, immediately but carefully scoop the cookies onto a cooling rack and dust with the cinnamon sugar mixture.

Freezing Directions:

Place cooled cookies in a single layer in a rigid freezer container. The baked cookies are very tender, so be careful when putting them into the container. Label, seal and freeze.

Serving Directions:

Thaw and serve. Cookies can also be warmed slightly if you like.

Notes:

The unbaked dough can be frozen and rolled out later, and the cookies themselves can be frozen. The baked cookies are very tender, so freeze them in a rigid freezer container. The dough must be chilled for several hours, so plan to make the dough the day before you will use it. Part of the beauty of this recipe is that the dough can be refrigerated for up to a week after it is made.

Nutritional Info:

Per Serving: 87 Calories; 4g Fat (41.3% calories from fat); 1g Protein; 12g Carbohydrate; trace Dietary Fiber; 11mg Cholesterol; 44mg Sodium.
Exchanges: 1 Fat; 1/2 Other Carbohydrates.

Italian Chicken Bites

Recipes:	1	2	3	4	5	6
Servings:	4	8	12	16	20	24
Ingredients:						
boneless, skinless chicken breasts, cubed	1 lb.	2 lbs.	3 lbs.	4 lbs.	5 lbs.	6 lbs.
Italian seasoned bread crumbs	1/2 C.	1 C.	1-1/2 C.	2 C.	2-1/2 C.	3 C.
grated Parmesan cheese	2 T.	1/4 C.	1/4 C. + 2 T.	1/2 C.	1/2 C. + 2 T.	3/4 C.
egg white	1	2	3	4	5	6

Assembly Directions:
Preheat oven to 400 degrees.
In a small bowl, combine the bread crumbs and the Parmesan cheese. In another bowl, beat the egg white. Dip the chicken pieces in the egg white and then coat with the crumb mixture.

Place chicken pieces on a 15x10x1 inch foil-lined baking sheet coated with nonstick cooking spray. Bake uncovered for 12-15 minutes turning once.

Freezing Directions:
Cool completely. Flash freeze and then put into labeled freezer bags.

Serving Directions:
Preheat oven to 400 degrees. Bake for 10 to 15 minutes or until hot.

Notes:
If you don't want to prebake the bites, you can combine the crumbs and cheese in a small bag, attach it to the bagged chicken cubes and then coat and bake them on the day that you serve them.

Serve with ranch dressing, barbecue sauce, or marinara sauce. Yum!

Nutritional Info:
Per Serving: 205 Calories; 4g Fat (18.7% calories from fat); 29g Protein; 11g Carbohydrate; 1g Dietary Fiber; 72mg Cholesterol; 518mg Sodium.
Exchanges: 1/2 Grain (Starch); 4 Lean Meat.

Honey BBQ Chicken Strips

Recipes:	1	2	3	4	5	6
Servings:	**4**	**8**	**12**	**16**	**20**	**24**
Ingredients:						
Worcestershire sauce	1/4 C.	1/2 C.	3/4 C.	1 C.	1-1/4 C.	1-1/2 C.
Seasoned salt	1/2 t.	1 t.	1-1/2 t.	2 t.	2-1/2 t.	1 T.
Garlic salt	1/2 t.	1 t.	1-1/2 t.	2 t.	2-1/2 t.	1 T.
Black pepper	1/8 t.	1/4 t.	3/8 t.	1/2 t.	1/2 t. + 1/8 t.	3/4 t.
Boneless, skinless chicken breasts, sliced into 1/2 inch strips	4	8	12	16	20	24
Barbecue sauce	1 C.	2 C.	3 C.	4 C.	5 C.	6 C.
Honey	1/2 C.	1 C.	1-1/2 C.	2 C.	2-1/2 C.	3 C.

Assembly Directions:

Preheat oven to 350 degrees.

In a large bowl, mix Worcestershire sauce, seasoned salt, garlic salt, and pepper. Place chicken in a large bowl with Worcestershire sauce seasoning and coat. Place chicken on foil-lined cookie sheet. Bake 10 minutes.

Meanwhile, combine barbecue sauce and honey in a measuring cup. After chicken has cooked 10 minutes, baste it with the honey barbecue sauce and return it to the oven. Bake an additional 10 minutes.

Freezing Directions:

Cool chicken pieces. Put into freezer bags. Seal, label, and freeze.

Serving Directions:

Thaw and reheat in microwave or oven.

Nutritional Info:

Per Serving: 319 Calories; 3g Fat (7.3% calories from fat); 29g Protein; 46g Carbohydrate; 1g Dietary Fiber; 68mg Cholesterol; 1162mg Sodium.
Exchanges: 4 Lean Meat; 3 Other Carbohydrates.

Chicken Snack Wraps

Recipes:	1	2	3	4	5	6
Servings:	8	16	24	32	40	48
Ingredients:						
Boneless, skinless chicken breasts	4	8	12	16	20	24
Oil	1/4 C.	1/2 C.	3/4 C.	1 C.	1-1/4 C.	1-1/2 C.
Honey	1 T.	2 T.	3 T.	1/4 C.	1/4 C. + 1 T.	1/4 C. + 2 T.
Lime juice	1 T.	2 T.	3 T.	1/4 C.	1/4 C. + 1 T.	1/4 C. + 2 T.
Paprika	1/4 t.	1/2 t.	3/4 t.	1 t.	1-1/4 t.	1-1/2 t.
Seasoned salt	1/2 t.	1 t.	1-1/2 t.	2 t.	2-1/2 t.	1 T.
Flour tortillas	8	16	24	32	40	48
On Hand:						
Lettuce						
Ranch dressing						
Shredded cheddar cheese						

Assembly Directions:

Cut each chicken breast into 4 strips. In a large mixing bowl, combine oil, honey, lime juice, paprika, and seasoned salt. Stir with a whisk until combined. Add chicken strips to the bowl and allow to marinate for at least one hour.

Stovetop: Remove chicken from marinade and place in a skillet. Discard marinade. Cook chicken over medium heat about 5 to 7 minutes on each side or until chicken is fully cooked.

Oven: Preheat oven to 350 degrees. Line a baking sheet with aluminum foil. Remove chicken from marinade and place on lined baking sheet. Discard marinade. Bake for 30 minutes or until chicken is fully cooked.

Grill: Grill over medium high heat until the meat is no longer pink inside and the juices run clear. Discard marinade.

Freezing Directions:

Cool chicken completely. Place chicken in freezer bag or container. Seal, label, and freeze. Attach bag of flour tortillas to the chicken.

Serving Directions:

Thaw chicken and tortillas. Reheat chicken in the microwave or in the oven. Chicken can be served cold. Warm tortillas for 30 seconds in the microwave. Place two chicken strips in the middle of the snack wrap. Add your toppings and roll up burrito style.

Nutritional Info:

Oil not included in nutritional analysis.
Per Serving: 178 Calories; 3g Fat (15.6% calories from fat); 16g Protein; 20g Carbohydrate; 1g Dietary Fiber; 34mg Cholesterol; 234mg Sodium.
Exchanges: 1 Grain(Starch); 2 Lean Meat; 0 Fruit; 1/2 Fat; 0 Other Carbohydrates.

Double Chocolate Brownie Cookies

Recipes:	1	2	3	4	5	6
Servings:	**30**	**60**	**90**	**120**	**150**	**180**
Ingredients:						
Sugar	1 C.	2 C.	3 C.	4 C.	5 C.	6 C.
Butter or margarine	1/2 C.	1 C.	1-1/2 C.	2 C.	2-1/2 C.	3 C.
Eggs	2	4	6	8	10	12
Unsweetened cocoa	6 T.	3/4 C.	1 C. + 2 T.	1-1/2 C.	1-3/4 C. + 2 T.	2-1/4 C.
Oil	2 T.	1/4 C.	1/4 C. + 2 T.	1/2 C.	1/2 C. + 2 T.	3/4 C.
Vanilla	1 t.	2 t.	1 T.	1 T. + 1 t.	1 T. + 2 t.	2 T.
Flour	2 C.	4 C.	6 C.	8 C.	10 C.	12 C.
Baking soda	1 t.	2 t.	1 T.	1 T. + 1 t.	1 T. + 2 t.	2 T.
Salt	1/4 t.	1/2 t.	3/4 t.	1 t.	1-1/4 t.	1-1/2 t.
Semi-sweet chocolate chips	1 C.	2 C.	3 C.	4 C.	5 C.	6 C.

Assembly Directions:

Preheat oven to 350 degrees. Spray baking sheets with cooking spray. Set aside.

In a large mixing bowl, combine sugar, butter, eggs, cocoa, oil, and vanilla. Beat at medium speed of electric mixer until well blended. Add flour, baking soda, and salt. Beat at low speed until a soft dough forms. Fold in chocolate chips by hand.

Drop dough by heaping teaspoons 2 inches apart onto prepared cookie sheets. Bake for 10 to 12 minutes or until set. Remove from cookie sheet and allow to cool.

Freezing Directions:

Place cookies in a freezer bag or freezer container. Seal, label and freeze.

Serving Directions:

Thaw and enjoy!

Nutritional Info:

Per Serving: 134 Calories; 7g Fat (42.6% calories from fat); 2g Protein; 18g Carbohydrate; 1g Dietary Fiber; 12mg Cholesterol; 100mg Sodium.
Exchanges: 1/2 Grain (Starch); 1-1/2 Fat; 1 Other Carbohydrates.

ried Ice Cream

Recipes:	1	2	3	4	5	6
Servings:	5	10	15	20	25	30
Ingredients:						
Vanilla ice cream	1 pint	1 quart	3 pints	1/2 gallon	5 pints	6 pints
Crushed cornflakes cereal[1]	1 C.	2 C.	3 C.	4 C.	5 C.	6 C.
Cinnamon	1/2 t.	1 t.	1-1/2 t.	2 t.	2-1/2 t.	1 T.
Egg whites	1	2	3	4	5	6
Peanut oil for frying						

Assembly Directions:

Scoop ice cream into 5 balls using a large spring loaded cookie scoop. Place on baking sheet and freeze at least 1 hour.

In a shallow dish, combine crushed cornflakes and cinnamon. In a second dish, beat egg whites until foamy. Roll ice cream balls in egg whites, then in cornflake mixture.

Freezing Directions:

Place in rigid freezer container until ready to fry, at least 3 hours. Seal, label, and freeze.

Serving Directions:

Heat peanut oil to 375 degrees. Using a slotted spoon or basket, fry ice cream balls one at a time for 10-15 seconds until golden brown. Drain immediately on paper towels and serve.

Notes:

[1] 2 C. flakes = 3/4 C. crumbs

You can also serve these in warm homemade tortilla bowls. Just shape small tortillas into a large muffin tin. Space out the tortillas so they aren't touching one another. Spray tortilla with cooking spray and sprinkle with cinnamon sugar. Bake at 350 for 8-10 minutes.

Nutritional Info:

Nutritional analysis does not include oil used in frying.
Per Serving: 165 Calories; 6g Fat (31.3% calories from fat); 4g Protein; 26g Carbohydrate; 1g Dietary Fiber; 23mg Cholesterol; 212mg Sodium.
Exchanges: 1 Grain (Starch); 1 Fat; 1 Other Carbohydrates.

Cinnamon Crunch Healthy Granola

Recipes:	1	2	3	4	5	6
Servings:	**30**	**60**	**90**	**120**	**150**	**180**
Makes:	**15 C.**	**30 C.**	**45 C.**	**60 C.**	**75 C.**	**90 C.**
Ingredients:						
Rolled oats	11 C.	22 C.	33 C.	44 C.	55 C.	66 C.
Cinnamon	2 T.	1/4 C.	1/4 C. + 2 T.	1/2 C.	1/2 C. + 2 T.	3/4 C.
Flaked unsweetened coconut	2 C.	4 C.	6 C.	8 C.	10 C.	12 C.
Raw sesame or sunflower seeds	1/2 C.	1 C.	1-1/2 C.	2 C.	2-1/2 C.	3 C.
Golden flax seed	1/2 C.	1 C.	1-1/2 C.	2 C.	2-1/2 C.	3 C.
Cornmeal	1/4 C.	1/2 C.	3/4 C.	1 C.	1-1/4 C.	1-1/2 C.
Raw wheat germ	1/2 C.	1 C.	1-1/2 C.	2 C.	2-1/2 C.	3 C.
Light brown sugar	1-1/2 C.	3 C.	4-1/2 C.	6 C.	7-1/2 C.	9 C.
Water	1/2 C.	1 C.	1-1/2 C.	2 C.	2-1/2 C.	3 C.
Oil	1 C.	2 C.	3 C.	4 C.	5 C.	6 C.
Vanilla	2 t.	1 T. + 1 t.	2 T.	2 T. + 2 t.	3 T. + 1 t.	1/4 C.

Assembly Directions:

In a very large bowl, combine oats, cinnamon, coconut, seeds, cornmeal, and wheat germ.

In a medium saucepan over low heat, combine brown sugar and water. Stir until sugar dissolves. Increase heat to medium and bring to a boil. Reduce heat to low and cook, stirring, for an additional minute. Remove from heat. Add oil and vanilla.

Pour syrup over dry ingredients, stirring to coat. Spray two 10x15 pans and pour granola into pans, spreading evenly.

Bake at 275 degrees for 55-60 minutes until lightly browned and toasted.

Cool in pans on wire racks. About 10 minutes after cooling, flip granola in chunks with a large spatula.

Freezing Directions:

Divide into suitable portions. Seal, label and freeze.

Serving Directions:

Thaw overnight in refrigerator. Use at your discretion.

Notes:

This granola tastes great! Chocolate chips, raisins and/or cranberries may be added after granola is cooled. Store snack sized bags in the freezer for a quick "to go" snack.

Nutritional Info: 1/2 C. per serving

Per Serving: 269 Calories; 15g Fat (47.7% calories from fat); 6g Protein; 30g Carbohydrate; 5g Dietary Fiber; 0mg Cholesterol; 7mg Sodium.
Exchanges: 1-1/2 Grain (Starch); 3 Fat; 1/2 Other Carbohydrates.

Dessert Recipes

Dessert Recipes

TIPS FOR DESSERT RECIPES

Yields

- 8" or 9" pie plates generally yield 8 servings.
- 9"x13" pans used for cakes or other desserts yield 15 2.5" x 3" pieces or 24 2.25"x2.25" pieces.
- 8"x8" pans used for cakes or other desserts generally yield 16 2" x 2" pieces.

Shopping & Cooking Tips

- People LOVE desserts! It's wonderful to have a few whole cheesecakes or pies in the freezer to give to a busy friend or pull out for unexpected company. With a piece of cheesecake going for over $5 now, what a treat!
- Watch for sales on pie plates. Sometimes it's nice to be able to take the entire pie out of the freezer and serve it in the glass plate but many of us only own 2 or 3 of these.
- Many desserts can be cut into individual serving sizes and frozen for a quick treat later. You don't want to keep thawing and refreezing a 9x13 pan of dessert just so that you can have a small piece each evening at bedtime. Bag the individual serving in a food storage bag and then put them all into a one gallon freezer bag.
- Have at least 2 sets of measuring spoons when cooking. One for dry ingredients and one for wet.
- Nuts can be stored in the freezer for up to 9 months. Use them in recipes straight from the freezer.
- When melting chocolate, whether on the stovetop, in the oven, or in the microwave, make sure everything is dry- even a small drop of water can make chocolate "seize."

Healthy Tips

- Homemade is always better! Most dessert recipes can be made healthier just by assembling them "from scratch". Feel free to sneak even more healthy ingredients (like wheat germ and dried fruit) into your desserts.
- Substitute ½ of the white flour with whole wheat flour.
- For baked goods, use half the butter, shortening or oil and replace the other half with unsweetened applesauce, mashed banana or prune puree.
- Reduce the amount of sugar by one-third to one-half. When you use less sugar, add spices such as cinnamon, cloves, allspice and nutmeg or flavorings such as vanilla extract or almond flavoring to enhance the sweetness of the food.

Website Recipes & Tips

- For more great 30 Day Gourmet dessert recipes, check out the recipes section of our website at: www.30daygourmet.com
- For more dessert freezing tips and recipes from our cooks, check out our message boards at www.30daygourmet.com
- Check out the *Freezer Desserts to Die For!, Healthy Freezer Cooking,* and *Freezer Cooking on a Budget* eBooks offered on our website for more great dessert recipes and tips.

It's great to have desserts on hand that can be pulled out of the freezer for surprise company.

Easy Pie Fillings

Recipes:	1	2	3	4	5	6
Servings:	**8**	**16**	**24**	**32**	**40**	**48**
Ingredients:						
Apple Pie Filling:						
Sugar	1 C.	2 C.	3 C.	4 C.	5 C.	6 C.
Salt	1/2 t.	1 t.	1-1/2 t.	2 t.	2-1/2 t.	3 t.
Cinnamon	1 t.	2 t.	1 T.	1 T. + 1 t.	1 T. + 2 t.	2 T.
Nutmeg	1/2 t.	1 t.	1-1/2 t.	2 t.	2-1/2 t.	3 t.
Flour	1-1/2 T.	3 T.	1/4 C. + 1-1/2 t.	1/4 C. + 2 T.	1/4 C. + 3-1/2 T.	1/2 C. + 1 T.
Butter/margarine	2 T.	4 T.	6 T.	8 T.	10 T.	12 T.
Cooking apples; peeled and sliced	4 C.	8 C.	12 C.	16 C.	20 C.	24 C.
Lemon juice	1/4 C.	1/2 C.	3/4 C.	1 C.	1-1/4 C.	1-1/2 C.
Cherry Pie Filling:						
Sugar	1 C.	2 C.	3 C.	4 C.	5 C.	6 C.
Flour	3 T.	1/4 C. + 2 T.	1/2 C. + 1 T.	3/4 C.	3/4 C. + 3 T.	1 C. + 2 T.
Salt	1/8 t.	1/4 t.	3/8 t.	1/2 t.	1/2 t. + 1/8 t.	3/4 t.
Butter/margarine	2 T.	1/4 C.	1/4 C. + 2 T.	1/2 C.	1/2 C. + 2 T.	3/4 C.
Sour pie cherries (fresh, or canned and drained)	4 C.	8 C.	12 C.	16 C.	20 C.	24 C.

Assembly Directions:

Apple: Mix sugar, salt, cinnamon, nutmeg, and flour in a small bowl. With a fork, blend butter into sugar mixture until it is crumbly. Place the lemon juice in a large bowl. As you peel and slice the apples, place them in the lemon juice and toss to coat well. When all apples have been coated with the lemon juice, pour apple slices into a colander and drain well. In a large bowl, mix drained apple slices and sugar mixture.

Cherry: In a large bowl, mix sugar, flour, and salt. With a fork, mix in butter until it is crumbly. Stir in pie cherries, stirring to coat well.

Freezing Directions for Both Pies:

Put fruit mixture in a labeled freezer bag or container. Remove excess air, seal and freeze.

Serving Directions for Both Pies:

Thaw filling, pour into pie shell, and seal top crust or sprinkle with crumbs. Bake at 425 degrees for 10 minutes, and then reduce heat to 350 degrees. Bake for 30-40 minutes until browned and bubbly.

Nutritional Info: Apple Pie Filling/No Crust

Per Serving: 163 Calories; 3g Fat (16.4% calories from fat); trace Protein; 35g Carbohydrate; 2g Dietary Fiber; 0mg Cholesterol; 167mg Sodium.
Exchanges: 1/2 Fruit; 1/2 Fat; 1-1/2 Other Carbohydrates.

Nutritional Info: Cherry Pie Filling/No Crust

Per Serving (excluding unknown items): 177 Calories; 3g Fat (14.6% calories from fat); 1g Protein; 38g Carbohydrate; 1g Dietary Fiber; 0mg Cholesterol; 75mg Sodium.
Exchanges: 1/2 Fruit; 1/2 Fat; 1-1/2 Other Carbohydrates.

Frozen Peanut Butter Bars

Recipes:	1	2	3	4	5	6
Servings:	**24**	**48**	**72**	**96**	**120**	**144**
Ingredients:						
Butter or margarine	1 C.	2 C.	3 C.	4 C.	5 C.	6 C.
Peanut butter, creamy	2 C.	4 C.	6 C.	8 C.	10 C.	12 C.
Graham cracker crumbs[1]	2-1/2 C.	5 C.	7-1/2 C.	10 C.	12-1/2 C.	15 C.
Powdered sugar	1-3/4 C.	3-1/2 C.	5-1/4 C.	7 C.	8-3/4 C.	10-1/2 C.
Chocolate chips, semi-sweet or milk chocolate	2 C.	4 C.	6 C.	8 C.	10 C.	12 C.
Milk	1/3 C.	2/3 C.	1 C.	1-1/3 C.	1-2/3 C.	2 C.

Assembly Directions:

In a large saucepan, melt butter and peanut butter together. Mix well. Remove from heat. Add crumbs and powdered sugar, mixing well. Spread peanut butter mixture in a 15x10x1 pan (for thinner bars) or 9x13 pan (for thicker bars). Chill. When the peanut butter layer is firm, melt chocolate chips with milk over low heat. Spread over chilled peanut butter mixture. Chill again.

Freezing Directions:

Cut into serving size pieces. Wrap individually and freeze in large rigid containers or one-gallon freezer bags.

Serving Directions:

Eat straight from the freezer or thaw slightly.

Notes:

[1] 14 graham crackers = 1 C. crushed

Hey, you peanut butter and chocolate lovers! It doesn't get any better than this! If you can keep from eating them, these are great to keep around for company, after school snacking and for a treat after the kids go to bed!

We have found that we can usually buy the graham cracker crumbs for the same price as the equivalent in graham crackers. Why do the work if you don't have to?

Nutritional Info:

Per Serving: 323 Calories; 21g Fat (55.4% calories from fat); 7g Protein; 32g Carbohydrate; 3g Dietary Fiber; trace Cholesterol; 202mg Sodium.
Exchanges: 1/2 Grain (Starch); 1/2 Lean Meat; 0 Non-Fat Milk; 4 Fat; 1 1/2 Other Carbohydrates.

Oreo® Truffles

Recipes:	1	2	3	4	5	6
Servings:	48	96	144	192	240	288
Makes:	4 dozen	8 dozen	12 dozen	16 dozen	20 dozen	24 dozen
Ingredients:						
Oreo® cookies	18 oz.	36 oz.	54 oz.	72 oz.	90 oz.	108 oz.
Reduced fat cream cheese, softened	8 oz.	16 oz.	24 oz.	32 oz.	40 oz.	48 oz.
Vanilla flavored candy coating	1 lb.	2 lbs.	3 lbs.	4 lbs.	5 lbs.	6 lbs.

Assembly Directions:

Crush Oreos® in food processor. In a large mixing bowl, use hands to combine the crushed cookies and cream cheese to form a stiff dough. Roll into 1 inch balls. Place the cookie balls on a waxed paper covered cookie sheet and put them in the freezer for 15 minutes. Meanwhile, melt the vanilla coating in the microwave in a deep bowl or 8 C. measuring bowl. Remove the cookie sheet from the freezer. One at a time, put the cookie balls on the tines of a fork and dip them until covered in the melted coating. Allow the excess coating to drip off, and put each completed truffle on a waxed paper covered cookie sheet until the coating is set.

Freezing Directions:

When the candy coating is set, put the truffles in a freezer bag or rigid container. Seal, label and freeze.

Serving Directions:

Thaw truffles for a few minutes on the counter, and serve. Keep any leftovers in the refrigerator.

Notes:

You can use peanut butter in place of the cream cheese.

Try chocolate coating or chocolate chips in place of the vanilla coating.

You can also use your favorite cookie instead of the Oreos®. Vienna Fingers® cookies with chocolate coating are great together.

At Christmastime, add red or green sprinkles just after dipping.

Nutritional Info: per truffle (using Oreos® and vanilla coating)

Per Serving: 113 Calories; 6g Fat (48.3% calories from fat); 1g Protein; 13g Carbohydrate; trace Dietary Fiber; 5mg Cholesterol; 106mg Sodium.
Exchanges: 1 Fat; 1 Other Carbohydrates.

Chocolaty Peanut Ice Cream Squares

Recipes:	1	2	3	4	5	6
Servings:	18	36	54	72	90	108
Ingredients:						
Oreo® cookies, crushed	18 oz.	36 oz.	54 oz.	72 oz.	90 oz.	108 oz.
Butter or margarine	1/2 C.	1 C.	1-1/2 C.	2 C.	2-1/2 C.	3 C.
Vanilla ice cream, softened	1/2 gallon	1 gallon	1-1/2 gallons	2 gallons	2-1/2 gallons	3 gallons
Salted peanuts	1-3/4 C.	3-1/2 C.	5-1/4 C.	7 C.	8-3/4 C.	10-1/2 C.
Butter or margarine	1/2 C.	1 C.	1-1/2 C.	2 C.	2-1/2 C.	3 C.
Evaporated milk	12 oz.	24 oz.	36 oz.	48 oz.	60 oz.	72 oz.
Chocolate chips	2/3 C.	1-1/3 C.	2 C.	2-2/3 C.	3-1/3 C.	4 C.
Powdered sugar	2 C.	4 C.	6 C.	8 C.	10 C.	12 C.

Assembly Directions:

Put the crushed Oreos® in the bottom of a 9"x13" pan. Melt the first measure of butter and mix into the crumbs. Press the mixture into the bottom of the pan to form a crust. Carefully spoon the softened ice cream onto the crust and smooth it out. Don't fill the pan to the top, as you need to leave room for the topping. Sprinkle peanuts on top of the ice cream. Put the pan in the freezer for the ice cream to harden while you make the topping.

To make the topping, put the second measure of butter and evaporated milk in a saucepan and start heating it. Add the chocolate chips and powdered sugar. Stir to mix well. Bring the mixture to a boil. Reduce heat and simmer for 10 minutes, stirring occasionally. Set topping aside and allow to completely cool. Remove dessert pan from the freezer, and spread the cooled topping over the dessert.

Freezing Directions:

Cover pan with foil or put in a two-gallon freezer bag. Seal, label and freeze.

Serving Directions:

Remove dessert from the freezer about 10 minutes before you want to serve it. Allow dessert to soften slightly, then cut into squares and serve.

Notes:

This is a great dessert to have on hand... everyone loves it! You can make it in two 8"x8" pans instead of a 9"x13" if you want. Once the whole dessert is frozen, you can cut it and wrap each individual piece in a sandwich bag or plastic wrap. Put all the wrapped pieces in a freezer bag. Then you can easily remove the needed number of servings.

Nutritional Info:

Per Serving: 205 Calories; 4g Fat (18.7% calories from fat); 29g Protein; 11g Carbohydrate; 1g Dietary Fiber; 72mg Cholesterol; 518mg Sodium.
Exchanges: 1/2 Grain (Starch); 4 Lean Meat.

eezer Cheesecake

cipes:	1	2	3	4	5	6
rvings:	12	24	36	48	60	72
ust Ingredients:						
aham cracker crumbs[1]	1-1/2 C.	3 C.	4-1/2 C.	6 C.	7-1/2 C.	9 C.
gar	2 T.	1/4 C.	1/4 C. + 2 T.	1/2 C.	1/2 C. + 2 T.	3/4 C.
tter/margarine; elted	3 T.	6 T.	9 T.	12 T.	15 T.	18 T.
ling Ingredients:						
eam cheese; room mperature	24 oz.	48 oz.	72 oz.	96 oz.	120 oz.	144 oz.
gs	4	8	12	16	20	24
nilla	1 t.	2 t.	1 T.	1 T. + 1 t.	1 T. + 2 t.	2 T.
gar	1 C.	2 C.	3 C.	4 C.	5 C.	6 C.
ur cream	16 oz.	32 oz.	48 oz.	64 oz.	80 oz.	96 oz.

embly Directions:
Preheat oven to 375 degrees. For each recipe, combine graham cracker crumbs, sugar and melted butter/margarine in a medium bowl, mixing well with a fork. Press mixture into a 9 inch spring-form pan across the bottom and just a bit up the sides. Set the pan on a small pizza pan and refrigerate while preparing the filling. In a large bowl, beat the cream cheese until it's light and creamy. Add the eggs, vanilla and sugar. Beat until creamy. Gradually add the sour cream. Continue beating until thoroughly combined. Pour filling into crust. Bake (on pizza pan) in preheated oven 50 minutes.

ezing Directions:
Cool the cheesecake. Remove the metal form, wrap in plastic wrap and freeze whole in a gallon freezer bag.

OR cut it into slices and freeze the slices individually.

rving Directions:
Thaw, serve and enjoy!

tes:
[1] 15 graham cracker squares = 1 C. crumbs

This truly is a "no fail" recipe. We tried lots of cheesecake recipes before we finally hit on this one several years ago. It's always great! You can serve it with strawberries and whipped cream on top or drizzle it with chocolate syrup.

tritional Info:
Per Serving: 444 Calories; 33g Fat (66.0% calories from fat); 8g Protein; 30g Carbohydrate; trace Dietary Fiber; 141mg Cholesterol; 303mg Sodium.
Exchanges: 1/2 Grain(Starch); 1 Lean Meat; 6 Fat; 1-1/2 Other Carbohydrates.

Crunchy Peanut Butter Ice Cream Cups

Recipes:	1	2	3	4	5	6
Servings:	24	48	72	96	120	144
Ingredients:						
Softened reduced fat vanilla ice cream	24 oz.	48 oz.	72 oz.	96 oz.	120 oz.	144 oz.
Non-dairy fat free whipped topping	2 C.	4 C.	6 C.	8 C.	10 C.	12 C.
Crunchy peanut butter	1/2 C.	1 C.	1-1/2 C.	2 C.	2-1/2 C.	3 C.
Chocolate pudding mix[1]	2 boxes	4 boxes	6 boxes	8 boxes	10 boxes	12 boxes
Grape Nuts® cereal	1-1/2 C.	3 C.	4-1/2 C.	6 C.	7-1/2 C.	9 C.

Assembly Directions:

In a large bowl, mix together the ice cream, whipped topping, peanut butter and dry pudding mix. Beat or stir until evenly combined. Using a spoon, fold in the Grape Nuts® cereal.

Freezing Directions:

Put foil cupcake liners in a muffin pan. Scoop the dessert into the foil liners for individual servings. Put the muffin pan into the freezer until the dessert is frozen. Remove from the freezer, and put the foil liners in a gallon freezer bag. Seal, label and freeze.

Serving Directions:

Remove the needed number of foil cups from the freezer. Allow to thaw slightly and serve.

Notes:

[1] Use the 4 serving size boxes of pudding, and do NOT make the pudding. Use the dry powder in the recipe.

This is an easy dessert that will be enjoyed by kids and adults alike.

Nutritional Info:

Per Serving: 115 Calories; 4g Fat (30.2% calories from fat); 3g Protein; 18g Carbohydrate; 1g Dietary Fiber; 4mg Cholesterol; 165mg Sodium.
Exchanges: 1/2 Grain (Starch); 1/2 Lean Meat; 1/2 Fat; 1/2 Other Carbohydrates.

Creamsicle Yogurt Pie

Recipes:	1	2	3	4	5	6
Servings:	8	16	24	32	40	48
Makes:	1 pie	2 pies	3 pies	4 pies	5 pies	6 pies
Ingredients:						
Non-dairy fat free whipped topping	8 oz.	16 oz.	24 oz.	32 oz.	40 oz.	48 oz.
Orange crème light yogurt	12 oz.	24 oz.	36 oz.	48 oz.	60 oz.	72 oz.
Graham cracker pie crust	1	2	3	4	5	6

Assembly Directions:
Thaw the frozen whipped topping. Fold the whipped topping and the yogurt together. Pour the filling into the graham cracker crust.

Freezing Directions:
Invert the plastic liner that came with the pie crust to use as a cover for the pie. Place the cover over the pie and fold down the foil edges to hold it in place. Label and freeze.

Serving Directions:
Thaw pie on the counter for 5 minutes so it's easier to cut. Cut and serve frozen. Put any leftovers back in the freezer.

Notes:
Make this with any flavor yogurt. Key Lime, Lemon, and Mixed Berry are the best. Try stirring some berries in the pie when using the Mixed Berry flavored yogurt.

You may want to add a few drops of food coloring to enhance the color.

This is an easy pie recipe to have on hand for company or summer "no oven" days.

Nutritional Info:
Per Serving: 216 Calories; 8g Fat (32.3% calories from fat); 3g Protein; 32g Carbohydrate; 1g Dietary Fiber; 1mg Cholesterol; 211mg Sodium.
Exchanges: 1/2 Non-Fat Milk; 1-1/2 Fat; 2 Other Carbohydrates.

Oatmeal Apple Cranberry Cookies

Recipes:	1	2	3	4	5	6
Servings:	36	72	108	144	180	216
Ingredients:						
Butter or margarine	1/2 C.	1 C.	1-1/2 C.	2 C.	2-1/2 C.	3 C.
Brown sugar	1 C.	2 C.	3 C.	4 C.	5 C.	6 C.
Eggs	2	4	6	8	10	12
Old-fashioned rolled oats	1 C.	2 C.	3 C.	4 C.	5 C.	6 C.
Dried cranberries	1-1/2 C.	3 C.	4-1/2 C.	6 C.	7-1/2 C.	9 C.
Chopped apples[1]	1-1/2 C.	3 C.	4-1/2 C.	6 C.	7-1/2 C.	9 C.
Flour	1-1/2 C.	3 C.	4-1/2 C.	6 C.	7-1/2 C.	9 C.
Salt	1/4 t.	1/2 t.	3/4 t.	1 t.	1-1/4 t.	1-1/2 t.
Baking powder	1/2 t.	1 t.	1-1/2 t.	2 t.	2-1/2 t.	1 T.
Baking soda	1/2 t.	1 t.	1-1/2 t.	2 t.	2-1/2 t.	1 T.
Cinnamon	1/2 t.	1 t.	1-1/2 t.	2 t.	2-1/2 t.	1 T.
Chopped walnuts	1 C.	2 C.	3 C.	4 C.	5 C.	6 C.

Assembly Directions:

Preheat oven to 375 degrees. Cream butter and brown sugar.

Add eggs and beat well.

Add oatmeal and fruits. Add dry ingredients and nuts. Mix well.

Drop by teaspoons onto sprayed cookie sheet. Bake for 8 to 10 minutes. Remove from baking sheet and allow to cool.

Freezing Directions:

Place cookies in freezer bags or rigid freezer containers. Seal, label, and freeze.

Serving Directions:

Thaw and enjoy!

Notes:

[1] 1 medium apple = 1 C. chopped

Freezing chopped apples and chopped walnuts in 1 C. portions makes a recipe like this VERY easy to assemble quickly.

These make great "grab and go" addition for your lunch box.

Nutritional Info: per cookie

Per Serving: 93 Calories; 5g Fat (46.4% calories from fat); 2g Protein; 11g Carbohydrate; 1g Dietary Fiber; 10mg Cholesterol; 74mg Sodium.
Exchanges: 1/2 Grain (Starch); 1 Fat; 1/2 Other Carbohydrates.

Pineapple Piña Colada Pie

Recipes:	1	2	3	4	5	6
Servings:	8	16	24	32	40	48
Makes:	1 pie	2 pies	3 pies	4 pies	5 pies	6 pies
Ingredients:						
Reduced fat cream cheese, softened	8 oz.	16 oz.	24 oz.	32 oz.	40 oz.	48 oz.
Skim milk	1/4 C.	1/2 C.	3/4 C.	1 C.	1-1/4 C.	1-1/2 C.
Vanilla instant pudding mix[1]	1 pkg.	2 pkgs.	3 pkgs.	4 pkgs.	5 pkgs.	6 pkgs.
Crushed pineapple, undrained	8 oz.	16 oz.	24 oz.	32 oz.	40 oz.	48 oz.
Non-dairy fat free whipped topping	8 oz.	16 oz.	24 oz.	32 oz.	40 oz.	48 oz.
Graham cracker crust	1	2	3	4	5	6
Coconut, toasted	1/4 C.	1/2 C.	3/4 C.	1 C.	1-1/4 C.	1-1/2 C.
On Hand:						
Sliced, fresh strawberries	1-1/2 C.	3 C.	4-1/2 C.	6 C.	7-1/2 C.	9 C.

Assembly Directions:
Beat cream cheese and milk in large bowl until well blended.

Add dry pudding mix and undrained pineapple. Mix well. Stir in whipped topping.

Spoon filling into crust. Top with toasted coconut.

Freezing Directions:
Replace plastic cover on graham cracker crust pie or cover pie well and freeze at least 2 hours before serving.

Serving Directions:
Thaw pie 20-30 minutes. Top with on hand fresh, sliced strawberries.

Notes:
[1] Use the 4 serving size boxes of pudding, and do NOT make the pudding. Use the dry powder in the recipe.

Nutritional Info:
Per Serving: 356 Calories; 14g Fat (35.2% calories from fat); 5g Protein; 52g Carbohydrate; 1g Dietary Fiber; 16mg Cholesterol; 556mg Sodium.
Exchanges: 1/2 Lean Meat; 1/2 Fruit; 2-1/2 Fat; 3 Other Carbohydrates.

Caramel Drizzle Freezer Pie

Recipes:	1	2	3	4	5	6
Servings:	8	16	24	32	40	48
Makes:	1 pie	2 pies	3 pies	4 pies	5 pies	6 pies
Ingredients:						
Graham cracker crust	1	2	3	4	5	6
Butter or margarine	3 T.	6 T.	9 T.	12 T.	15 T.	18 T.
Shredded coconut[1]	3/4 C.	1-1/2 C.	2-1/4 C.	3 C.	3-3/4 C.	4-1/2 C.
Chopped pecans[2]	1/2 C.	1 C.	1-1/2 C.	2 C.	2-1/2 C.	3 C.
Sweetened condensed milk	7 oz.	14 oz.	21 oz.	28 oz.	35 oz.	42 oz.
Reduced fat cream cheese, softened	4 oz.	8 oz.	12 oz.	16 oz.	20 oz.	24 oz.
Non-dairy fat free whipped topping, thawed	8 oz.	16 oz.	24 oz.	32 oz.	40 oz.	48 oz.
Caramel ice cream topping	1/2 C.	1 C.	1-1/2 C.	2 C.	2-1/2 C.	3 C.

Assembly Directions:

Melt butter/margarine in skillet over medium heat. Add coconut and pecans, stirring to coat. Sauté until coconut and pecans are lightly toasted, about 5 minutes. Set aside.

In a large mixing bowl, beat condensed milk and cream cheese until fluffy. Fold in whipped topping.

Spoon 1/2 of cream cheese mixture into graham cracker crust. Drizzle with 1/4 C. of caramel ice cream topping. Repeat layers. Top pie with coconut and pecan mixture.

Freezing Directions:

Replace plastic cover on graham cracker crust pie or cover pie well and freeze for at least 2 hours before serving. You can also cut individual pieces and freeze separately in quart size freezer bags.

Serving Directions:

Thaw pie slightly and serve.

Notes:

[1] 7 oz. bag yields 1-1/2 C.
[2] 1 lb. pecans = 3-3/4 cups chopped

Nutritional Info:

Per Serving: 473 Calories; 24g Fat (45.2% calories from fat); 6g Protein; 59g Carbohydrate; 2g Dietary Fiber; 17mg Cholesterol; 421mg Sodium.
Exchanges: 1/2 Lean Meat; 4-1/2 Fat; 3-1/2 Other Carbohydrates.

Rocky Road Freezer Pie

Recipes:	1	2	3	4	5	6
Servings:	8	16	24	32	40	48
Makes:	1 pie	2 pies	3 pies	4 pies	5 pies	6 pies
Ingredients:						
Butter or margarine, melted	1/4 C.	1/2 C.	3/4 C.	1 C.	1-1/4 C.	1-1/2 C.
Vanilla wafers, coarsely chopped[1]	24	48	72	96	120	144
Reduced fat cream cheese, softened	8 oz.	16 oz.	24 oz.	32 oz.	40 oz.	48 oz.
Skim milk	1 C.	2 C.	3 C.	4 C.	5 C.	6 C.
Chocolate instant pudding mix	4 oz.	8 oz.	12 oz.	16 oz.	20 oz.	24 oz.
Non-dairy fat free whipped topping, divided	8 oz.	16 oz.	24 oz.	32 oz.	40 oz.	48 oz.
Miniature marshmallows	3/4 C.	1-1/2 C.	2-1/4 C.	3 C.	3-3/4 C.	4-1/2 C.
Peanuts	1/2 C.	1 C.	1-1/2 C.	2 C.	2-1/2 C.	3 C.
Semi-sweet chocolate chips	1/3 C.	2/3 C.	1 C.	1-1/3 C.	1-2/3 C.	2 C.

Assembly Directions:

Melt the butter/margarine in the microwave. Mix chopped vanilla wafers with melted butter. Press into bottom of spring form pan and refrigerate while making filling.

Beat cream cheese in large bowl until creamy. Gradually beat in milk. Add dry pudding mix and beat until blended. Stir in 2 C. of frozen whipped topping, miniature marshmallows, peanuts and chocolate chips.

Spoon filling into spring form pan. Top with remaining frozen whipped topping.

Freezing Directions:

Freeze at least 4 hours. Once frozen, unmold and rewrap in plastic wrap then put in gallon sized freezer bag. You can also cut individual pieces and freeze separately in quart size freezer bags.

Serving Directions:

Thaw pie slightly and serve.

Notes:

[1] 12 oz. box = about 88 wafers

Nutritional Info:

Per Serving: 407 Calories; 21g Fat (46.2% calories from fat); 8g Protein; 47g Carbohydrate; 2g Dietary Fiber; 16mg Cholesterol; 521mg Sodium.
Exchanges: 1/2 Lean Meat; 3-1/2 Fat; 3 Other Carbohydrates.

Creamy Frozen Mocha Dessert

Recipes:	1	2	3	4	5	6
Servings:	12	24	36	48	60	72
Ingredients:						
Instant coffee granules	2 t.	1 T. + 1 t.	2 T.	2 T. + 2 t.	3 T. + 1 t.	1/4 C.
Hot water	1 T.	2 T.	3 T.	1/4 C.	1/4 C. + 1 T.	1/4 C. + 2 T
Chocolate sandwich cookie crumbs[1]	1 C.	2 C.	3 C.	4 C.	5 C.	6 C.
Chopped pecans, divided[2]	3/4 C.	1-1/2 C.	2-1/4 C.	3 C.	3-3/4 C.	4-1/2 C.
Butter or margarine, melted	1/4 C.	1/2 C.	3/4 C.	1 C.	1-1/4 C.	1-1/2 C.
Reduced fat cream cheese, softened	16 oz.	32 oz.	48 oz.	64 oz.	80 oz.	96 oz.
Sweetened condensed milk	14 oz.	28 oz.	42 oz.	56 oz.	70 oz.	84 oz.
Chocolate flavored syrup	1/2 C.	1 C.	1-1/2 C.	2 C.	2-1/2 C.	3 C.
Non-dairy fat free whipped topping, thawed	8 oz.	16 oz.	24 oz.	32 oz.	40 oz.	48 oz.

Assembly Directions:
In a small cup, dissolve coffee granules in hot water. Set aside.

In another bowl, combine cookie crumbs, 1/2 C. pecans, and butter. Pat into the bottom of a 9x13 baking dish.

In a mixing bowl, beat cream cheese until light and fluffy. Blend in coffee mixture, milk and chocolate syrup. Fold in whipped topping and spread over crust. Sprinkle the remaining pecan on top.

Freezing Directions:
Wrap completely in heavy-duty aluminum foil, or put dessert in a two gallon freezer bag. Seal, label, and freeze.

Serving Directions:
Thaw slightly and serve.

Notes:
[1] 14 sandwich cookies = 1 C. crumbs
[2] 1 lb. pecans = 3-3/4 cups chopped

One recipe can be made in two 8x8 pans.

Nutritional Info:
Per Serving: 377 Calories; 20g Fat (46.8% calories from fat); 8g Protein; 43g Carbohydrate; 1g Dietary Fiber; 33mg Cholesterol; 371mg Sodium.
Exchanges: 1/2 Lean Meat; 3-1/2 Fat; 2-1/2 Other Carbohydrates.

Frozen Latte Dessert

Recipes:	1	2	3	4	5	6
Servings:	9	18	27	36	45	54
Ingredients:						
Heavy whipping cream	2 C.	4 C.	6 C.	8 C.	10 C.	12 C.
Instant coffee granules	1 T.	2 T.	3 T.	1/4 C.	1/4 C. + 1 T.	1/4 C. + 2 T.
Chocolate flavored syrup	1/2 C.	1 C.	1-1/2 C.	2 C.	2-1/2 C.	3 C.
Flour	1 C.	2 C.	3 C.	4 C.	5 C.	6 C.
Powdered sugar	1/3 C.	2/3 C.	1 C.	1-1/3 C.	1-2/3 C.	2 C.
Butter, chilled	1/2 C.	1 C.	1-1/2 C.	2 C.	2-1/2 C.	3 C.
Chopped walnuts[1]	1/2 C.	1 C.	1-1/2 C.	2 C.	2-1/2 C.	3 C.

Assembly Directions:
Preheat oven to 350 degrees. In a large bowl, combine heavy cream, instant coffee granules, and chocolate syrup and put in refrigerator.

In a medium mixing bowl, combine flour and powdered sugar. Cut butter into flour/sugar mixture until mixture resembles large crumbs. Add nuts and press into 9x9 pan. Bake in preheated oven 15 minutes until lightly browned. Cool completely.

Beat chilled cream mixture until stiff peaks form. Spread over cooled crust.

Freezing Directions:
Wrap completely in heavy-duty aluminum foil, or put dessert in a two gallon freezer bag. Seal, label, and freeze.

Serving Directions:
Thaw slightly and serve.

Notes:
[1] 2 oz. walnuts = 1/2 C. chopped

Freeze at least 4 hours before serving.

Nutritional Info:
Per Serving: 420 Calories; 34g Fat (70.4% calories from fat); 5g Protein; 27g Carbohydrate; 1g Dietary Fiber; 100mg Cholesterol; 133mg Sodium.
Exchanges: 1 Grain (Starch); 6-1/2 Fat; 1 Other Carbohydrates.

Pumpkin Cream Cheese Roll

Recipes:	1	2	3	4	5	6
Servings:	12	24	36	48	60	72
Ingredients:						
Eggs	3	6	9	12	15	18
Sugar	1 C.	2 C.	3 C.	4 C.	5 C.	6 C.
Flour	3/4 C.	1-1/2 C.	2-1/4 C.	3 C.	3-3/4 C.	4-1/2 C.
Canned pumpkin	3/4 C.	1-1/2 C.	2-1/4 C.	3 C.	3-3/4 C.	4-1/2 C.
Ground cinnamon	1-1/2 t.	1 T.	1 T. + 1-1/2 t.	2 T.	2 T. + 1-1/2 t.	3 T.
Baking powder	1 t.	2 t.	1 T.	1 T. + 1 t.	1 T. + 2 t.	2 T.
Ground ginger	1 t.	2 t.	1 T.	1 T. + 1 t.	1 T. + 2 t.	2 T.
Salt	1/2 t.	1 t.	1-1/2 t.	2 t.	2-1/2 t.	1 T.
Ground nutmeg	1/2 t.	1 t.	1-1/2 t.	2 t.	2-1/2 t.	1 T.
Lemon juice	1 t.	2 t.	1 T.	1 T. + 1 t.	1 T. + 2 t.	2 T.
Finely chopped pecans	1 C.	2 C.	3 C.	4 C.	5 C.	6 C.
Powdered sugar						
Filling Ingredients:						
Reduced fat cream cheese, softened	8 oz.	16 oz.	24 oz.	32 oz.	40 oz.	48 oz.
Butter, softened	1/4 C.	1/2 C.	3/4 C.	1 C.	1-1/4 C.	1-1/2 C.
Powdered sugar	1 C.	2 C.	3 C.	4 C.	5 C.	6 C.
Vanilla	1/2 t.	1 t.	1-1/2 t.	2 t.	2-1/2 t.	1 T.

Assembly Directions:
Preheat oven to 375 degrees.

Line a 15x10x1 baking pan with waxed paper. Coat lined pan with nonstick cooking spray and set aside. In a mixing bowl, beat eggs for 5 minutes. Add the sugar, flour, pumpkin, cinnamon, baking powder, ginger, salt and nutmeg. Mix well. Add lemon juice. Spread batter evenly in pan. Sprinkle with chopped pecans.

Bake at 375 degrees for 15 minutes or until cake springs back when touched lightly. Cool for 5 minutes. Dust a thin, cotton kitchen towel with powdered sugar. Cover cake with towel and carefully flip cake onto towel. Peel off waxed paper. Roll cake up in towel, jellyroll style, beginning with a short end. Cool completely.

In a large mixing bowl, combine the filling ingredients and beat until smooth. Unroll cake carefully. Spread filling over cake to within 1/2" of edges. Roll up again and place seam side down. Refrigerate for at least an hour before serving.

Freezing Directions:
Cool completely. Wrap cake roll in plastic wrap. Place in gallon size freezer bag.

Serving Directions:
Thaw and serve.

Nutritional Info:
Per Serving: 300 Calories; 15g Fat (44.2% calories from fat); 5g Protein; 38g Carbohydrate; 2g Dietary Fiber; 57mg Cholesterol; 296mg Sodium.
Exchanges: 1/2 Grain (Starch); 1/2 Lean Meat; 2-1/2 Fat; 2 Other Carbohydrates.

Pumpkin Pecan Dessert

Recipes:	1	2	3	4	5	6
Servings:	**12**	**24**	**36**	**48**	**60**	**72**
Ingredients:						
Canned pumpkin	30 oz.	60 oz.	90 oz.	120 oz.	150 oz.	180 oz.
Evaporated milk	12 oz.	24 oz.	36 oz.	48 oz.	60 oz.	72 oz.
Sugar	1 C.	2 C.	3 C.	4 C.	5 C.	6 C.
Eggs	3	6	9	12	15	18
Vanilla	1 t.	2 t.	1 T.	1 T. + 1 t.	1 T. + 2 t.	2 T.
Yellow cake mix (18.5 oz. box)	1	2	3	4	5	6
Frosting Ingredients:						
Reduced fat cream cheese, softened	8 oz.	16 oz.	24 oz.	32 oz.	40 oz.	48 oz.
Powdered sugar	1-1/2 C.	3 C.	4-1/2 C.	6 C.	7-1/2 C.	9 C.
Vanilla	1 t.	2 t.	1 T.	1 T. + 1 t.	1 T. + 2 t.	2 T.
Non-dairy fat free whipped topping, thawed	12 oz.	24 oz.	36 oz.	48 oz.	60 oz.	72 oz.

Assembly Directions:

Preheat oven to 350 degrees. Line a 9x13x2 inch baking pan with waxed paper. Coat with nonstick cooking spray and set aside.

In a large mixing bowl, combine the pumpkin, milk and sugar. Beat in eggs and vanilla. Pour into prepared pan. Sprinkle with dry cake mix and drizzle butter all over. Sprinkle with pecans.

Bake at 350 degrees for 50 minutes or until lightly browned. Cool completely in pan. Invert onto a large serving platter and carefully remove waxed paper.

In a large mixing bowl, beat the cream cheese, powdered sugar and vanilla until smooth. Fold in whipped topping. Spread over baked dessert. Freeze until firm.

Freezing Directions:

Wrap dessert in plastic wrap and put into gallon freezer bag or cut individual pieces and freeze separately in quart size freezer bags. Label, seal and freeze.

Serving Directions:

Thaw slightly and serve.

Notes:

One recipe can be made in two 8x8 pans.

Nutritional Info:

Per Serving: 483 Calories; 12g Fat (22.2% calories from fat); 8g Protein; 85g Carbohydrate; 3g Dietary Fiber; 67mg Cholesterol; 457mg Sodium.
Exchanges: 1/2 Lean Meat; 1 Vegetable; 2 Fat; 5 Other Carbohydrates.

Individual Cheesecakes

Recipes:	1	2	3	4	5	6
Servings:	**12**	**24**	**36**	**48**	**60**	**72**
Ingredients:						
Reduced fat cream cheese; softened	16 oz.	32 oz.	48 oz.	64 oz.	80 oz.	96 oz.
Reduced fat sour cream	1 C.	2 C.	3 C.	4 C.	5 C.	6 C.
Eggs	2	4	6	8	10	12
Vanilla	1-1/2 t.	1 T.	1 T. + 1-1/2 t.	2 T.	2 T. + 1-1/2 t.	3 T.
Lemon juice	1 t.	2 t.	1 T.	1 T. + 1 t.	1 T. + 2 t.	2 T.
Sugar	2/3 C.	1-1/3 C.	2 C.	2-2/3 C.	3-1/3 C.	4 C.
Vanilla wafers	12	24	36	48	60	72
On Hand:						
Strawberry or cherry pie filling	15 oz.	30 oz.	45 oz.	60 oz.	75 oz.	90 oz.

Assembly Directions:

Preheat oven to 350 degrees.

In a mixing bowl, beat cream cheese until it is smooth and free of lumps. Add sour cream, eggs, vanilla, lemon juice, and sugar. Beat until smooth.

Line a muffin pan with foil liners. Place one vanilla wafer in the bottom of each foil liner. Divide mixture evenly among the muffin cups.

Bake for 20 minutes or until a toothpick inserted in the center comes out clean. Cool completely.

Freezing Directions:

Place cheesecakes on a baking sheet. Flash freeze until solid. Put into labeled freezer bags or containers. Seal and freeze.

Serving Directions:

Thaw overnight in the refrigerator. Top each cheesecake with a tablespoon of pie filling. Serve.

Notes:

You can also top these with fresh fruit, chopped candy bars and whipped topping. They are very versatile.

Nutritional Info:

Per Serving: 219 Calories; 9g Fat (36.5% calories from fat); 6g Protein; 29g Carbohydrate; trace Dietary Fiber; 54mg Cholesterol; 249mg Sodium.
Exchanges: 1/2 Lean Meat; 1-1/2 Fat; 2 Other Carbohydrates.

Homemade Ice Cream Mix

Recipes:	1	2	3	4	5	6
Servings:	8	16	24	32	40	48
Makes:	4 C.	8 C.	12 C.	16 C.	20 C.	24 C.
Ingredients:						
Whole or 2 percent milk	3 C.	6 C.	9 C.	12 C.	15 C.	18 C.
Sweetened condensed milk	14 oz.	28 oz.	42 oz.	56 oz.	70 oz.	84 oz.
Vanilla	1 T.	2 T.	3 T.	1/4 C.	1/4 C. + 1 T.	1/4 C. + 2 T.

Assembly Directions:
Pour the milk into a medium-sized bowl. Add the sweetened condensed milk and the vanilla. Use a whisk to mix the ingredients together.

Freezing Directions:
Pour the mixture into a rigid container or a freezer bag. Seal, label and freeze.

Serving Directions:
Thaw the mix overnight in the refrigerator. Stir and use the mix in your ice cream maker, according to the manufacturer's directions. Freeze any leftovers.

Notes:
This recipe is nice because it does not use raw eggs. It's simple, and has wonderful flavor! A 4 quart size ice cream maker holds a double batch of this recipe. By keeping this mix in the freezer, you're ready to make ice cream any time you want!

Nutritional Info: whole milk
Per Serving: 220 Calories; 7g Fat (30.0% calories from fat); 7g Protein; 32g Carbohydrate; 0g Dietary Fiber; 29mg Cholesterol; 108mg Sodium.
Exchanges: 1/2 Non-Fat Milk; 1-1/2 Fat; 2 Other Carbohydrates.

Nutritional Info: 2 percent milk
Per Serving: 209 Calories; 6g Fat (26.0% calories from fat); 7g Protein; 32g Carbohydrate; 0g Dietary Fiber; 24mg Cholesterol; 109mg Sodium.
Exchanges: 1/2 Non-Fat Milk; 1-1/2 Fat; 2 Other Carbohydrates.

Favorite Chocolate Chip Cookies

Recipes:	1	2	3	4	5	6
Servings:	60	120	180	240	300	360
Makes:	5 dozen	10 dozen	15 dozen	20 dozen	25 dozen	30 dozen
Ingredients:						
Butter or margarine	2 C.	4 C.	6 C.	8 C.	10 C.	12 C.
Packed brown sugar	2 C.	4 C.	6 C.	8 C.	10 C.	12 C.
Sugar	1-1/2 C.	3 C.	4-1/2 C.	6 C.	7-1/2 C.	9 C.
Eggs	3	6	9	12	15	18
Vanilla	2 t.	1 T. + 1 t.	2 T.	2 T. + 2 t.	3 T. + 1 t.	1/4 C.
Flour	6 C.	12 C.	18 C.	24 C.	30 C.	36 C.
Salt	1-1/2 t.	1 T.	1 T. + 1-1/2 t.	2 T.	2 T. + 1-1/2 t.	3 T.
Baking soda	1-1/2 t.	1 T.	1 T. + 1-1/2 t.	2 T.	2 T. + 1-1/2 t.	3 T.
Semi-sweet chocolate chips	12 oz.	24 oz.	36 oz.	48 oz.	60 oz.	72 oz.

Assembly Directions:
Preheat oven to 350 degrees.

In microwave, melt butter in large bowl. Mix in sugars by hand until smooth. Add eggs and vanilla.

In separate measuring cup, combine flour, salt, and baking soda. Using mixer, stir into sugar mixture. Add chocolate chips by hand.

Drop dough by teaspoonful onto a sprayed cookie sheet. Bake for 9-10 minutes.

Freezing Directions:
Cool completely. Put into labeled freezer bags or containers. Seal, label, and freeze.

Serving Directions:
Thaw and enjoy.

Notes:
Using a small spring-loaded cookie scoop makes the job go very quickly. You can also freeze the dough in balls to bake later. It's best to flash freeze the balls of dough first and then put them into freezer bags. A dozen fits nicely into a quart size bag. There's no need to thaw the frozen dough before baking. Just add a minute or two onto the baking time.

You can make your own "slice and bake" cookies by shaping these into logs, wrapping them in plastic wrap, and putting them in freezer bags.

Nutritional Info:
Per Serving: 177 Calories; 8g Fat (40.1% calories from fat); 2g Protein; 25g Carbohydrate; 1g Dietary Fiber; 9m Cholesterol; 162mg Sodium.
Exchanges: 1/2 Grain (Starch); 1-1/2 Fat; 1 Other Carbohydrates.

Strawberry Freezer Jam

Recipes:	1	2	3	4	5	6
Servings:	80	160	240	320	400	480
Makes:	48 oz.	96 oz.	144 oz.	192 oz.	240 oz.	288 oz.
Ingredients:						
Crushed, fresh or frozen strawberries	2 C.	4 C.	6 C.	8 C.	10 C.	12 C.
Sugar	4 C.	8 C.	12 C.	16 C.	20 C.	24 C.
Dry pectin (1.75 oz. pkg.)	1	2	3	4	5	6
Water	3/4 C.	1-1/2 C.	2-1/4 C.	3 C.	3-3/4 C.	4-1/2 C.

Assembly Directions:

Mix crushed strawberries with the sugar and let mixture stand for 10 minutes.

Stir the pectin into the water in a small saucepan. Bring to a boil over medium-high heat, and boil for 1 minute.

Stir the boiling water into the strawberries. Keep stirring for a full 3 minutes. This will dissolve all of the sugar granules.

Freezing Directions:

Pour into jars or freezer containers. Let the sealed jam sit at room temperature for 24 hours then freeze or refrigerate. Jam will keep in the refrigerator for up to 1 month.

Serving Directions:

Thaw and serve.

Notes:

Aside from being a lot cheaper than purchased jam, it's also great in smoothies and milkshakes! The same recipe also works well for blackberries.

Nutritional Info:

Per Serving: 43 Calories; trace Fat (0.5% calories from fat); trace Protein; 11g Carbohydrate; trace Dietary Fiber; 0mg Cholesterol; 1mg Sodium.
Exchanges: 1/2 Other Carbohydrates.

Summertime Ice Pops

Recipes:	1	2	3	4	5	6
Servings:	6	12	18	24	30	36
Fruity Yogurt Ice Pops:						
Fresh or frozen fruit, blueberries, raspberries, strawberries, sliced bananas	2 C.	4 C.	6 C.	8 C.	10 C.	12 C.
Sugar	1/4 C.	1/2 C.	3/4 C.	1 C.	1-1/4 C.	1-1/2 C.
Plain or vanilla yogurt	2 C.	4 C.	6 C.	8 C.	10 C.	12 C.

Assembly Directions:
Place 2 C. of the fruit (any combination is fine), sugar and yogurt into a blender. Cover and blend until fruit is smooth.

Freezing Directions:
Pour mixture into 6 popsicle molds and freeze at least 5 hours.

Serving Directions:
Enjoy straight from the freezer!

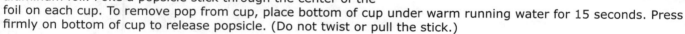

Notes:
Since most cooks only own one set of 6 molds, another option is to freeze the mixture in 6 small (5 oz.) paper cups. Fill them ¾ full and cover the top of each cup with a strip of aluminum foil. Poke a popsicle stick through the center of the foil on each cup. To remove pop from cup, place bottom of cup under warm running water for 15 seconds. Press firmly on bottom of cup to release popsicle. (Do not twist or pull the stick.)

Nutritional Info:
Per Serving: 93 Calories; trace Fat (2.9% calories from fat); 5g Protein; 18g Carbohydrate; 1g Dietary Fiber; 1mg Cholesterol; 63mg Sodium.
Exchanges: 1/2 Non-Fat Milk; 1/2 Other Carbohydrates.

Recipes:	1	2	3	4	5	6
Servings:	6	12	18	24	30	36
Pudding Ice Pops:						
Cold skim milk	2 C.	4 C.	6 C.	8 C.	10 C.	12 C.
Instant pudding mix (4 serving size)	1 box	2 boxes	3 boxes	4 boxes	5 boxes	6 boxes

Assembly Directions:
Pour milk into medium bowl. Add pudding mix. Beat with wire whisk 2 minutes. Spoon into molds or cups.

Freezing Directions:
Pour mixture into 6 popsicle molds and freeze at least 5 hours.

Serving Directions:
Enjoy straight from the freezer!

Notes:
ROCKY ROAD: use chocolate instant pudding and stir in 1/2 cup miniature marshmallows and 1/4 cup each Semi Sweet real chocolate chips and chopped peanuts.
TOFFEE CRUNCH: use vanilla instant pudding and stir in ½ cup chopped chocolate-covered toffee bars.
COOKIES & CREAM: use vanilla instant pudding and stir in 1/2 cup chopped chocolate sandwich cookies.

Nutritional Info: plain
Per Serving: 92 Calories; trace Fat (2.4% calories from fat); 3g Protein; 20g Carbohydrate; 0g Dietary Fiber; 1mg Cholesterol; 289mg Sodium.
Exchanges: 1/2 Non-Fat Milk; 1 Other Carbohydrates.

Appendix

Multiplication Chart For Recipes

1	2	3	4	5	6
1/8 t.	1/4 t.	1/4 + 1/8 t.	1/2 t.	1/2 + 1/8 t.	3/4 t.
1/4 t.	1/2 t.	3/4 t.	1 t.	1-1/4 t.	1-1/2 t.
1/2 t.	1 t.	1-1/2 t.	2 t.	2-1/2 t.	1 T.
1 t.	2 t.	1 T.	1 T. + 1 t.	1 T. + 2 t.	2 T.
1-1/8 t.	2-1/4 t.	1 T. + 3/8 t.	1 T. + 1-1/2 t.	1 T. + 2-1/2 t. + 1/8 t.	2 T. + 3/4 t.
1-1/4 t.	2-1/2 t.	1 T. + 3/4 t.	1 T. + 2 t.	2 T. + 1/4 t.	2 T. + 1-1/2 t.
1-1/2 t.	1 T.	1 T. + 1-1/2 t.	2 T.	2 T. + 1-1/2 t.	3 T.
2 t.	1 T. + 1 t.	2 T.	2 T. + 2 t.	3 T. + 1 t.	1/4 C.

1	2	3	4	5	6
1 T.	2 T.	3 T.	1/4 C.	1/4 C. + 1 T.	1/4 C. + 2 T.
1-1/2 T.	3 T.	1/4 C. + 1-1/2 t.	1/4 C. + 2 T.	1/4 C. + 3-1/2 T.	1/2 C. + 1 T.
2 T.	1/4 C.	1/4 C. + 2 T.	1/2 C.	1/2 C. + 2 T.	3/4 C.
2-1/2 T.	1/3 C.	1/4 C. + 3-1/2 T.	1/2 C. + 2 T.	3/4 C. + 1-1/2 t.	3/4 C. + 3 T.
3 T.	1/4 C. + 2 T.	1/2 C. + 1 T.	3/4 C.	3/4 C. + 3 T.	1 C. + 2 T.
3-1/2 T.	1/4 C. + 3 T.	2/3 C.	3/4 C. + 2 T.	1 C. + 1-1/2 T.	1-1/3 C.

1	2	3	4	5	6
1/4 C.	1/2 C.	3/4 C.	1 C.	1-1/4 C.	1-1/2 C.
1/3 C.	2/3 C.	1 C.	1-1/3 C.	1-2/3 C.	2 C.
1/2 C.	1 C.	1-1/2 C.	2 C.	2-1/2 C.	3 C.
2/3 C.	1-1/3 C.	2 C.	2-2/3 C.	3-1/3 C.	4 C.
3/4 C.	1-1/2 C.	2-1/4 C.	3 C.	3-3/4 C.	4-1/2 C.
1 C.	2 C.	3 C.	4 C.	5 C.	6 C.
1-1/4 C.	2-1/2 C.	3-3/4 C.	5 C.	6-1/4 C.	7-1/2 C.
1-1/3 C.	2-2/3 C.	4 C.	5-1/3 C.	6-2/3 C.	8 C.
1-1/2 C.	3 C.	4-1/2 C.	6 C.	7-1/2 C.	9 C.
1-2/3 C.	3-1/3 C.	5 C.	6-2/3 C.	8 C.	9-2/3 C.
1-3/4 C.	3-1/2 C.	5-1/4 C.	7 C.	8-3/4 C.	10-1/2 C.
2 C.	4 C.	6 C.	8 C.	10 C.	12 C.
2-1/4 C.	4-1/2 C.	6-3/4 C.	9 C.	11-1/4 C.	13-1/2 C.
2-1/2 C.	5 C.	7-1/2 C.	10 C.	12-1/2 C.	15 C.
2-2/3 C.	5-1/3 C.	8 C.	10-2/3 C.	13-1/3 C.	16 C.
2-3/4 C.	5-1/2 C.	8-1/4 C.	11 C.	13-3/4 C.	16-1/2 C.
3 C.	6 C.	9 C.	12 C.	15 C.	18 C.
3-1/4 C.	6-1/2 C.	9-3/4 C.	13 C.	16-1/4 C.	19-1/2 C.
3-1/3 C.	6-2/3 C.	10 C.	13-1/3 C.	16-2/3 C.	20 C.
3-1/2 C.	7 C.	10-1/2 C.	14 C.	17-1/2 C.	21 C.
3-2/3 C.	7-1/3 C.	11 C.	14-2/3 C.	18-1/3 C.	22 C.
3-3/4 C.	7-1/2 C.	11-1/4 C.	15 C.	18-3/4 C.	22-1/2 C.
4 C.	8 C.	12 C.	16 C.	20 C.	24 C.

1	2	3	4	5	6
4-1/4 C.	8-1/2 C.	12-3/4 C.	17 C.	21-1/4 C.	25-1/2 C.
4-1/3 C.	8-2/3 C.	13 C.	17-1/3 C.	21-2/3 C.	26 C.
4-1/2 C.	9 C.	13-1/2 C.	18 C.	22-1/2 C.	27 C.
4-2/3 C.	9-1/3 C.	14 C.	18-2/3 C.	23-1/3 C.	28 C.
4-3/4 C.	9-1/2 C.	14-1/4 C.	19 C.	23-3/4 C.	28-1/2 C.
5 C.	10 C.	15 C.	20 C.	25 C.	30 C.

Equivalency Chart

DRY MEASURE

Pinch = a little less than 1/4 teaspoon
3 teaspoons = 1 Tablespoon
2 T. = 1 oz. = 1/8 C.
4 T. = 2 oz. = 1/4 C.
5-1/3 T. = 2.7 oz. = 1/3 C.
8 T. = 4 oz. = 1/2 C.
10-2/3 T. = 5.4 oz. = 2/3 C.
12 T. = 6 oz. = 3/4 C.
16 T. = 8 oz. = 1 C.
4 C. = 1 quart
4 quarts = 1 gallon
16 oz. = 1 lb.

LIQUID MEASURE

a dash = a few drops
3 teaspoons = 1 Tablespoon
2 T. = 1 oz.
4 T. = 2 oz. = 1/4 C.
5-1/3 T. = 2.7 oz. = 1/3 C.
8 T. = 4 oz. = 1/2 C.
10-2/3 T. = 6 oz. = 3/4 C.
16 T. = 8 oz. = 1 C.
2 C. = 1 pint = 1/2 quart
4 C. = 2 pints = 1 quart
4 quarts = 16 C. = 1 gallon = 128 oz.

Bread Cubes and Crumbs

4 slices of bread = 2 C. fresh soft crumbs
4 slices of bread = 3/4 C. dry crumbs
6 oz. dried bread crumbs = 1 scant cup
16 oz. loaf = 14 C. one inch cubes

Cereal

21 oz. box corn flake cereal = 7 cups
2 C. flakes = 3/4 C. crumbs
15 oz. box crisp rice = 11 cups of cereal
13 oz. box of crisp rice = 6 C. crumbs
42 oz. box rolled oats = 10 C.

Flours/Meal

1 lb. white flour = 3-1/2 C. or 4 C. sifted
1 lb. whole wheat flour = 3-1/4 C. or 3-1/2 sifted
1 C. flour = 4 oz.
14 oz. cracker meal = 3-3/4 C.

Leavening Agents

16 oz. baking soda = 2-1/3 C. = 37 T.
16 oz. baking powder = 2-1/3 C. = 37 T.
14 oz. can baking powder = 1-3/4 C. = 28 T.
5-1/2 oz. baking powder = 1 C.
.25 oz. active dry yeast = 1 T.
1 oz. of active dry yeast = 3-1/3 T.
16 oz. of active dry yeast = 3-1/3 C.
.60 oz. compressed yeast = 4 t.

Cracker & Cookie Crumbs

28 soda or saltine crackers = 1 C. fine crumbs
16 oz. crackers = 6 C. fine crumbs
15 square graham crackers = 1 C. crumbs
16 oz. graham crackers = 70 crackers
1 roll of snack crackers = about 1-1/3 C. crumbs
16 oz. of snack crackers = about 5-1/3 C. crumbs
24 round butter crackers = 1 C. fine crumbs
14 oz. box of cracker meal = 3-3/4 C. crumbs
22 vanilla wafers = 1 C. crumbs
14 Oreos® (with middle) = 1 C. crumbs

Butter/Margarine/Shortening

1 T. = 1/2 oz. = 1/8 stick
4 T. = 2 oz. = 1/4 C. = 1/2 stick
8 T. = 4 oz. = 1/2 C. = 1 stick
16 T. = 8 oz. = 1 C. = 2 sticks
32 T. = 16 oz. = 2 C. = 4 sticks = 1 lb.
3 lb. can of shortening = 6 C.

Sweeteners

12 oz. honey = 1 C.
16 oz. honey = 1-1/2 C.
16 oz. corn syrup = 1-1/2 C.
11 oz. molasses = 1 C.
11 oz. maple syrup = 1 C.
16 oz. white sugar = 2-1/3 C.
4 lbs. white sugar = 10 C.
16 oz. brown sugar = 2-1/4 C. packed
16 oz. powdered sugar = 3-1/2 C.

Equivalency Chart

DAIRY PRODUCTS

Shredded and Cubed Cheese
16 oz. = 4 C. cubed or shredded
4 oz. = 1 C. cubed or shredded
Heavy Whipping Cream
1 C. or 8 oz. carton = 2 C. whipped
Parmesan or Romano Cheese, grated
6 oz. = 1 C.
16 oz. = 2-2/3 C.
24 oz. = 3 C.
Cottage Cheese
6 oz. = 1 C.
16 oz. = 2-2/3 C.
Sour Cream
16 oz. = 1-3/4 C.
9 oz. = 1 C.
Cream Cheese
3 oz. = 6 T. or about 1/3 C.
8 oz. = 1 C.
1 lb. or 16 oz. = 2 C.
Sweetened condensed milk
14 oz. can = 1-1/4 C.
Evaporated Milk
14-1/2 oz. can = 1-2/3 C.
6 oz. = 2/3 C.
Dry milk powder
16 oz. = 4 cups dry or 4-5 quarts of liquid
Buttermilk Powder
12 oz. = 3-3/4 qts. of liquid buttermilk
1/4 C. buttermilk powder = 1 C. buttermilk

FRUITS

Apples
1 lb. = 3 medium
1 medium = 1 C. chopped
Applesauce
16 oz. = 2 C.
Bananas
1 lb. = 3 med. = 2-1/2 C. diced or 3 C. sliced
1 medium = 1/3 C. mashed
Strawberries/Raspberries
1 lb. = 2 C. sliced
Blueberries
1 lb. = 3 C.
Cranberries
1 lb. = 4 C.
Limes
1 medium = 1-1/2 to 2 T. fresh juice
Raisins
1 lb. = 3-1/2 C.
6 oz. = about 1 C.
Pineapple
1 lb. = 2-1/2 C. diced
Lemons
1 medium = 3 T. juice or 1 T. grated rind
5-8 lemons = 1 C. fresh juice
Oranges
1 = 1/3 C. fresh juice

MEATS

Bacon
8 slices = 1/2 C. cooked and crumbled
16 oz. = about 18 slices
Beef
1 lb. ground = 2-1/2 C. browned
10 lbs. ground = 25 C. browned
1 lb. beef cuts = 3-1/2 C. sliced
Bulk Sausage
1 lb. raw = 2-1/2 C. cooked and crumbled
Chicken, boneless, skinless
7-1/2 lbs. raw = about 25 pieces
1 lb. raw = 2 C. raw ground = 2-2/3 C. raw diced
5 lbs. raw = 12 C. cooked, diced
1 large breast = 3/4 C. cooked, diced
2-1/2 lbs. = 7-8 large pieces
Chicken Thighs
5 lbs. = about 25 pieces
Whole Chicken
2-1/2 lb. chicken = 2-1/2 C. cooked, diced meat
3-1/2 to 4 lb. chicken = 4 C. cooked, diced meat
4-1/2 to 5 lb. chicken = 6 C. cooked, diced meat
Crab meat (real or imitation)
1 lb. cooked and boned meat = 2 cups
Ham
1 lb. whole ham = 2-1/2 C. ground ham
1 lb. whole ham = 3 C. cubed
Turkey Breast
5 lb. raw breast = 10 C. cooked, diced meat
1 lb. drumstick or thigh = 1-1/8 C. diced
Whole Turkey
Each pound of turkey = approx. 1 C. cooked meat
Tuna Fish
6 oz. = 3/4 C. lightly packed

MISCELLANEOUS

Jams/Jellies/Preserves
6 oz. = 2/3 C.
10 oz. = about 1 C.
16 oz. = 94 t. = 32 T. = 2 C.
Nuts
16 oz. = 4 C.
2 oz. = 1/2 C.
Cocoa Powder
8 oz. = 2 C.
16 oz. = 4 C.
Chocolate Chips
6 oz. = 1 C.
Shredded Coconut
16 oz. = 5 C.
Peanut Butter
16 oz. = 1-3/4 C.
Ice Cubes
11 cubes = 1 C. liquid
Mayonnaise
1 quart = 32 oz. = 4 C.
Marshmallows
16 oz. = 9 C.

Equivalency Chart

ONE OUNCE OF WEIGHT TO MEASUREMENT OF HERBS AND SPICES

Allspice, ground	5-1/2 T.	Mustard; dry, ground	6 T. + 1 t.
Basil	1/2 C.	Nutmeg; ground	5 T.
Bay leaf, whole	7 T.	Onion powder	4-1/2 T.
Black pepper; ground	1/2 C.	Oregano	6 T.
Celery Seed	1/4 C.	Paprika	5 T.
Chili Pepper	1/2 C. + 1-1/2 t.	Parsley flakes	1/2 C. + 1-1/2 t.
Cinnamon	5-1/2 T.	Poppy Seeds	3-3/4 T.
Cloves, ground	5-1/2 T.	Red pepper flakes	1/2 C. = 1-1/2 t.
Cumin seed	6 T.	Rosemary	1/2 C.
Curry powder	5-1/2 T.	Sage	1/2 C. + 1-1/2 T.
Dill Weed	6 T.	Savory	6-3/4 T.
Dill Seed	4-1/2 T.	Sesame Seed	5 T.
Garlic powder	6-1/3 T.	Tarragon	6-3/4 T.
Ginger	6 T.	Thyme	6-1/3 T.
Marjoram	1/2 C.	Turmeric	5 T.

VEGETABLES

Carrots
1 lb. = 3 C. sliced = 2 C. diced = 6-8 medium
1 medium carrot = 1/2 C. grated
Cooking Onions
1 lb. = 3 medium = 3 C. sliced or chopped
1 medium onion = 1 C. chopped = 2/3 C. sautéed
Green Onion 7 medium green onions = 1/2 C. sliced
Green Beans 1 lb. fresh = 3 C. = 2-1/2 C. cooked
Green Pepper 1 large = 1 C. diced
Broccoli 1 lb. fresh or frozen = 2 C. flowerets
Cabbage 1 lb. = 4 C. shredded
Cauliflower 1 lb. = 1-1/2 C. cooked = 3 C. florets
Celery
1 medium bunch = 2-1/2 to 3 C. sautéed
1 medium bunch = 3 C. diced = 3-1/2 C. sliced
3 large ribs = about 1-1/2 C. diced
1 Cup diced = 2/3 C. sautéed
1 rib = 1/2 C. sliced or diced
Corn
2-3 fresh ears = 1 C. kernels
1 lb. frozen = 3 C. kernels
Peas 4 oz. = 1 C.
Potatoes
1 lb. = 3 medium = 2-3/4 C. diced = 3 C. sliced
1 lb. = 2 C. mashed
5 lbs. = 10 C. diced or mashed
Sweet Potatoes
1 lb. = 3 medium = 2-1/2 - 3 diced
Spinach and other greens
1 lb. raw = 10-12 C. torn = 1 C. cooked
10 oz. frozen = 1-1/2 lb. fresh = 1-1/2 C. cooked
Sweet Bell Peppers
1 medium = 1/2 C. finely chopped
1 lb. = 5 medium or 3-1/2 C. diced
Mushrooms
4 oz. fresh = 1 C. whole = 1/2 C. cooked
1 lb. = about 20 large or 40 medium whole
Tomatoes 1 lb. = 4 small = 1-1/2 C. cooked
Garlic 1 medium clove = 1/2 t. minced
Water Chestnuts 8 oz. sliced or whole = 1 C. drained

DRY BEANS/GRAINS/PASTA/NUTS

Lentils
6 oz. dry = 1 C.
Kidney Beans
11 oz. dry = 1 C. dry = 3 C. cooked
15 oz. can = 1-3/4 C.
16 oz. dry = 5 C. cooked
Barley
3/4 C. pearl barley = 3 C. cooked
1 C. quick cooking barley = 2-1/2 C. cooked
Long Grain White Rice
16 oz. dry = 2-1/2 C. dry = 10 C. cooked
1 C. dry = 7 oz. dry = 3 C. cooked
Quick Cooking Brown Rice
1 C. dry = 2 C. cooked
12 oz. box = 5-1/3 C. fully cooked
       = 4-1/2 C. half cooked
White Converted Rice
1 C. dry = 4 C. cooked
Oatmeal
42 oz. dry = 10 C. dry
Spaghetti
2 oz. = 1 serving = 1/2" diameter dry portion
16 oz. = 4-5 C. dry = 10 C. cooked
Elbow Macaroni
4 oz. dry = 1 C. dry = 2-1/2 C. cooked
16 oz. dry = 4 C. dry = 9 C. cooked
Egg Noodles
4 oz. dry = 1 C. dry = 3 C. cooked
16 oz. dry = 4 C. dry = 12 C. cooked
Tiny Pasta (acini pepe, orzo, ditalini, alphabets)
8 oz. dry = 1-1/3 C. dry

Freezing Time Chart

The following list should give you a good idea of the basics when freezing most ingredients used in **30 DAY GOURMET** cooking. Remember, nothing goes "bad" in the freezer. It may just lose quality over time. Packaging mak[...] all the difference. To determine how long to freeze a recipe that has a combination of different ingredients, the item[...] that freezes well for the least amount of time determines how long to freeze the entire recipe.

FOOD	FREEZER LIFE
Baked Goods:	
Bread dough; yeast, unbaked	2 weeks
Baked bread	12 months
Rolls:	
unbaked	2 weeks
1/2 baked	12 months
fully baked	12-15 months
Muffins:	
unbaked	2 weeks
baked	3 months
Waffle/pancake batter	2-4 weeks
Waffles/pancakes, cooked	6 months
Dairy Products:	
Butter:	
salted	3 months
unsalted	6 months
Margarine	5 months
Hard cheese	3 months
Cream cheese	3 months
Milk	1 month
Eggs, raw and out of shell	6 month
Produce:	
All Vegetables	12 months
Exceptions:	
Asparagus	8-12 months
Onions	6 months
Jerusalem artichokes	3 months
Potatoes	3-6 months
Beets	6 months
Green beans	8-12 months
Leeks	6 months
Winter squash	10 months
Mushrooms	8 months
Corn on the Cob	8-10 months
Herbs	6 months
Vegetable Purees	6-12 months
Prepared Vegetable Dishes	3 months
Miscellaneous:	
Pasta, cooked	3-4 months
Pasta, mixed into dishes	3-4 months
Rice, cooked	3-4 months
Rice, mixed into dishes	3-4 months

FOOD	FREEZER LIFE
Beef:	
raw ground beef/stew beef	3-4 months
fresh beef steak	6-12 months
fresh beef roast	6-12 months
fresh beef sausage	3-4 months
smoked beef links or patties	1-2 months
cooked beef dishes	2-3 months
fresh beef in marinade	2-3 months
Pork:	
ground pork	3-4 months
fresh pork sausage	1-2 months
fresh pork chops	4-6 months
fresh pork roast	4-6 months
bacon	1 month
pepperoni	1-2 months
smoked pork links or patties	1-2 months
canned ham	don't freeze
ham, fully cooked	
whole:	1-2 months
half or slices:	1-2 months
pre-stuffed pork chops	don't freeze
cooked pork chops	2-4 months
uncooked casseroles w/ham	1 month
cooked casseroles w/ham	1 month
fresh pork in marinade	2-3 months
Poultry:	
fresh ground turkey	2-3 months
fresh turkey sausage	1-2 months
fresh whole turkey	12 months
chicken or turkey:	
fresh pieces	9 months
cooked pieces	4 months
cooked nuggets	3-4 months
pre-stuffed chicken breasts	don't freeze
cooked poultry dishes	4-6 months
fresh chicken in marinade	2-3 months
Fish:	
fresh pieces	6-12 months
cooked pieces	2-3 months
cooked fish dishes	2-3 months
fish in marinade	2-3 months
Miscellaneous:	
vegetable or meat soups/ stews	2-3 months
ground veal and lamb	3-4 months
gravy and meat broths	2-3 months
cooked meat pies	3-4 months
cooked meatloaf	1-3 months

Blanching Chart For Vegetables

ays choose good, quality, fresh vegetables. Clean and trim off inedible parts. Cut to desired uniformly sized pieces.

CROWAVE BLANCHING

Choose a round microwaveable bowl or container.
Place 1/4 C. of water in the container.
Into the container, place no more than 4 C. of leafy vegetables (like spinach) or 2 C. of other vegetables.
Cover the container with microwaveable plastic wrap.
Make sure that if you have a turntable, it can move freely.
Microwave according to the chart below on highest power setting.
After blanching, spread vegetables out in a single layer on a tray or baking sheet and cool 5 minutes. They are now suitable for freezing by themselves, or in a freezer recipe.

OVETOP STEAMING

Prepare vegetable as above.
Use a pan that a wire mesh basket or steamer basket will fit into (at least 8 qt. size).
Bring 1 inch of water to a rolling boil in the pan.
Place no more than 1 pound of vegetables in the basket and place over the steaming water.

- Time according to the chart below.
- Remove the basket of vegetables from the pot and plunge into cold or ice water, or run cold water over them. This stops the cooking action.
- Drain well. The vegetables are now ready for freezing or using in a freezer recipe.

BOILING WATER BLANCHING

- Clean and prepare vegetables as above.
- In a large pot, bring at least 1 gallon of water for every pound of vegetables to a rolling boil.
- Plunge the vegetables in the water 1 pound at a time.
- When the water begins to boil again, start timing according to the chart below.
- At the end of the blanching time, remove vegetables from the water with a slotted spoon, steamer basket, or strainer with a handle.
- Cool hot vegetables as for stovetop steaming. The vegetables are now ready for use in the freezer.

BLANCHING CHART			
VEGETABLE	**MICRO-STEAM**	**STOVETOP STEAM**	**BOILING WATER**
beets	n/a	n/a	30-45 min.
broccoli	5 min.	3-5 min.	2-4 min.
brussels sprouts	4 min.	6 min.	4 min.
cabbage wedges	3 min.	4 min.	3 min.
carrots	2-5 min.	4-5 min.	2-5 min.
cauliflower	5 min.	5 min.	3 min.
celery	3 min.	4 min.	3 min.
corn on the cob	n/a	n/a	6-8 min.
corn cut from cob	4 min.	6 min.	4 min.
green beans	3 min.	4 min.	3 min.
peas, all types	4 min.	6 min.	4 min.
potatoes, cut	10 min.	12 min.	10 min.
spinach/other greens	n/a	3 min.	2 min.
sweet potatoes	Any method will work. Cook until soft.		
zucchini, cubed	2-3 min	2-3 min	2-3 min
NO BLANCHING NEEDED FOR: mushrooms, onions, peppers, tomatoes, shredded zucchini			

Cooking Terms & Definitions

One of the goals of this manual is for it to be so simple that only the most basic cooking skills are needed. If you are unfamiliar with any o the cooking terms used in this manual, you should be able to find their meanings written below:

Baste: Refers to spooning or brushing juices, pan drippings, stock, broth, butter, oil or marinade over meats, poultry or fish. You can use a brush, bulb syringe, bulb baster, or spoon for this job.

Beat: This means to mix rapidly to make a mixture smooth and light. In beating, air is incorporated into the mixture. Beating by hand should be done with a whisk, a fork, or a wooden spoon. Use your wrist in a quick up and down circular motion. An electric mixer is one of the greatest cooking tools! Use a round bowl for beating, not a square or rectangular container. You will not get the corners mixed adequately.

Blanch: This means to boil rapidly in a good quantity of water. It destroys harmful enzymes in vegetables, helps to make peeling tomatoes or fruits easier, sets the color, and seals in juices and vitamins. See the blanching chart on page 223 for more complete instructions.

Blend: This means to mix two or more ingredients together so thoroughly that they become one product. This is most completely done with an electric blender or mixer.

Boil: This means to heat a liquid until bubbles constantly come to the surface. A slow boil means the bubbles lazily come to the surface. In a hard boil, the bubbles are large and rapidly break the surface.

Broil: Broiling is a cooking method using intense heat on one side. Broiling can be done in the stove, or on a grill. It is usually a quick cooking method that needs to be watched carefully to prevent burning.

Brown: The purpose of browning is to quickly sear the meat, sealing in juices and giving color to the food. Medium to high heat is usually used. Sometimes the heat is lowered to complete the cooking!

Broth: This is a liquid containing the flavors and aroma of chicken, beef, fish, or vegetables. The meat or vegetables are simmered in water, then the solids are strained out, leaving broth. Broth may be made from purchased granules or cubes that have been dissolved in water. Condensed broth is also available.

Chop: Chopping is cutting a solid object into pieces with a sharp knife. To chop efficiently, hold the blade of a large knife at both ends, bringing it up and down firmly over the food to be chopped.

Cream: This means to beat two or more ingredients together until smooth and creamy.

Cut in: Work butter, shortening, margarine, or lard into a flour mixture until it looks like coarse crumbs.

De-grease: Removing grease or fat from a broth, soup, or sauce is called de-greasing. You can skim the fat off the top with a spoon or skimmer, or chill the liquid until the fat rises to the surface and hardens. The hard fat can be removed with a slotted spatula and discarded.

Dice: This is similar to chopping, but it usually results in fairly sm pieces.

Dredge: This usually means to drag a solid food like meat, fruit, vegetables through other dry ingredients like sugar or flour. This presses the dry ingredients into the food.

Drippings: These are the juices, fats, and browned bits of food le in a pan after cooking. The drippings are good for making sauces and gravies.

Flash Freeze: or Open Freeze. To firm up foods before fully freez by putting them on a pan in the freezer until just firm and then packaging them for long term storage. Usually done with fragile foods.

Fold: Folding is done when a substance that has a lot of air in it, like whipped cream or beaten egg whites, is mixed into a heavier ingredient, like a batter. A rubber spatula or large spoon can be used to carefully lift and mix.

Grate: This usually means to rub a solid food, like vegetables or cheese against a grater. A grater has sharp blades that cut the so food into smaller pieces.

Marinate: This means to cover food in a seasoned liquid that contains some form of acid, like fruit juice, wine, or vinegar. This done to tenderize and flavor a food.

Mince: This means to chop very, very fine.

Pinch: As a measurement, it is a very small amount. What you c hold between your thumb and index finger.

Puree: This means to mash something until it is a uniformly smoo product. This is done with a blender, food processor, or food mill.

Reduce: Boil or simmer a liquid to reduce its volume and intensif its flavor.

Sauté: This is a slower form of frying, requiring lower heat and le fat.

Simmer: Simmering is a *very* slow boil. The bubbles should bar break the surface of the liquid.

Steam: This means to cook or heat food over boiling water, with the food not touching the water. This is a very healthy way to coo Usually uses a steamer basket inside a pan and a lid.

Stock: This is an intensely flavored broth. The liquid is simmered until much of it evaporates, leaving a stronger flavored product.

Whisk: This means to beat with a whisk or whip until the food is mixed.

Freezer Selection & Maintenance

nether you are considering purchasing a brand-new freezer, or looking for a reliable used model, there are a few important things
consider. Plan to purchase your appliance from a dealer who services what he sells. Look for a well-known brand so that parts
not hard to find for repairs. If your freezer is new, fill out the warranty card and send it into the manufacturer right away. Keep
Owner's Manual!

nstruction

reezer cabinet should be made of a wrap-around, one-piece
ucture. The compressor should be hermetically sealed so
t it requires no maintenance from you. It should have
eling feet on the cabinet. The controls should be positioned
that *you* can reach them easily, but toddlers can't. Freezer
or seals are usually magnetic. Make sure that the seal is
nt on all edges. If you close a piece of paper in the door it
uld be held tightly. If you have children, you might consider
chasing a freezer with a built-in lock. This will prevent food
m "disappearing" and more importantly, will prevent the
ezer door from being left open "accidentally".

ost-Free" vs. "Frost-Full"

frosting is a burdensome chore for most homeowners.
st-free models eliminate the problem by utilizing small
aters that melt the ice periodically. Because of the drying
ion and heat, it is especially important to properly package
d headed for a frost-free appliance. Frost-free models cost
und 50% more to operate than standard freezers. They
also more expensive to purchase. Because it costs more
operate and to purchase a frost-free model, you will have
determine if the cost is worth it. Most people only have to
rost a freezer once or twice a year. Look for the Federal
de Commission (FTC) label on the appliance. The label will
you how many kilowatt-hours the appliance will use. The
aller the number listed, the less energy is used.

pacity

eck the capacity of the freezer and buy the size that is most
ted to your eating patterns. A nearly full freezer runs much
re efficiently than a half full one. If you purchase a freezer
t is too large for your use, it may have a lot of air space that
u have to cool. The freezer has to work harder to keep air cool
n food, so frozen air takes more energy than frozen food!

Upright Freezers

Uprights range in size from 12 to 30 cu ft. A sliding basket
or drawer is very handy for bulky items. Some come with ice
makers, but they are usually optional, and they do take up
room. A benefit of upright freezers is that they take up less
floor space than a chest freezer of the same capacity. Also, the
food is easily stacked and distributed on the shelves, and it is
easier to find what you need without digging. This is a great
benefit for the shorter folks among us! The temperature in the
door storage spaces will be a bit warmer than the temperature
in the back.

Chest Freezers

The sizes for these models run from 5 to 28 cu. ft. They
generally cost less to buy than upright models. You also have
more usable space in a chest freezer, because you can pack
it clear to the top if you like. Utilizing baskets or boxes can
help keep foods organized. Chest freezers are also more cost
efficient to operate. The frozen food is packed more tightly
together, so it holds the chill in. Also, since heat rises, opening
the lid of a chest freezer allows less cold air to escape than
opening the door of an upright freezer. In a chest freezer, the
top center section will generally be a little warmer than the rest
of the freezer.

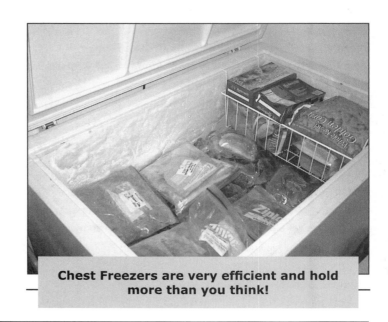

**Chest Freezers are very efficient and hold
more than you think!**

Freezer Selection & Maintenance

Installment

Most people do not have the luxury of a large freezer in or near the kitchen. The room it takes up is a big consideration for where to place a freezer. Also, you want to make sure you don't have it in a spot that is too warm or too cold. If your freezer is in the kitchen, it will have to work harder because of the surrounding temperature. Any spot that is relatively cool, out of direct sunlight, dry, and well ventilated is a suitable one for a freezer. The freezer will actually run better if it is in a room that remains above 40°F. Think about where you will plug it in. A freezer should be plugged into its own, grounded outlet. A freezer should also have its own circuit so that an overload from another appliance does not shut it off. The outlet should be in a position that it is as protected as possible. No one (pets included) should be able to become tangled in the cord. An unseen pulled plug spells disaster for your frozen foods! You should not push a freezer tightly up against a wall, or into a corner. A freezer needs room to dispel heat into the air. It is a very good idea to decide *where* the freezer will go, before you decide on a size or type. It is a good idea to set the leveling feet so that it tips back slightly. This will cause the door to swing shut automatically.

Temperature Settings

0°F is a temperature that will keep the foods you store well protected. Even though water freezes at 32°F, destructive enzymes are not kept from harming your foods at that temperature. The lower the temperature, the longer the food will store well. A temperature of -5°F will keep quality even longer, but be aware that your electric bill will rise as the temperature lowers!

If you will be away from home for more than a couple of days, have a neighbor or friend check up on your freezer to make sure it is still running.

Defrosting

Follow the manufacturer's instructions (if you have them) for defrosting or do a web search for "freezer defrosting". If your freezer is running well and the seal is in good shape, you should not have to defrost more than once or twice a year. You should defrost before the ice is 1/2" thick on the interior walls. This job will take anywhere from 2 to 3 hours, so allow plenty of time.

Here is a method that will work in the absence of the original manufacturer's instructions.

1. Plan to defrost your freezer at a time when it is fairly empty already.
2. Remove the frozen food and place it in coolers, or wrap the food containers in several sheets of newsprint and pack it tightly into cardboard boxes or crates.
3. You need to shut off the power to the freezer, or unplug the appliance.
4. If you are working on a chest freezer, be sure to prop the lid open so that it can't come crashing down.
5. Place some old towels on the floor in front of the freezer and a rolled up towel on the bottom of an upright freezer next to the rubber door seal. This will keep water from pouring out the bottom.
6. Clean the freezer as quickly as possible. Some manufacturers say to place pans of hot water in the freezer and close the door. Then, remove the frost as it loosens and replace the water as it cools. Make sure the freezer is completely cool before restarting it. Other manufacturers do not recommend using pans of hot water in their freezers because the refrigerant pressure could build up in the evaporator, making restarting the freezer difficult. These manufacturers recommend allowing the frost to thaw naturally or with the aid of a fan.
7. You can also use a rag dipped in very hot water to drench and melt the ice. A bulb baster works well too. Draw boiling hot water into it, then squirt it over the ice. Just be very careful not to burn yourself. Repeat the hot water drenching until you are down to the bare surface.
8. If your freezer has a drip tray underneath it, empty it every once in a while to keep it from overflowing. If you need to, sop up the melted ice with a rag or sponge and squeeze the water into a bucket or tub.
9. Do not use an ice pick, screwdriver, hammer, or knife to break apart the ice. Besides the danger to yourself, you will probably damage the inside of your freezer! You might just mark up the inside, or you might even break right through a coolant line, which will release toxic fumes into the air and kill your freezer.
10. Dry out the compartment with a clean dry towel.

Freezer Selection & Maintenance

[Ext]erior Cleaning

[Wh]en you are finished defrosting a freezer, it is a great time [to cl]ean and deodorize it also. If you can, drag the whole [app]liance away from the wall. Vacuum up the dirt and mop [up t]he remaining grime. Remove the grate in the back that [cov]ers the compressor and fan. This is usually at the very top, [or v]ery bottom of the appliance. Use a vacuum cleaner with a [nozz]le attachment to remove the accumulated dust around the [com]pressor and fan. Replace the cover. Use an all-purpose [clea]ner to safely clean the outside of the freezer. Vacuum [the]dust off the condenser coils. When you are done and [eve]rything is clean and dry, turn the power to the freezer back [on]or plug it back into its outlet. Turn the freezer back on and [mak]e sure the temperature control is set where you want it to [be.] Wait 15-30 minutes to allow the freezer to become chilled [befo]re returning the food to the freezer. If food packages are [wet], scrape or wipe them to remove frost or moisture.

[Int]erior Cleaning

[For]food residues, use a paste made of baking soda and water. [Use] it like a scouring powder to scrub the food off. Rinse the [bak]ing soda mixture off with clean warm water and a sponge or [ra]g. A baking soda and water solution is also a good rinse for [the]entire freezer. Besides the cleaning it will get, the baking [sod]a also helps to remove odors.

[Stu]bborn Odors

[If t]here are stubborn odors in the freezer that the baking soda [will] not remove, try these options one at a time so that there [will] not be any chemical reactions between them. Rinse out [the]freezer with clear water if needed and wipe it dry before [tryi]ng another method.

- Vinegar and water solution - mix one cup of vinegar with one gallon of water.
- Household chlorine bleach - mix a half cup of bleach with one gallon of water.
- Leave crumpled up black and white newsprint in the freezer with the door shut.
- Place charcoal briquettes in a tub or pan and leave them in the freezer with the door shut.
- Make a mild solution of dish washing liquid and water. Wash with the mixture, then rinse with clean water.

Sometimes the odor is impossible to remove. Food that has been in the freezer too long, food that has been improperly packaged, or food that has spoiled in a power outage can cause lasting odors. If smelly moisture is absorbed by the freezer insulation, it may have strong permanent odors. You can either have the insulation replaced by an appliance repairman, or live with the problem. If you choose to put up with the odor, try to double wrap all of the foods in the freezer. When you take the food from the freezer, discard the outer wrapper. Hopefully *it* will contain the odor, not the inner wrap and food beneath it.

There are 60+ entrees in this upright freezer. Don't you wish they were yours?

Power Failure!

It's happened to all of us! The storm comes through and we lose power the day AFTER we stocked our freezer. Or worse yet, we run down to the basement and discover that "someone" has left the freezer door open. What do we do? Is the food safe? Does everything need to be thrown away "just to be sure"?

The following information comes from the USDA. One idea that they didn't offer (probably because they don't have kids) is to use the lock and key that most likely came built into your freezer. This will keep your kids from eating 20 popsicles in one day and "accidentally" leaving the door open.

In the event of a power outage, freezer failure or open freezer door, the food may still be safe to use. Without power, a full upright or chest freezer will keep everything frozen for about 2 days. A half-full freezer will keep food frozen 1 day. If the power will be coming back on fairly soon, you can make the food last longer by keeping the door shut as much as possible and covering the unit with blankets and quilts. Make sure that you do not block the air vent. If the freezer is not full, quickly group packages together so they will retain the cold more effectively. Separate meat and poultry items from other foods so that if they begin to thaw, their juices won't drip onto other foods.

For short term power outages – less than 6 hours – just leave the door closed until the power returns. If the power is off for more than 6 hours, you may want to put block ice or bags of ice in the freezer or transfer foods to a friend's freezer until power is restored. Use an appliance thermometer to monitor the temperature.

To determine the safety of foods when the power goes on (or you first discover the open door), check their condition and temperature. If food is partly frozen, still has ice crystals or is as cold as if it were in a refrigerator (40 degrees), it is safe to refreeze or use. It is not necessary to cook raw foods before refreezing (see tips below). Discard foods that have been warmer than 40 degrees for more than two hours. Discard any foods that have been contaminated by raw meat juices. Dispose of soft or melted ice cream for quality's sake.

Without power, a refrigerator will keep food cool for 4-6 hours depending on the kitchen temperature. A full, well-functioning freezer unit above a refrigerator should keep food frozen for 2 days. A half full one will keep food frozen for about 1 day. If you have access to it, block ice can keep food on the refrigerator shelves cooler.

Refreezing Foods

As a general rule, if the power has been off for quite a while and then comes back on, food still containing ice crystals or that feel refrigerator-cold can be refrozen. Do not be surpris if a little quality is lost in refreezing. Discard any thawed foo that has risen to room temperature and remained so two ho or more. Immediately throw out anything with a strange color or odor. Before you begin to refreeze food, be sure to turn the freezer to its coldest temperature. Mark the foods a "refrozen". Space the food out on the shelves so that air ca flow freely around the packages. When all the foods are soli refrozen, return the temperature setting to its normal positio

Meats - To refreeze meats, repackage them in freezer bags, tightly sealed rigid freezer containers. Do not refreeze grou meats that have thawed. Only refreeze ground meat packag that are still solidly frozen. Icy cold packages of thawed me can be cooked thoroughly, then repackaged for the freezer.

Cured Meats - Ham, bacon, hard salami, and pepperoni ca be re-frozen if they are still cold to the touch.

Poultry – Repackage icy poultry in moisture-vapor proof packaging before refreezing. Leave the original wrapping on it, but place it inside a freezer bag or rigid freezer container. Discard any poultry that has come to room temperature. If poultry juices have dripped onto other foods, treat them like thawed poultry - throw them out! If the poultry is still cold, cook and eat it right away, or cook it and freeze immediately

Fish - Do not refreeze fish unless it is still solidly frozen. If fish is thawed, but very cold to the touch, cook it and consu immediately. Throw out any fish that has come to room temperature.

Fruits - Use thawed fruits to make jams, jellies, preserves, cooked pie fillings.

Vegetables - You can refreeze vegetables that still have ice crystals in them. If the vegetables are thawed but still in go condition, you can cook and eat them.

Miscellaneous - Completely thawed baked goods, dinner entrees, juices and cheese should not be refrozen. If they a still cold, they should be refrigerated and eaten as soon as possible. Do not eat dinner entrees that have thawed to roo temperature.

Index

Index continued...

Index continued...

Index continued...

Notes

Notes

Notes

Notes

Notes

Notes

Notes